"...WHERE LOVE BEGINS"

Also by Helga Sandburg

NOVELS

The Wheel of Earth
Measure My Love
The Owl's Roost
The Wizard's Child

FOR YOUNG PEOPLE

Blueberry
Gingerbread
Joel and the Wild Goose
Bo and the Old Donkey
Anna and the Baby Buzzard

REMINISCENCE AND SONG (ADULT)

Sweet Music

POETRY

The Unicorns
To a New Husband

SHORT STORIES

Children and Lovers: *Fifteen Stories*

NON-FICTION

Above and Below (with George Crile, Jr.)
A Great and Glorious Romance: *The Story of Carl Sandburg and Lilian Steichen*

Helga

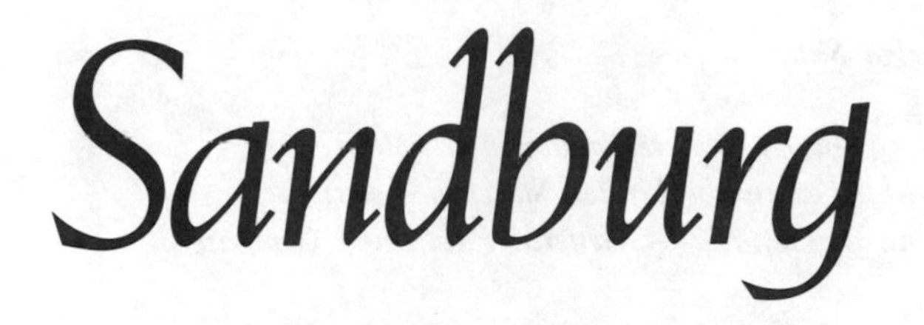

"...WHERE LOVE BEGINS"

c.1

DONALD I. FINE, INC.
New York

 Published in the United States of America by Donald I. Fine, Inc. and in Canada by General Publishing Company Limited.

Library of Congress Cataloging in Publication Data

Sandburg, Helga.
". . .where love begins
1. Sandburg, Helga—Biography. 2. Sandburg, Carl, 1878-1967—Biography—Family. 3. Authors, American—20th century—Biography. 4. Fathers and daughters—United States—Biography. I. Title.
PS3569.A48Z476 1989 811'.54 [B] 88-45858
ISBN 1-55611-134-7 (alk. paper)

Designed by Irving Perkins Associates

Manufactured in the United States of America
10 9 8 7 6 5 4 3 2 1

The following pages constitute an extension of the copyright page.

The author and the publisher wish to thank the following for permission to quote from the sources listed: Maurice C. Greenbaum and Frank M. Parker, Trustees of the Sandburg Family Trust, for the unpublished writings of Carl Sandburg. Alfred C. Edwards, Trustee of the Estate of Robert Lee Frost, for letters and excerpts from letters of Robert Frost; G. d'Andelot Belin and Brinton P. Roberts, Trustees under the Will of Amy Lowell, for an excerpt from a letter of Amy Lowell; Houghton Mifflin Company for an excerpt from a poem by Amy Lowell from *The Complete Poetical Works of Amy Lowell* by Amy Lowell. Copyright © 1955 by Houghton Mifflin Company, copyright © 1983 renewed by Houghton Mifflin Company, Brinton P. Roberts and G. d'Andelot Belin; The American Foundation For the Blind, Inc., for excerpts from a letter of Helen Keller; Lady Chaplin for the little drawing by Charlie Chaplin; Helen Sarett Stockdale for an excerpt from a letter of Lew Sarett; Eric Sevareid for an excerpt from a broadcast from overseas; Mrs. James Reston for an excerpt from her letter; Joanna Taub Steichen for excerpts from her letters; The Estate of Babette Deutsch Yarmolinsky for a letter of Babette Deutsch which includes her poem; The Estate of Mary Hemingway for excerpts from her letters; Margaret Sandburg for excerpts from her letters; Janet Sandburg for four of her poems; The Dial Press for excerpts from songs from *Sweet Music, A Book of Family Reminiscence and Song* by Helga Sandburg, copyright © 1963; Josef Krames for pertinent help on photographs. Harcourt Brace Jovanovich for the use of the following poems and songs and writings of my father: excerpts from "At a Window" and "The Junk Man" from *Chicago Poems* by Carl Sandburg, copyright © 1916 by Holt, Rinehart and Winston, Inc., renewed 1944 by Carl Sandburg, reprinted by permission of Harcourt Brace Jovanovich, Inc.; excerpts from "Potato Blossom Songs and Jigs" and "Wilderness" from *Cornhuskers* by Carl Sandburg, copyright © 1918 by Holt, Rinehart and Winston, Inc., renewed 1946 by Carl Sandburg, reprinted by permission of Harcourt Brace Jovanovich, Inc.; excerpts from "Tawny," "Savoir Faire" and "Finish" from *Smoke and Steel* by Carl Sandburg, copyright © 1920 by Harcourt Brace Jovanovich, Inc., renewed 1948 by Carl Sandburg, reprinted by permission of the publisher; excerpts from "Slabs of the Sunburnt West" and "Without the Cane and the Derby" from *Slabs of the Sunburnt West* by Carl Sandburg, copyright © 1922 by Harcourt Brace Jovanovich, Inc., renewed 1950 by Carl Sandburg, reprinted by permission of the publisher; excerpts from "The Quaker's Wooing," "I Ride an Old Paint" and "Mama Have You Heard the News?" from *The American Songbag* by Carl Sandburg, copyright © 1927 by Harcourt Brace Jovanovich, Inc., renewed 1955 by Carl Sandburg, reprinted by permission of the publisher; excerpts from "Explanations of Love," "Good Morning, America," "Counting" and "Monkey of Stars" from *Good Morning, America* by Carl Sandburg, copyright © 1928, 1956 by Carl Sandburg, reprinted by permission of Harcourt Brace Jovanovich, Inc.; excerpts from pages 3 and 1009 from *Remembrance Rock* by Carl Sandburg, copyright © 1948 by Harcourt Brace Jovanovich, Inc., renewed 1976 by Lilian Steichen Sandburg, Margaret Sandburg, Janet Sandburg and Helga Sandburg Crile, reprinted by permission of the publisher; excerpts from "The Man with the Broken Fingers" and "Mr. Attila" from *Complete Poems of Carl Sandburg,* Revised and Expanded Edition, copyright © 1950 by Carl Sandburg, renewed 1978 by Margaret Sand-

FOR MY GRANDCHILDREN,
SASCHA,
TRISTAN,
MARCEL
AND
HELGA SKY
AND
BIRCH

There is a place where love begins and a place where love ends—and love asks nothing.

From "Explanations of Love"
CARL SANDBURG, 1928

CONTENTS

Part One

THE TIME OF MY CHILDHOOD

HER NAME is Helga. I see her there as through a glass darkly. It is as if I, the woman, stand in moonlight and she, the baby, the growing girl, the young woman, in the sun. I cannot speak to her because she does not know me or that I am here all these years later. But I know her well and all the answers to where she will go and what she will do. It is the window of memory.

The voice. Her father's, its cadence, the rising and falling. The baby hears it. The Rootabaga tales, his cornfairy stories. I was born in November of 1918 and am three and a half when *Rootabaga Stories* is published. It is dedicated "To Spink and Skabootch" my sisters, Margaret, then ten and Janet, five. Not to Helga, me. Can I remember hearing them read to me? Yes, by my mother. She is Paula, his name for her. And he is Carl. When more of the children's tales follow in a year, *Rootabaga Pigeons,* they are "To Three Illinois Pigeons." There is a cadence to that voice which lingers in memory. It whispers if he wishes, so that in an auditorium of ten thousand the silence holds its breath waiting for his next word. That comes later in his life. Now it rumbles and roars (and that is a clear remembrance) as he stamps the floor of his attic room, "Can't a fellow have a little peace and quiet in his own home!"

The guitar. There has been one in the house since 1910 when Carl's triumphant letter came to Paula's hand, telling about the instrument he had purchased and how "there will be songs warbled and melodies whistled to the low Mexican thrumming." A memory—his whistling like a bird, but no bird I'd ever heard—a wondrous entertaining whistle. The guitar is a part of our lives. And the songs he collects as he goes about the land will in time be put into *The American Songbag.*

Remembering is a dream that comes in waves. The positions of staircases and walls and paths are as vivid as the figures that come and go. Nowadays my father is beneficent when he appears in memory and dream. It was not always so. And that is true of my mother too. In the days of Helga's childhood, the materials for the dreams begin to accumulate. When does memory start? I am pushing the cat in a doll carriage up and down the flagstone walks of my mother's garden. The willing creature is clothed in doll dress and bonnet. The iris blooms tower. It is dusk and an early moon. There are fireflies and crickets about. My sisters and parents are on the porch and a stranger, a large woman, and her driver. Helga is two and does she remember or has she heard the story?

Supper is over and everyone listens. (Of the large woman, her peer and friend, Ezra Pound, says, "Don't make fun of Amy. She's the only hippopoetess in our zoo.") The guitar sounds under the voice. It is a song Carl came upon in a once-slave plantation in Georgia (he was reading for the local poetry society) and his family knows it.

Bill's wife was baking bread, this morning,
Bill's wife was baking bread, this evening,
Bill's wife was baking bread
When she got word that Bill was dead,
This morning, this evening, so soon!

Amy Lowell writes a poem after she leaves and returns to Brookline and she sends it to Carl, "I hope you will like it. . . . Remember me to Mrs. Sandburg and my friends, Margaret, Janet, and Helmar." A part goes:

. . . To-night I saw an evening moon
Dodging between tree-branches
Through a singing silence of crickets,

And a man was singing songs to a black-backed guitar. . . .
The moon stops a moment in a hole between leaves
And tells me a new story,
The story of a man who lives in a house with a pear-tree
before the door, . . .
There is a woman in the house, and children,
And, out beyond, the corn-fields are sleeping and the trees
are whispering to the fire-flies.
So I have seen the man's country, and heard his songs
before there are words to them.
And the moon said to me: "This now I give you," and
went on, stepping through the leaves.
And the man went on singing, picking out his
accompaniment softly on the black-backed guitar.

My father is forty-two, sitting there in the moonlight, waiting for the rain, his wife believing in every word he writes and says. Paula. He gave her the name. She was Lilian Steichen when they met. Paula. Writing to him in the early days of their marriage, ". . . when you do arrive, what a company of geniuses you will be—Poet—Essayist—Agitator—Orator—Organizer—Lover of Humanity—and Lover of the Wonder-Girl!" The last was herself.

Miss Lowell knows his books *Chicago Poems* and *Cornhuskers.* This evening he reads poems from the manuscript of his next, *Smoke and Steel.* Others of his peers recognize him too. "Lord love you as a good man in the cause of men," says William Marian Reedy. Carl Van Doren, "I wonder whether you saw Clement Shorter's recent remark that he considered Thomas Hardy and you the two greatest living poets." Louis Untermeyer has looked at the new manuscript at Harcourt Brace, the publisher, ". . . even that hurried look made me gasp. And that's something I seldom do these mad days. Carl, you came so damn fast you took our breath away. But, by God, you're still coming! You not only outstripped us all, you haven't even stopped running." From Henry Holt and Company, where those first two books were published, Lincoln MacVeagh, "I'd eat my hat to publish for you. Why not admit it?" From *Harper's Bazaar,* Henry Blackman Sell, "One of the finest things in my life is knowing you, Carl, and that's no bull."

My father and mother and for that matter, the family there, Margaret (polite and listening and enthralled), Janet (harum-scarum and about), and Helga (behind a door somewhere, perennially and permanently shy), and Amy Lowell, all know he's on his way. Miss Lowell has written of him in her critique of six American poets. He likes that.

We can leave them there in the moonlight with the guitar and the poetry. Janet and Helga before long are kissed and put to bed. Margaret may stay up as long as she likes, a natural night owl and raised unconventionally. Amy Lowell and her driver will leave and Carl and Paula will talk into the night, as the rain mists down. His voice rises and falls, in cadence, and there is a murmuring now and then from my beautiful mother.

There are a hundred poems to Paula. There they are in his books. And a few to Margaret and Janet. And two for Helga. There she is in the sunlight of the kitchen.

The milk-drops on your chin, Helga,
Must not interfere with the cranberry red of your
cheeks
Nor the sky winter blue of your eyes.
Let your mammy keep hands off the chin.
This is a high holy spatter of white on the reds and
blues. . . .

My father is a wanderer. A roamer. He will always be a traveler, leaving his family and out on the land. He first went off when he was a little over nineteen and lived in Galesburg, Illinois, and said goodbye to his mother and father and brother and sisters in June of 1897. The nation was in a depression and men had no jobs and little bands rode the boxcars and gathered in "hobo jungles" by the tracks. Young Charlie (Paula had not liked the name Charles for him and picked Carl, strong and simple, she felt, and he accepted it) set out then on an adventure. He had $3.25 in cash, at least so goes the story he relates to us, proud. For four months he hoboed over the landscape, riding the cars like the bums, taking little jobs for cash along the way—blacking stoves, waiting at lunch counters, cutting weeds, as a railroad section man, on a threshing crew in Kansas. He saw the Rocky Mountains and Pikes Peak. He was rawboned and hardy and had a strong sense of curiosity that travel satisfied.

He takes another trip in Helga's time. I am two. Our home is in a small town, Elmhurst, on the outskirts of Chicago. He has been asked to lecture in Los Angeles for literary clubs. Friends will put him up. He means to make the most of it. He is tall and rangy and strong. He stays in what he and Paula call "baseball trim." His once raven black hair is grayed. He sees himself as a poet. He gives readings (Paula does not go along) every winter at Le Petit Gourmet in Chicago. His friend and enthusiastic critic, Harry Hansen, describes him as "a tall gaunt figure, with good-sized cheekbones, and a heavy jaw that seems to stick forward when he is especially wrought up. . . . His hair, fast turning gray, falls over his forehead. He is addicted to suits of heavy material, suits that will wear well, shirts that are bargains. . . . He reads very slowly, in a marvelous voice that you can never forget . . ."

His movements are awkward. So I remember. He has never been on a dance floor for all I know. For his daughters he will do happy clog steps. (Later he will waltz me, an adolescent, adoring!) Even his playing of the guitar is not done with a conventional sense of rhythm. He handles the instrument as he does his prose—mastering it in his own (lyric?) style.

Now he puts on his long gray overcoat and his visored cap and with a valise holding his books and manuscripts and a change of shirts and socks in one hand, and the guitar in its cheap case in the other, he boards the Rock Island Railroad in Chicago. He travels part of the nearly 3,000 miles by Pullman, taking an upper berth. The Rock Island takes him to Des Moines and Omaha, the Union Pacific to Salt Lake City and the Santa Fe to Williams, Arizona, where he makes a small detour.

How do poems come to a poet who knows he is one? They are waiting to be written and all of his life he will read the ones he writes now to audiences. It is a windy Friday night as he gets off the train. In the morning the Santa Fe shuttle brings him to the Grand Canyon rim. Before long he begins and there he is in the poem. How confident he is of his genius.

A rider came to the rim
Of a slash and a gap of desert dirt—
A long-legged long-headed rider
On a blunt and a blurry jackass—
Riding and asking, "How come? How come?" . . .

And the man took a stub lead pencil
And made a long memo in shorthand
On the two blurry jackass ears:— . . .

He stays overnight at a Grand Canyon hotel, during the day roaming the paths. When finished, his poem will run ten pages.

And another will come of the trip. In Los Angeles he strikes up a curious and fleeting friendship with Charlie Chaplin, eleven years younger, unmarried. By that spring of 1921, Chaplin has produced three films and Carl has lavishly reviewed the last, "As an artist he is more consequential in extent of audience than any speaking, singing, writing or painting artist today."

And now another character enters the story and for him my father has the same kind of pure and extravagant praise and total admiration as for Chaplin. Paula's only brother, Edward Steichen, had been famous on the continent as a photographer-painter-artist when she and Carl first met in 1908. Uncle Ed and my father became like blood brothers. Uncle Ed's frequent visits to our home are as welcome as those from Santa Claus or the Tooth Fairy. He dazzles my sisters and me and his talk with my parents lasts till daybreak. His first marriage now is over and done and he will soon return to the States for good. At present he lives in Voulangis outside Paris where he has a studio and garden. On his last visit to us, he brought new photographs of Isadora Duncan and her pupils at the Parthenon (he made love to one of the beautiful pupils, who later noted that he desired her hand as well)—and then delicate portraits of grasshoppers and flowers and apples and spider webs and Auguste Rodin's sculptures, all done at the Voulangis studio.

When *The Gold Rush* is released in August of 1925, Uncle Ed will do a portrait of Chaplin for *Vanity Fair.* And Steichen will go on the staff of that magazine, making fashion photographs and portraits of the famous and will get a lot of money. It seems to me that Chaplin as well as Uncle Ed were inclined to swings between moods of gayety and gloom. I have read of the dark side of Charlie. Although I never saw that side of my uncle, his granddaughter, among others, has spoken of it. And vanity. Chaplin shared that with Steichen. Those about him played to it. Helga along with her mother play to the vanity of Carl. (Count my bright sister Margaret out. Janet? She's not even interested.)

The "blood brothers" will each do his interpretation of Charlie. Carl's is a poem about one of the charade skits Chaplin performs one evening for a party. He calls it "Without the Cane and the Derby (for C.C.)."

The room is dark. The door opens. It is Charlie playing
for his friends after dinner, "the marvelous urchin,
the little genius of the screen," (chatter it like a
monkey's running laughter cry.)
No . . . it is not Charlie . . . it is somebody else. It
is a man, gray shirt, bandana, dark face. . . .

Now is the fall that *Rootabaga Stories* is slated for publication and Carl wants Chaplin to write a few introductory words. He asks him and waits and finally gives up. But the poem about Charlie's skit will sell to *Vanity Fair* for fifty dollars.

And so my father leaves Hollywood behind and heads for San Francisco. There in Chinatown, he wanders the book stalls, picks up Hokusai and Hiroshige reproductions and tinseled Chinese decorations in pinks and tangerines and greens and blues and lavenders and reds and lots of gold. He buys Chinese curios. I see my father there (looking through the glass back there). Don't I know his ways? Who is with him (wondering, these years later), as he roams, curious and restless? New friends? Newspaper people? A lady or so (a daughter's late question)?

He is driven down the coast to Monterey Bay where he

watches the fishermen and soon will note down six verses of a local Italian ballad for his book. It begins

In Carmel Bay the people say
We feed the Lazzaroni
On caramels and cockle-shells
And hunks of abalone . . .

As he gets back on the train, he is Texas-bound, swinging southwest toward Waco and Austin. A blizzard strikes. He gets off in Santa Fe to wait it out. An old friend will welcome him for the night. Alice Corbin Henderson, once assistant editor at *Poetry: A Magazine of Verse* in Chicago. (She is the one who first saw the group of "Chicago Poems" Carl handed in that startled the literary world and began his emergence as the "Poet of Free Verse.") He comes to her adobe house on a rutted road. William Penhallow Henderson is her husband, an artist. Through the years at their fireside will sit the poets and writers—Vachel Lindsay, Robert Frost, D.H. Lawrence, Edna St. Vincent Millay, Willa Cather, others.

Carl hears more songs that night to slip into his valise, including the Spanish and English translation of "La Cucaracha." Other songs come at the next stops. John Lomax takes him into the Silver King Saloon and he hears for the first time "C.C. Rider" and "The Sunshine Special." And then later at the home of Frank Dobie, secretary of the Texas Folklore Society, Mexican love songs and trail driver ballads. He has them in shorthand in his valise, saved for the book.

Home. At the supper table reading the long western poem begun at the Grand Canyon, calling it "Slabs of the Sunburnt West." It will be the final one in a fourth book of poems having that title and dedicated "To Helga" (I will be three). The finished Chaplin poem will go in too. And he brings out his Chinatown treasures and announces that friends will be sending on dark-colored Indian serapes and Navajo clay figures that will be for us, the "kids." He puts whatever pay he has earned into my mother's hands, as always. And also a small paper he has collected and to be kept for me.

There are two beds for Carl in the house. He shares a large double one with my mother in their bedroom. But he also has a narrow iron army cot for himself in his workroom. If he writes late toward dawn, he sleeps here. This work place is his lair, with its own individual odor, redolent of cigar smoke, coffee and the scent of man. His spittoons are here, not in the rest of the house. He empties them himself, a masculine task. And here he lifts me upside down sometimes to walk on the low ceiling. He has walked me on all the ceilings of the house. My father likes to rough-house with his daughters. He calls them his "homeyglomies," writing home from his travels that he misses their babbling, their pulling on his ears, their sliding down the banisters, and his walking them on the ceilings.

What ties a marriage, a household, together? Delight? Grief? Intensity? Time apart? Admiration? Passion? Children? Paula, Mother, had been twenty-four when they met briefly in late December of 1907 in the rallying halls of the Social Democrat Party in Milwaukee. They exchanged letters for almost three months, both imbued with "revolutionary passion" which tinged his poetry and prose. They called each other "comrade." Then, at my grandparents' house outside Milwaukee, in Menomonee Falls, Carl came to visit for a week. After that the letters came in floods between them. The country's spirit had been awakened at the turn of the century and the two were part of it. They were first-generation immigrants. In their childhood households, the languages of the old country had been spoken. They read Keats and Browning, Darwin and Veblen, and spoke their new tongue with studied selection and awareness. They married in June of 1908. What were their dreams? How had they seen their life together? Did they see her giving speeches and serving by his side as a comrade and organizer for the Social Democrat Party? Did they see themselves helping the Poet find his Place? Did he see himself with a stalwart worthy son or two to carry his name? Was it simply that she at twenty-four and he at twenty-nine had been ready to mate and felt their luck that the other came along?

Back then, in that early time, Carl had always been away, giving talks for the party, collecting dues, occasionally doing a literary lecture. Had he missed her as she missed him? He wrote in that first year, "Home is more of a Home when the open is stormy. I want you for the sun and the flowers, Paula, but I want you for the rain & the dark too."

And my father, Carl, does not forget that early pledge as the dark and stormy comes. As the summer of 1921 slips by and fall arrives, a malevolent dragon that has lain concealed gets ready to reveal itself. In time the beast will assume a more placid shape, harnessed, but when first sighted in mid-November, it seems a heartbreaking creature. Its name is *epilepsy* from the Greek: to seize upon. Medically, it is *cerebral dysrhythmia,* a disturbance of the brain's normal rhythm. My brilliant ten-year-old sister Margaret is one of the first Montessori pupils. She is the light of her father's eyes. The first warning of the dragon is an episode of falling asleep in school. Before long, the seizures become frequent and violent.

Does my father love my mother a thousandfold more as she takes on the battle like St. George—her spear medical knowledge, maternal devotion and outraged determination?

When Uncle Ed hears of Margaret's bravery with the dragon, he writes at once, "I will turn over my cross of the Legion d'Honneur to her."

And Carl? A poem called "Marny" begins:

Smolder of dreams in your slow, proud eyes,
Flicker of roses maroon in your shadows of hair,
You, the youngblood, the lightfoot,
Took the road and went away to find answers
Unto the words unanswerable.
You lay before us when we, for tears,

Held our lips and could not tell you how dreams and roses go and where. . . .

I am four. A flame has lighted my father. The household feels it. He is impatient with noisy daughters and their playfellows. "Quiet!" "Hush," pleads and counsels my mother. It is summer, 1923, sixty years after Abraham Lincoln freed the slaves in the territory still at war with the Union. Carl is absorbed in his workroom. Before him are boards with notes thumbtacked to them. He has hauled up orange crates and apple boxes and set them on end, using the inside partitions for shelves for cigar boxes of pencils and paper clips and odds and ends. His typewriter is on one of the crates. Cigar ends and ashes are in the Mason jar cover over here. Dust is about. No one may clean in here. He wants everything left just where he has put it.

We live in a little white house with a fence around it. Up in his room at the top of the house, the summer sun blazes through the curtainless windows. The still air is heated. He carries the typewriter on its crate down the steep back stairs and out into the vacant lot behind the house. Here cows used to graze. And here is an old small barn. He gets out the dusty chair that he keeps inside the barn door for this purpose. Here, in the early spring, Mother and my grandmother Oma, with me and my sisters, gathered dandelion heads for the dry white wine the women make. Later, in the fall, there will be Concord grape wine settling in the cellar. Sometimes a child is sent out to my father, bringing him a glass of milk or a pot of coffee. He responds absently. He has hung his shirt on a nail on the barn side. Current notes are tacked beside it onto the slabs as the day moves on. He sits in the sun in the weeds and the long meadow grass, his skin sweating and browning. In the spring, he had spaded up some ground and put in sweet corn. Now the tassels rustle when a breeze moves. My father's book is writing itself. It is on the way. One chapter will be the sixty-sixth of one hundred and sixty-eight, and tell only of corn and how it grew in Illinois in the time of young Abraham Lincoln.

At the supper table, Carl will tell his family of the "grand golden spiders" out there by the barn. And he reads an early poem that we are used to.

I ask you for white blossoms.
I bring a concertina after sunset under the apple trees.
I bring out "The Spanish Cavalier" and "In the Gloaming,
O My Darling."

The orchard here is near and home-like.
The oats in the valley run a mile.
Between are the green and marching potato vines.
The lightning bugs go criss-cross carrying a zigzag
of fire: the potato bugs are asleep under their
stiff and yellow-striped wings: here romance
stutters to the western stars, "Excuse . . . me . . ."

At this time my father is keeping away from people, writing a friend, "I am working like a dog at a root, on a job that when it is finished will alibi me for many social shortcomings."

Fall. The sugar maples in the yard turn golden yellow. Then snow blows and a storm howls outside the workroom windows. The house is quieter. Helga and Janet are in kindergarten. Margaret, thin and subdued after a fast, calculated by the doctors to control the dragon, is reading off in a corner. The younger daughters return. Squeals of laughter and screams of protest and the barking of Pooch, the dog.

Carl stamps on the floor boards. "Pipe down!" He pounds

his way to the back stairway. He yells. "Quiet! Jesus Christ in the foothills!" He hears from his publisher, Alfred Harcourt, by Thanksgiving, ". . . if it keeps up, it will be the brightest feather in our cap—a regular plume!"

Can I say that Helga is in any way mistreated as a child? Or her sisters? He roars. But he walks me on the ceiling. He spins me through the countryside before him on his bicycle, past cornfields and gardens, his voice in my ear. Again he holds squealing Janet up as she weeps and refuses to stop and his rage is enormous. But he catches her as she slides down the banister and sets her to dash up again and slide down.

Another spring and in between his lecturing his work on the book continues. He arrives at his publisher's office with a valise full of the beginning manuscript on *Lincoln: The Prairie Years.* In time the books on Lincoln will mount to six volumes (seven with the one on Mary, the wife) and will gain a Pulitzer. He writes from Harcourt's office, "Paula. . . . Am going slow and coming along. Prayers for and love to you all."

Summertime. And the blaze of the back lot again, as the writing goes on. After supper, darkness comes on and my father stands with Mother at the porch rail overlooking the garden. Fireflies glint here and there and he says there has never been such a year for glow worms. The sugar maples are in full leaf. The cat has delivered a litter in the barn loft and Janet and Helga have discovered them. Before long they will be dressed along with the dolls and wheeled in our carriages. We whisper, "Daddy's a-working!" Nodding our heads, solemn. By the flagstones of Mother's gardens are heliotrope, nasturtiums, larkspur, bachelor buttons, marigolds, cosmos, asters, poppies.

Set out on the grass in the shade are cedar chairs and rockers with reed backs. Paula never seeks the sun the way Carl does. The skin of her face stays untanned all of her days.

She sits in one of the chairs. Near her the kittens sprawl and Pooch, the dog, sleeps. She breaks beans in a pan or cross-stitches a child's pinafore or darns a basketful of socks, watching her daughters on the wood swing or the Ford tire hung on a rope or dangling from the metal rings that hang from a branch of the spruce in the side yard. The rabbits doze in their fenced pen against the barn side.

Fall and winter. "It's a sweet and noble book," Harcourt praises. My father responds, "The book marches; it has good second wind . . ." And publication is set for the fall of 1925. But first spring and Carl is lecturing out in Waco, Texas. Mother writes him, "Garden is lovely with lilacs and honeysuckle and the children are asking for you every day. . . . Everything fine here. Margaret . . . finer than she has been for some years. This may not last long—but I'm enjoying every minute of it while it does last."

Then a telegram is put in Carl's hand out there in Waco. The book is sold to a magazine, *Pictorial Review.* "YOUR SHARE SERIAL MONEY TWENTY ONE THOUSAND SIX HUNDRED DOLLARS GET DRUNK AND BE HAPPY LOVE ALFRED HARCOURT."

He pens a wire home at once. "FIX THE FLIVVER AND BUY A WILD EASTER HAT." She replies from her heart, "YOUR WIRE WITH BIG NEWS CAME SUNDAY OVERJOYED MUST TAKE LONG VACATION FROM ALL WORK THIS SUMMER ALL JUBILATING HERE IN GAY EASTER BONNETS EVERY OPPORTUNITY ASSURED MARGARET NOW HIGH HOPES AND BUSHELS OF LOVE PAULA."

The malevolent dragon is now at bay.

There sits my curious father, enthralled with his galley and page proofs at his publishers, passing the time with friends, restless, looking ahead into his life. And my incredible mother with her brood of daughters ranging from six to fourteen, at a little lake resort in Williams Bay, Wisconsin. Will he take the "long summer vacation" she wired him about? Never. Do we miss him? Not much, his hoodlum daughters. But his wistful Paula perhaps, "Carl . . . I hope you will somehow manage to get some rest after the book gets into page proofs . . . Love from us all—and special kisses from each and all. Paula and children." There we are, for the first time on a vacation, now that there is money for it. We all (including Mother) wear skirted bathing suits and rubber bathing caps in the water. Janet and I dog paddle in ring floaters. Margaret, diligent, has taken beginner's swimming lessons and learned the breast stroke. In two weeks we are back in Elmhurst.

At the end of October, another wire goes to her, "LINCOLN BOOK COMMITTED TO THE EVERLASTING DEEP STARTING HOME DEEP LOVE TO YOU AND EVERYBODY CARL." And so that is that. And I am seven years old when the two-volume *Abraham Lincoln: The Prairie Years* is published on Lincoln's Birthday in 1926. The reviewers praise the book and many ask whether he will continue with more volumes and cover the story of Lincoln's Washington and war years. Carl isn't sure, "Whatever I may undertake in the way of a 'sequel' will not start for five years and may be of as different an order that it won't be thought of as a sequel."

Looking at the child Helga through the glass darkly, she is in brilliant sunlight and absorbed in the procession of rabbits and kittens and puppies that come into her days. Her father is loving but her relationship to him is that of a third child. She learns her prose and her habits from the older sibling, Margaret, who spends time with her and is always about and is a committed "bookworm." Helga's commitment is to the animals. There she is with Bimbo, in heaven the two of them, on the grass and the dog lies on a blanket and Helga is dressed as a "nurse" and administers to her patient. She will never forget being photographed on a pony stationed outside the schoolyard. An undying memory. Now Margaret is in a different situation. An early Montessori child, her parents' first, she converses at ease with adults and has none of Helga's ingrained shyness, her leaping under tables and behind doors at the approach of outsiders.

Helga's debt to her sister. The "bookworm," unrestrained by organized education, reads all of Walter Scott, all of Dumas *père,* Chinese and Indian and Japanese and British history, whatever. And she does not read these books aloud to Janet and me. She will lose her audience. She re-tells them, as much as we can handle. She decorates them, as time goes on, illustrating them with our circus toys. D'Artagnan is the ringmaster. Aramis is the hussar. Louise de la Valliere is the lady equestrienne. Or cutting out paper dolls. Here is Quentin Durward, the gallant, and these are his high boots and his cloak to dress him properly. "And now, how do you suppose the Count of Monte Cristo came by his name!" We enact plays. We are Tom Sawyer and Aunt Polly one day. We are Cathy and Heathcliff the next. If the plot is mislaid for the moment, we make it up. We are in the books, living them.

And now another dragon is lurking about to distress Paula. This is a milder one and it concerns Janet. I am in the second grade and am hurling myself into class projects—booklets to be assembled, posters to be colored and then the complicated job of just writing my name or a complete sentence. Janet is a year ahead of me in the third grade. She will be ten in June. At that time, I am promoted to third grade and Janet's promotion to fourth is "on condition." She is going under with *F*'s. Paula is studying out how she will deal with this new treacherous small beast.

Does Janet notice the little dragon? No, nor does Helga. These two are close—two years and five months apart. They go hand in hand. They never argue or shout at each other (this cannot be said of Helga and Margaret, as time moves on!). In the schoolyard or escaping the taunts or tricks of bullies who lie in wait for them on their way home, Helga slings her lunchpail in defense of her sister. They know the same jumprope rhymes to recite at recess. Paula buys them identical dresses, sews their smocks or aprons in the same pattern. Janet has a sweet and slightly stubborn nature. She is not retarded. In another setting, she might have led a different life. But with a father heading straight into fame, her slow development is a more complex problem. Do you see the picture? Paula is standing on the porch and her expression mirrors her concern. She watches her younger daughters in their hand-stitched jumpers squealing with delight as they pedal their tricycles down the walkway. Paula, camera in hand, is photographing laughing Helga in clown suit and shaking the tambourine and pretty Janet, proud in her Brownie outfit and clashing her cymbals together. They are having a wonderful time, while Paula studies it out.

Meanwhile, do not think that Carl is absent from the house more than half the time. When he is home there is always the guitar and the songs. When he is called for supper and descends the stairs, he is humming, singing. The songs are a part of Helga's being and of her sisters'. "Daddy! Supper!" goes the call. A roar replies. And shortly the voice on the stairs, "Everybody works at our house but my old man!" or "Where, oh, where is Old Elijah!" And there is peace. It is a house of peace and love. This is Paula's way. Discord does not exist. She has patience. She rules the decisions on the children. She cares for his income. She set the pattern in the brief time before their marriage and it remains. She does as she pleases about renovation, painting, plantings. He does not demur.

Another happiness in the household. Uncle Ed. The tie between my father and my mother's brother is so close that any story about one includes the other. Uncle Ed is back in the States now with a studio in the Beaux Arts Building in New York. He is Chief of Photography for Condé Nast, who publishes *Vogue* and *Vanity Fair.* He comes to visit and announces that he is pleased because when the question of salary came up, as he was lunching with publisher and editor, he asked a big sum. Nast said it was more than he'd ever paid a photographer. Uncle Ed pointed out that he'd been featured in a recent copy of *Vanity Fair* as "the greatest living portrait photographer." Since his work was to be mainly portraiture of prominent people and since the statement did not come from himself—well, "Nast gave in!"

Uncle Ed likes his work. He photographs Katharine Cornell as Elizabeth Barrett Browning, Lillian Gish as Ophelia, John Barrymore as Hamlet. And there are new photographs that he brings with him now and a new lady is with him, the subject of them. In one striking color portrait there is a gray-eyed, soft-mouthed actress who wears a knitted dress of navy-and-orange. Her auburn hair is loosed from its coil and her arms are crossed as she leans on a Chinese pillow. Before her is a red apple from which she has taken a bite. Dana Desbora Glover met my uncle at the New York School of Photography in 1921 and since then he's been "living with her." So Paula tells Helga.

And the family takes to the new member of our tribe. You see, Paula, with a Phi Beta Kappa key and a Bachelor of Arts degree in Philosophy and with an early interest in the classics and the poets and a lifetime concern with science, has not even the slightest interest in fashion. Our Dana is straight from New York and she is elegant and very fashionable. She has a low laugh, a musical voice and always will fit easily into our household when she comes to visit with Uncle Ed. Occasionally, at Christmases, she will send "fashionable" skiing outfits or sporty clothes. Being midwesterners and living in the countryside, we will not take to them easily. But we do not say that to our Dana.

Meantime there we are in the springtime of 1926 and Paula is handling the little new dragon.

And how does Paula do it? Triumphantly and unconventionally. She has located another summer resort that she fancies, called Tower Hill, with a lake (and a big one, Lake Michigan) and surrounded with grand sand dunes. This is the land where she wants to rear her daughters. Its wildness suits her. And it suits Carl. She removes Helga and Janet in early May of 1926 from their school in Elmhurst and brings them here. She is beginning to accept it that the two girls will be in the third grade together in the coming fall. The promotion "on condition" has not held. Does Janet mind? Not a bit. Does Helga? They have other matters to concern them. Paula has found and plans to purchase a cottage, white and sturdy and on a sandy rise covered with beach grass. Catbirds squall from the underbrush. A brown thrasher is nesting in the woods up behind. Wrens have taken over the eaves; it is called "Wren Cottage." The screened porch where the girls sleep on iron bunk beds faces the lake.

Helga feels her luck at seven years. Against advice, she scratches at the poison ivy itches. There are pricks on her fingers from the sand burrs she removes from the laces of her tennis shoes. Her face burns and her legs too from the sun. The dog, Bimbo, thumps his tail on the sand-gritted floors.

The lake looks like blue honey and the sun glances off it in golden flecks. She has been turned loose into the summertime hot sand.

Carl writes from his travels, "I do a lot of figuring and dreaming about the coming summer in the sand for Us & Co. Carl." And a wire, "ALL GOING WELL BUT WOULD RATHER BE ON THE SANDHILLS WITH YOU AND DEAR ONES."

But the tall dune we dub "Pikes Peak," is there. The daughters roam it, the highest knob around for miles. Up its brushy side in the blaze of sun, they claw their way. And yelling, rolling and sliding, descend the blistering hot sandy face. At its base they hunt arrowheads uncovered by the moving sand, chipped out by the Potawatomi Indians not too long ago. The triangular shapes sometimes have colors of ochre and rose through them. Helga recognizes the three-leaved poison ivy now and has taught Bimbo to remove sand burrs from her socks and laces with his teeth. At night gigantic dark silk moths, their wing spans over six inches sometimes, beat like small soft birds at the screens of the rooms, sometimes making rags of their wings. During the days she follows the butterflies, the swallowtails, mourning cloaks, monarchs that come in clouds in migration time. And the fall-drunken ones clustered upon the fruit rotting in the sun of our farmer neighbor's orchard. And always the dazzling lake. Where the waves wash the shore, among the grains of gravel and sand, are tiny stone-like fossils of ancient crinoids. The girls collect them. Many still have their central holes and can be strung on a thread to make a necklace.

Daddy. He comes and is shown about. Admires the crinoid necklaces and the arrowheads and approves of his daughters' brown skins. He has been busy and Harcourt is happy. He wants to do the songbook. The slips of papers and envelopes with their shorthand song annotations have been emptied from his long pockets and are beginning to form a shape he likes. The Victor Talking Machine Company is putting out a record of some of the songs. On one side he sings "The Boll Weevil" and on the other, an arrangement of spirituals. The odd little record will spread about the world. John Gunther off in Prague, "Dear Carl, A few weeks ago I arrived in Belgrade . . . The first evening there I had dinner with a pleasant young American. . . . He had just received some new phonograph records from America. . . . I listened, and felt profoundly moved. . . . I said, 'My God—it sounds just like old Carl Sandburg!' And by George—it was. Yours ever." The present manuscript has sixty songs. By the time of publication there will be three hundred and five.

Fall. Paula is packed. We pile into the Ford for our return to Elmhurst for the winter. On the way, we stop for towering colorful seven-layered ice cream cones and sing the songs that have been filling the house and others we've learned from him:

Goodbye, I'm on my way to dear old Dublin Bay,
That's why I'm feeling gay,
O, my sweet Molly, olly, olly, olly, oll!
My Colleen's fair to see,
She's waiting there for me,
Her heart with love a-bubbling . . .

School again. Helga and Janet are plunging along, both in third grade, but in different classrooms with different teachers. A stopgap move. Although Paula signs all the report cards firmly, "Mrs. Carl Sandburg," she asks him once during a year to put his signature on them. He is the father.

May 1927. Lindy has landed at Le Bourget airfield outside Paris. Henry Ford introduces the Model A and the Model

T is in the past now. Paula, true to herself, plucks Helga and Janet from school before the term is out and returns them to their duneland paradise. She is beginning to think of staying at the lake forever. The Lincoln windfall money is hers to use. When does she speak of her plan to Carl? He is dashing off to New York again for "three or four weeks closing up my songbag," he writes a friend.

Summertime. The book is in its last birth throes. There are four musicians and arrangers, three men and a woman, to whom Carl makes special acknowledgments. The woman, Hazel Felman, is a family friend along with her husband, Dr. Jake Buchbinder. One of the letters that go to her from Wren Cottage, "Dear Hazel—The Chronicle in the day's log is that two songs are lost. We know the hour they were here, Sunday 3.30 p.m., God's time. And we know they are gone. And only one other thing we know; we have searched every goddam corner into which they could have crawled or fallen. It is what the Insurance Policies call An Act of God. The two are, first, that fine music box stunt CUCKOO WALTZ, and second, OLD BRASS WAGON. Do you happen to have copies? If you could send them they would be copied and returned on day of receipt. If you don't have copies please weep with all others concerned. There is a malignant and dark Personal Devil hanging around and operating. Yours cursing—Carl." The songs come.

He is working full-time in the cottage now. Letters go out in the summertime blaze of sun, "Sometimes I think the reason that kind of book has not been done before is because so many tackle it and die on the job." And suddenly, early in that hot July, Carl has what Paula, talking to me, Helga, later in life, calls an "episode." At the time, she believed it might have been an epileptic seizure and that a new malevolent dragon might have hovered over Wren Cottage. It was, however, never to be seen near Carl again.

But at the time the book comes to a standstill. The daughters are warned to do their shouting out in the dunes. They are impressed. Carl is taking it easy, "I have run on high too much and am under strict orders to double my sleep and be a lazy bum." Paula calls in a local carpenter who speedily puts together under her direction a small gray-shingled one-room cabin for Carl's use. It is a hundred yards from Wren Cottage with a chimney and wood stove for cool weather. She sets up army cots and brings in chairs and a table or two for work and his tray of food. A large flat stone is the doorstep. A plank walkway leads from the cottage where Paula or some helping secretary can come and go, bringing him what he wants when he wants it. He names the cabin "The Shanty" or "The Shack" or "The Studio."

Carl invites friends out from Chicago "to make the run out here." He challenges them to a Horseshoe Tournament. And there are swim suits and cots to sleep on and "a big hardwood Liar's Log where you are invited to tell tall ones." And he adds, "I am under orders to shun work, to play and be irresponsible as the birds, the bees, and the bums." He works a little. He is lonely for adult companionship.

Walks with her father. These are a pattern of his life. Helga (along with anyone else in the family that is about and wants to go) follows his footsteps on the trails that he always finds wherever we live. He carries the flashlight, swinging it in his hand to help those following. In falling snow. In wildly blowing warm wind. In lightning preparing for a storm. In summertime twilight chatter of frogs and katydids. In the brilliant greenish-colored air after the sun has set in its splendid wound in the west over the lake. In the mourning of foghorns up the distant shore. Under a piece of a moon in a high haze. Sometimes we sing as we walk. And he talks, his voice rising and falling in its particular cadence.

And he is funny too. He tells tall tales and extends a "joke" as long as possible, milking the punch line.

And then a bit of education. Paula was a star elocution pupil when a child and she and a schoolmate were sent about to the lower grades in the Sixth Ward in Milwaukee to declaim lengthy poems for the edification of younger aspirants. My father had been involved in elocution too, since his college classes, since the time when he rose as a young man, stuttering, to address small audiences of Wisconsin Social Democrats and let them wait till he got it right. And so, education. "Green and blue eggs?" asks my mother when I use "lay" for "lie." And, "Enunciate!" storms my father, "Ga-rahge, not g'rage! Put a pebble on your tongue and go down to the shore like Demosthenes!" He hunts up tomes he's picked up in his travels and presents them to me. "Read these. They're in your department." *The Life of the Earthworm* (Fabre), *The Insect and Spider Book,* and so on. And again reading at the table endlessly, playing his words and those of others against the vulnerable minds of my sisters and myself.

The family gathers by a beach fire when his horseshoe companions arrive. It is night. Earlier everyone went swimming in the sunset glowing waters. And there was a mile hike up the shore. The moon is lifting itself through the branches of the pines on the dunes behind us. Carl has brought the guitar and Helga's face glows. She is close by his side and she sings clear and loud. Her key is correct and she is aware of it. Margaret knows all the words in case anyone forgets. And Janet is as tone-deaf as Paula, although she sings along unaware. Paula never joins in, but her serene smile is there. She likes the family together. And she has favorite songs.

"I had a true love but she left me,
Oh, oh, oh, oh,

And I now am broken-hearted,
Oh, oh, oh, oh."
"Well, if she's gone I wouldn't mind her, . . .
You'll soon find one that'll prove much kinder,
Fol de rol de hey ding day."

September. Carl writes Harcourt, "I have been sleeping an average of nine hours a night for six weeks and broke training last night for the first time to see the fight [Tunney-Dempsey!]; I gained in weight; I cut out all meats, liquor, pastries; have handled an ax an hour a day . . . and have laid around lazy whenever I felt like it. Now I believe I can make the grade on the Songbag." And he was gone. All the family took a deep breath. We could shout again!

Paula. True to herself, she enrolls Helga and Janet in a school in Three Oaks, a nearby town. Helga will be nine in November and Janet was eleven the past June. Margaret, just sixteen, is about to make a stab at formal education. Paula is trying her out at a Catholic school—Nazareth Academy in La Grange, Illinois. Margaret likes the girls at school, but misses home. "I thought you said you would surprise me by coming out one of these days, Daddy," she writes. And, "Why don't Janet and Helga write to me?" And she signs herself from the Rootabaga tales, "Peter Potato Blossom Wishes."

The first copies of *The American Songbag* arrive. Carl writes in Margaret's, ". . . for fun or for grief there is nothing like singing . . ." In Janet's, ". . . sing! girl, sing! . . ." In mine, ". . . may you be a thrush, a mockingbird—is the wish of your everloving Father." And again, just generally in one volume, "For My Daughters—may you all sing long as you live—Daddy."

And a note goes to him from our house, "I was so glad to hear yow were coming home. I didn't know yow were coming at first. With very Loving love and 2,000 bushels of kisses, 20 hugs and a hello! from Helga."

Something important is happening in our lives. A move. And all because of the dividend from the Lincoln book. The Songbag and the poetry sell. But the Lincoln is a meal ticket. My mother (as we know, Carl will go along with whatever she decides) is purchasing a five-acre lot a few miles down the shore from Tower Hill. Carl will name it "Paw Paw Patch" after a while. Paula is drawing the plans and studies them with satisfaction. The family views her with awe and acceptance. Her vigor shines in her eyes and as she stands out in the February winds, her gray hair glistens and curls. She is beautiful.

The local carpenter keeps a record of his time in a small notebook in his vestpocket. He carries the beams himself as the structure rises. Later a neighbor says it looks like a Swedish hotel. There are three stories, the top one split into Carl's bedroom and a work room with a small black woodstove which he will stoke with driftwood gathered on his walks and with twisted newspapers. A tin pipe zigzags up from it into a flue. There are a multitude of windows (Carl has written, "I was foolish about windows . . . I was hungry for windows . . ."). Wherever there is an empty wall, bookshelves are nailed in. They hold up the house. Paula orders linoleum put on the floors so the dogs can run in and out freely. A fireproof concrete-and-steel vault is dug in under the terrace of the house and lined with bookshelves. Helga is put in charge of remembering the combination when by mistake, the double-steel door (the outer one thick and with a turntable lock and a massive handle) gets locked. And on the top of the house is a deck where Carl, the sun-lover, can work. He writes a friend that he plans to protect himself "from the disease called civilization—amid the sandhills of Michigan."

My father is fifty. After the summertime Songbag illness scare, he is careful. Both Paula and he know that he was working too intensely. They want him back in "baseball trim." The two, Paula and Carl, take long beach walks, with daughters and dogs tagging along. A friend, Fred Black from the Ford Motor Company in Dearborn, offers a diversion. He wants to take Carl up in a "Ford three-motor ship." He is referring to an airplane and my father goes. We hear about it, but somehow there is no question of any of us participating in the event. We don't even think of it.

Mother is forty-five. Janet. She studies on it. Why not try some special education? Margaret is doing splendidly at Nazareth Academy, although this eldest daughter writes that she is homesick and also, ". . . tell Janet and Helga that I won't write ever to them because they don't write me." My sister is ashamed of us, she says. But Janet. The move to the new home is approaching. Janet has her own rate of development which differs from mine and it continues to bother Paula.

There is a special private institution in Berwyn, Pennsylvania—Devereux School, where perhaps Janet will be happy. They consent at $1,000 a year. She will begin there in April. The doctor who suggests the school advises that while he knows that separation is hard on a mother, he still thinks a child's interests are best served by offering special training. He doesn't know my sister. Or our mother.

School stationery is ordered for Janet. The required linen napkins have labels sewed into the corners. The silver napkin ring and knife and fork and spoon are engraved. And then this middle daughter is packed and on her way with Paula. They stop off to say hello to Carl, who sits at his third-floor corner of the Chicago *Daily News* building, wearing his green visor against the light. He is busy and will not be home for a while, but he writes a letter about the visit. "Dearest Paula—. . . your face was lovely—and Janet was superb. She is your Work of Art; you've done some of the modeling!" And he adds that he's had an invitation to sail on Lake Erie with a friend and also that a new Model A Ford of "Arabian-sand" color will be coming to grace Paw Paw Patch shortly. And he has a little book with him that he will bring along for his youngest. It is all about the true Mary of the story and is published by Mr. and Mrs. Henry Ford.

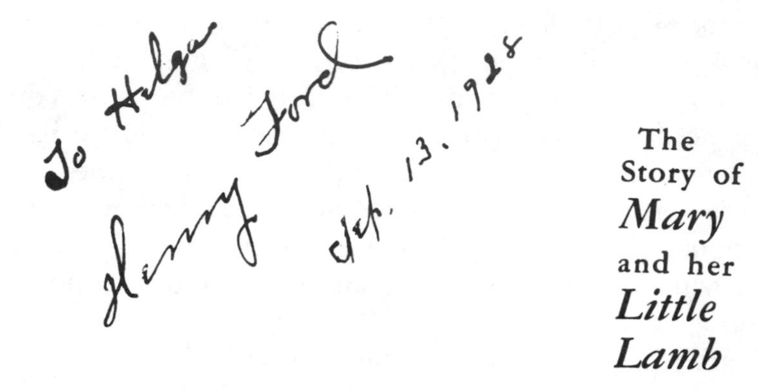
To Helga
Henry Ford
Sept. 13. 1928

The Story of *Mary* and her *Little Lamb*

Bosco. He is the family's new dog, to replace Bimbo, who was run over by a car in an Elmhurst street. He comes along in the move to Paw Paw Patch. It is the first of May 1928. Carl has a new book of poetry in manuscript. *Good Morning, America.* He advises Harcourt that he is under pressure because of the move, "I am taking along all of my books, notes, manuscripts and this means not merely hours but days; a nine years accumulation has to be handled." And a letter turns up during his packing. One he had not sent and he decides to do so now. It is to Helen Keller in praise.

She responds, ". . . Many and many a time, when you least

suspected it, your spirit has spoken to mine in a kindred language, and lo! the silent dark about me shone with the light of your mind. . . . last winter I discovered that some angel had transcribed a number of your poems into Braille. How eagerly my hands lingered over the pages, only wishing that there were more of them to caress and absorb. This is no metaphor; for I literally absorb the poets I love . . ."

And he, "I tried to read your letter out loud to my family and some friends at dinner one evening in my home. As I got into the last three paragraphs of your letter I knew all of a sudden that if I went on reading it I would be crying, and knowing this, I stopped reading and said, 'I won't read the rest of the letter. You can read it for yourselves if you want to'. . . ."

Helen Keller had a handicap of sorts. Does Janet? Our sunny girl who in time will become a sunny woman? Not so. But now her mind is on home and family and she does not like Devereux. She is homesick and Paula will go there and bring her where she belongs. And that is that.

Margaret hones in the same way for the peace and love that makes up our household and is unique to it. "Dearest Helga, I was so glad when I received your letter. . . . because I knew that you remembered me, and remembered that I said I wanted a letter from at least one of my two sisters . . ." Early June and she writes me the good news, "Aren't you happy now? Janet is coming home next week and I am the week after."

As for her youngest daughter, Paula, in her wonderful quiet way, lets Helga out of school early that spring, without being promoted to fifth grade. The next fall she will find a tutor for Janet, who will promptly go into fifth, while Helga, bless her, will remain with the same teacher and a new set of faces in the fourth. And that is that.

Carl. It is June 1928. He is setting out for Harvard, Harcourts and Uncle Ed's. Does Paula go along? No. Her days are busy. She seems to have little need for close personal friends. Her way of life suits her. At this time, she is supervising the planting of cedars and poplars along the duneside to hold down the eroding movement of the sand. There she is, as soon as she's put him on the train, under the June sky, directing the hired hand as to where she wants the saplings set. Her face wears a tranquil absorbed look. She spends her evenings consulting catalogs of tree farms and nurseries. She receives shipments of seedlings, cuttings, transplants. She knows just what to do with them.

My father has never planted a tree. He is reading his poem "Good Morning, America" in Cambridge before the Phi Beta Kappa Chapter of Harvard University. It is a murky Friday afternoon. The poem is the lead and title one in the book Harcourt is putting out in three months. It takes up twenty-five pages and he will be made an honorary member of the society. We all know because he has mentioned it often at the supper table that our mother *earned* her key in 1903 when she was twenty years old.

Good morning, America.
Good morning, Mr. Who, Which, What.
Good morning, let's all of us tell our real names.
Good morning, Mr. Somebody, Nobody, Any-
body-who-is-Anybody-at-all.
Good morning, Worms in the Dust, Eagles
in the Air, Climbers to the Top of the Sky. . . .

And he is on his way to New York and Harcourts where the book will soon be put to bed at the printers. Then Carl will head out to his "brother's." Uncle Ed is making so much money at his new position with Nast that he, like his sister, has purchased a piece of land. Carl will look it over and give a first-hand report to Paula. And get the news.

The latest happening with Edward Steichen has to do with a Brancusi sculpture called *Bird In Space.* It is tall, slim, bronze, abstract and famous. On leaving Voulangis, my uncle had brought it into the States. The customs people refused it duty-free entry as a "Work of Art." After much hassling, they let it in under the heading "Kitchen Utensils and Hospital Supplies" and asked $600 duty, estimating that as forty percent of its value. Uncle Ed paid. But when he mentioned the incident at a party before Mrs. Harry Payne Whitney, she said that if he would let her, she would like her lawyers to take the case over. And they did."*Brancusi* vs. *the United States*." Museum directors and critics and artists were there when the case came up. It was decided that it was not in the province of the government to define Art. The opinion of recognized art authorities would rule. The $600 was returned to Uncle Ed.

He is in high spirits. And he and Dana and their new Irish wolfhound puppy, Fingal, escort Carl on a walk about the new place. Uncle Ed calls it "Umpawaug." There he will put two acres into flowers. There he will dam for a lake. Like his sister's, his fingernails are rimmed with soil. Out under the June sky, he directs the hired man who sets up a block of young delphinium plants while he marks the stakes. He sees the dream, the long rows of spikes of varied shadings from white through purple. Hummingbirds will swoop and dive about the perfume! He will even name one variety, an early five-foot sky-blue one "Carl Sandburg." The Umpawaug Plant Breeding Farm is to Uncle Ed what Paw Paw Patch is to Paula.

Summertime and my uncle, on his way somewhere, stops by to inspect our Paw Paw Patch, heaven come true. The sun blazes. We gather to descend the long beach stairs to the sands below, all in swim suits except Uncle Ed, who disdains water, and Mother, who has her camera along and wants to record this rare day with her brother. Bosco leads the way, dashing ahead, barking. In the same way that I always have my hand upon Bosco or any of our dogs to tame them to my command, I do this with Uncle Ed, my hand upon him, possessive, my voice in his ear, when he comes on his rare visits. Kneeling against him, seeing to it that I am the one next to him in the picture. And then he, the photographer and director, advises all to scramble down onto the sand on our stomachs, lining up for Mother. There they are—Helga, Uncle Ed, Bosco, Carl, Janet—tongues out panting and our paws, along with Bosco's, before us in the warm sand. Will we forget the day? No, for there are Mother's pictures. My Uncle approves of Paw Paw Patch.

Fall. November and north winds blowing straight from the North Pole. An event. Is Carl there? No. It is the twenty-seventh of the month and Helga is spending the night, as she does sometimes, in his attic bed. Nobody minds. She likes the smell there. And the isolation from the household. The difference. Binoculars and a flashlight are under the pillow and her coat is on the chair. In the small hour of the morning, Mother rouses her and the family assembles outside on the deck. We are level with the treetops and the dome of the sky is clear. We have already learned up there the beautiful star names and have seen them. Aldebaran, Antares, Vega, the bright Capella. And the constellations. Pegasus, Orion, Sagittarius, Ursa Major and Minor. All pointed out by Paula. The lunar eclipse begins at two-thirty and ends an hour later. Before the year is out Paula, stirred by the event, buys a second-hand two-inch telescope to help the eye sightings. Helga keeps a small notebook of comments on the wonders. Later, down in her father's bed, she listens to the shuddering of pines outside, the lap of waves, the creak of house-boards. The moonlight is flooding over the dunes.

Before long, the *Graf Zeppelin* comes by on its round-the-world trip from Germany with its twenty passengers. It floats over the lake and we climb along the slanted shingled roof of the house to watch. After that, Paula gets her local carpenter back again and has a crow's nest installed with stairs leading up and benches and a table. We are not caught unaware again.

And winter. Our first at Paw Paw Patch. We have toboggans and skis now and race up and down the hills. Carl, is he out there with us? No. That is not his role. He is committed to his work and is absorbed by it. We are a part of it in the sense that he reads to us at the table at night and we know what he is about. Paula does, bless her. It is his fifty-first birthday in 1929 and he writes, "I have been toiling on Lincoln and have actually got his feet planted in Washington . . ." He speaks of how he is off for a long lecturing tour west. After that, "from the first of May and then on for six months or more," he will be at home at work where by now he has "a mammoth Civil War and Lincoln library."

While he is gone, letters come to Paula. And packages of more of the serapes and Mexican glass and books. She sends a wire that they arrive and "HELGA WROTE CARE SACRAMENTO . . . CARDINALS SO TAME THEY FEED ON SHELF OUTSIDE DINING PORCH WINDOW ALL HAPPY AND WELL LOVE PAULA. And he reports, ". . . have been riding on the desert, watching Charlie Chaplin work and play, and rustling through old book shops." She? Restless, lonely, sending always a love note, "Dearest—all well here and looking for your return. Every day a box arrives—or a package. Now we are counting the days until *You* arrive. None of your trips ever seemed so long as this one. Love & love from all of us—and wishes for your safe return home to the Paw paws and the Blow and the White Horses. Paula."

Is Helga lonely the way she is? No. Her life is filled. There are woods about where creatures roam and fly. She sends her own reports on the crow and "mr. Mathosala, that turtle" and "We are having a very nice time out here and I wish yow were here. Lovingly."

For reasons lost in the dim of time, Carl has given his youngest a nickname during this time that sticks throughout their lives.

ATLANTA BILTMORE
ATLANTA, GA.

April 15, 1929

Dear Swipes—
My heart is glad to have
your letter. And the news
about turtles and crows makes
me homesick. Love to your
beautiful mother, your sweet
sisters, and your angel-faced
self— Daddy

It is a unique bond—father and daughter. How can I speak of it? His endearing loving way. The tyranny of the head of the household. I, this girl Helga, seen through the glass there in the sunlight, seeks, like Cordelia, to please, to love. It is a mystical bond. And he praises her. It is his way in the household. Praise is power. "Take a poem and memorize it, Swipes. Then when there are guests, you can stand up there and do something."

> *This I beheld or dreamed it in a dream*
> *There came a cloud of dust upon a plain*
> *And underneath the cloud or in it . . .* and so on

Shy but determined, she remembers and, "My girl, Helga, has learned a poem . . ." and so on. At any length, it is paradise.

Letters go to the traveler in care of his publisher, "It is very lonesome here without yow. I can hardly wait for the eighth of March when yow will come back. It's so nice to hear the crows cawing again. It seems like summer. I wish yow were here to take nice walks with me. I send yow many many kisses and a nice big hug. Helga."

And of course the anger. In the family, Carl is noted for his amazing temper. Ripping his shirt. Smashing a chair. Inanimate objects in the wrong place or behaving incorrectly, infuriate him. He never strikes a child or wife or dog. A male in a house of females. Take this evening scene. Helga has neglected to polish his shoes, a chore that is hers. Roaring. Tears. Loud sounds. In her bedroom, she casts herself upon the sheets. She is dismayed and unloved and her life is over. In the morning there is an envelope at the bedside with her name in her father's clear hand, "Dearest Helga,

Please forget it—then I won't need to be forgiven. With love, Daddy." And there you are. She is back and smitten with adoration again.

The household is aware that we cherish him also because he is our breadwinner. Paula tells him so repeatedly. All of us are everlastingly grateful for Paw Paw Patch! She writes him off on that long western trip, ". . . I'm thanking our lucky stars and You that we can be in this lovely Winter Playground! Love and love to my Dearest, Paula."

Bosco is run over (it is not too hard, for we have two of his sons now, as our dog family increases) and when Paula reports on it to Carl, she says that Helga is crying and will not stop and all because her daddy will be unhappy over the loss. I write him too. And Carl's reply to Paula ends, "It's good we have Bosco's sons. Tell Sweet Helga I'm guilty & know it, not answering her *gorgeous* letter . . ."

Why it happens is perhaps inexplicable but the tie between my father and myself is powerful and everlasting. As the woman here in the moonlight looking back at that time and with him gone now, I think we are all pilgrims. I would not change any event involving sorrow, fury or delight during my life with him.

He advises me as a child on my coming days. "It is better to be wildly, exquisitely, unhappy, Swipes, than to be just plain ordinary happy-happy. Stay away from the little deaths."

Into the summertime of those days come arrivals. Some are dogs—a collie is presented to Helga by one of Carl's horseshoe-pitching Chicago friends. And then Martha, twenty-nine, with soft brown hair and glowing smile, a Quaker, arriving in July of 1930. The stock market has crashed and she comes with a suitcase and a few dollars in her pocket and she will stay. My father's eccentric feelings about noise and cleaning, the raft of dogs, the size of the house not to mention the wash, have caused others to throw up their hands. She wears a hat and gloves and knocks on the door. The pay is fifteen dollars a week and another three if she will do the extra big wash. But of course. She will stay, a part of the household, for over a decade.

Carl, returning from travel, finds Martha breaking beans in the kitchen, shakes her hand, hopes she will stay. Later he will say he could never have finished the Lincoln job if she hadn't been there, not minding his yelling, doing his shirts up properly, fixing plain proper food. Paula is forty-eight and gets on with Martha from the start. Helga at eleven, at last has someone to tell her the secrets (Paula has higher ambitions for her daughters) of how to sort clothes to wash, the running of the machine and the wringer, the proper hanging of sheets, the way to iron a man's shirts, the value of a hope chest, the importance of avoiding parked cars in which couples are sitting because men can be dangerous at those times. Also about the betrayal possible from that temperamental sex.

The new collie has been wandering and we have a son of his now too. The dog tribe waxes and wanes in numbers. Carl is presented with two young red Irish setters he calls Dan and Cullie. They go up into his study on the third floor and lie about there. And when he comes down in the evenings, singing on the stairs, he is preceded by their wild delighted barking. Carl spends time on walks with them and they learn quickly to retrieve the sticks he throws.

Through the window there in the sunlight of long ago, Helga is absorbed in her imagination. She is Tarzan (not Jane) and Jack (the collie's son), Dan, Cullie, and the rest of the dogs are lions pacing at her side. Trotting through the woods again, she is Mowgli and they are Akela's clan of wolves hunting Shere Khan. She will join a circus and all the dogs now shake hands, roll over, jump through hoops, sit on pedestals or stand on tree branches. She has read *Under Two Flags,* and becomes Cigarette and the sled she rides down the hill is a dark horse and she is dying for a principle. She has hitched the dogs in a tandem team. They haul the toboggan over the ice floes of Lake Michigan which is Jack London's frozen north and she is John Thornton. Jack is Buck.

There now are guinea pigs, mice, and piebald and white rats in various pens and cages about the cellar and garage. Helga prowls through the jungle with Davy, his rat coat sleek, his long pink tail hanging down, his whiskers resting on her neck. He is a mongoose—Rikki-Tikki-Tavi in Kipling's *The Jungle Book,* and has just killed the cobra, Nag. And there are captured creatures of the wild who have come to investigate the premises. A raccoon, a pair of possums, a nest of baby rabbits, a few turtles, a hawk with a broken wing, a young crow.

Paw Paw Patch is isolated in the wintertime. In the summers, vacationers come out from Chicago. Helga, surrounded by the untamed duneland, grows introspective through solitude. Her time is not monitored by father or mother as she passes through her childhood. Picture her also with her head often in a book. She gets what she pleases from the local library or the shelves of the house. Dreiser's *Sister Carrie* (Dreiser had tried to get *Chicago Poems* published very early on) is here (published in 1900, Carl's copy) and *Plutarch's Lives* and *The Girl of the Limberlost* (Margaret's). From the library comes *The Sheik* and *Bongo: The Jungle Boy.* The last two she reads (and others like them) when her father is away. If he is about and enters her bedroom suddenly, unannounced, to say goodnight, and they are revealed, they may become damaged as they fly across the room. "Your mind's too fine, girl, to clutter it up with trash! Life is too short for this damn tripe!" She has evolved circumventions. The flashlight for reading under the covers. The placing of the offending volume within the covers of an accepted one. So there.

Carl is away. An occasional honor, a degree of Doctor of Letters somewhere. And if he is home, all are aware of the work in progress, the long Lincoln (four volumes) under way. Helga hears the footsteps in his bedroom above hers in the night. Smells the cigar smoke drifting from the open windows. Hears the rumble of the Underwood. She avoids open confrontation when he comes roaring in the afternoons to the top of the stairs, where below the women are cooking, cleaning, waiting on the sick, quieting the pack of dogs, "Can't a feller once in a while get a little peace and quiet!" And stamping on his workroom floor, "Yah! Yah! Yah! Keep on hollering down there!"

He reads in the evenings at the meal, not necessarily from his current work. One time it is the translation of *The Trial of Jeanne d'Arc.* In the summertimes, when the children of vacationers are sporting out there, Helga watches and waits for the proper moment when a phrase is finished, a paper put aside, a reference examined, to beg to be excused (along with Janet, her right hand) so they can dash off to play a game of Murder in the old ice-house or Run-Sheep-Run or One Old Cat down at the beach where the sun is beautifully sinking. "I am losing half my audience," he says, raising his eyebrows as we flee.

Paula, at this time, is preoccupied, writing him, away, about Margaret, "Her general condition is fine—more alive than ever—but attacks every other night." And those two are off to Rochester and the Mayo doctors again for a two-week try at a new diet that may control the dark dragon. Martha will take care of the mail, of sending pajamas and shirts to "Mr. Sandburg" when his wire arrives asking for them. She reports, "I have two lovely little girls & we are a happy little family, the doggies are fine . . . So good nite. Love, Martha."

A fourteen-page letter goes to Carl about coping with the dragon there in Rochester, about the seizures, the ketogenic diet, the bromide intoxication, the hallucinations ("little pink epilepsies swimming in blood on the ceiling" . . . rats, snakes, more), the sleep following, and finally of Paula's undiminished hope. And love, "No one but you can put so much love and solace in a few words . . . Dearest. . . . We send you as always bushels and bushels of love. Paula."

Carl. There he is in the blaze of Coral Gables' Florida February sunlight, his mind sometimes on the two up north. And on money. The provider. He is just getting word from his boss at the *Daily News* that his $50 a week will be cut to $37.50, an " 'economy measure' ordered by Col. Knox." There is a secretary and a familiar desk at the *News.* But because of the book in progress and time on it needed, he quits, writing Harcourt, "I'd rather have the book done by 1935 or 1936 than by 1937 or 1938." It will take him till 1939.

Trouble compounds. It is now 1932. The twelfth of September. Our Janet is sixteen and has just started her freshman year in high school. She sees her tutor daily. I am nearly fourteen and a year behind Janet, where Mother likes me to be. The town postmaster is driving on his way home past our Three Oaks School yard. At the same time, Janet remembers that she has left her lunch pail behind and dashes back for it. She is knocked down in the street and is unconscious in a heap, blood at her head. She is carried to a doctor's house a block away. Mother arrives. Our Chicago friend, Dr. Jake Buchbinder, is called and advises that Janet be taken to our home and kept quiet. Her skull must knit and she will recover. An ambulance brings her to Paw Paw Patch.

Paula worries. Janet improves. The doctor is urged to let her return to school soon. She can go to her tutor's house across the street and lie down when she wishes. One month after the accident, she is back in school. It doesn't work. Continual headaches. She will stay at home awhile. The dilemma again. And so in the next fall, Janet is enrolled in still another school, New Troy, as a freshman. Finally, when all is said and done, Helga and Janet are happily in the same school. Janet is a year behind Helga which bothers no one but Paula. Eventually Janet will graduate in May of 1938, sorry to leave school life. Carl writes in one of his books to her, "For my proud, whimsical, shy daughter Janet."

The dark year of 1932 at last ends for the family. It is a gloomy one for others. Lindy's baby boy is kidnapped. A popular hit is "Brother, Can You Spare a Dime?" Hitler is soon appointed chancellor of Germany. Carl writes Harcourt, "I am still rumbling along, working every day, troubled by the matter of scale and proportion, the balances of the book. . . . I'll be 55 in three more days and I doubt whether I'll live to be another number divisible by 11."

Part Two

THE TOM THUMB DAIRY

TIME GOES on. It is spring of 1935. I, Helga, am sixteen. My mother is fifty-two. From here, in the moonlight, I wonder what jostled Paula then into wanting land. Perhaps she feels she has done all she can for her daughters. Janet is nearly nineteen, Margaret nearly twenty-four. A feeling for the earth stirs in my beautiful mother's blood.

What does she do but buy up the piece of land adjacent to Paw Paw Patch on the inland side of our dune. She is going to dig up the sand and order a truckload of manure and fence in the place and make a garden prosper! Helga is finished with play and make-believe. This is reality. She hurls herself into the project at Paula's side.

It is a breathless spring. At the nearby feed store, they buy packets of seed. The rows are laid out with stakes and string. Paula makes blueprints—here the rows of vegetables, here the *x*'s where each apple, peach, apricot, plum, cherry, nectarine, will put down roots. There will be Kieffer, Anjou, Bartlett, Lincoln, Shelden, Seckel pears. And McIntosh, Jonathan, Grimes Golden and Fall Pippin apples. And Moorpark and Superb apricots. And Red Roman and Boston nectarines. And Great Yellow and Burbank Elephant Heart and Italian Prune and Greengage plums. And Burbank Black Giant and Windsor Sweet cherries, and Montmorency Sour cherries. And Golden Jubilee and Red Bird Cling and Early Elberta and Hale Haven and Belle of Georgia peaches. The grape posts will stand here and their wires be strung for the Delaware, Catawba, Niagara and Concord vines. And when the small orchard blooms in white and pink in a tremor of rain, Paula stands at the gate and gazes and we feel her passion move.

She has called the carpenter back. He puts up an eight-by-twelve tool shed. We have a hand cultivator with a big wheel now and an interchangeable plow blade, marker and harrow.

It is a small paradise. Helga is dizzy with glory. Summer arrives. And six giant gray Toulouse geese. And Peking ducks. And a flock of White Rock pullets. An addition is built onto the shed. Rabbits are next—New Zealand Whites. Paula and Helga become proficient at the swift kill and the skinning, plucking and eviscerating of whatever is for the table.

And while the adolescent girl goes about cleaning the hutches and the roosts, while she moves behind the cultivator up and down the rows and picks the crops, an idea begins to flicker. Martha is approached and agrees. Helga wants her hands on the warm smooth soft hair of a huge creature. She wants to feel the rubbery nose, to smell the sweet breath, to hear the low voice. She has a heavy maternal desire for a Jersey cow.

Paula listens. The plea is longwinded and earnest. Paula will be the advocate. And Carl? "No. A cow's expensive. How about a goat? What's the girl going to do when the cow's got to be bred? Lead her down back roads for ten miles? A goat can be put in the back of the flivver."

Me, I yearn to lead a Jersey cow down long hot back roads. But Mother and I get out the paper and look up ads. We set out. Would the life of the family have changed in the way it did if the two hadn't happened onto a rambling place on a hillside with a clean barn and a handsome lot of dairy goats standing quietly about? Paula asks to taste the milk. The lady of the house goes to the kitchen for a cup and a small pail and places a white linen napkin over the latter. She leads a doe into a small room where it leaps onto a milking stand, puts its head through the stanchion and munches its cud while being milked. My mother pronounces the milk nectar. We return with three does—Leona, Sophie and Felicia.

Helga is in heaven. Her Jersey cow concept has tripled. The does are bedded down in the tool shed that night and

Paula sits at her desk and draws up a small blueprint to convert the tool shed into "The Tom Thumb Dairy," with six stalls. We are returning to the little hillside farm to bring back additions.

It is September of 1935. Carl writes Harcourt a report. "At home it is the nicest allround summer the gang has had at this place. Paula and Helga are lit up and tireless. . . . Over 200 quarts of string beans, corn, spinach and broccoli are put up and in the cellar, and perhaps a peck of dry lima beans, more to come. For a month and more we have had cantaloupe unlimited and the end not in sight. Of squash and pumpkin there will be enough for many weeks after frost, besides parsnips for February and March. A pig will come next, they tell me." And then, "The farm here progresses beyond words. The most colossal barn in the great state of Michigan, a regular Old Testament edifice is under construction. It will hold when completed more goats, kids and revolutionary pamphlets than any other barn in Michigan."

It is a dusky morning of that same summer. The pink shadows of dawn have not yet shown themselves. Helga slips from her bed to dress. Although hushing her footsteps descending the stairs, secretive, she is caught. Carl and Paula are still talking together in the dining room. He is back from a journey. Their time clocks differ from mine. They are at home in the night. The dawn is my hour. My mother has mending before her, one of his sweaters, or a farm catalog she has been leafing through. Dishes are still about—coffee cups and plates. Strewn among them are manuscripts and a Swedish newspaper, *Svenska Dagbladet,* and the crudely formed dice that my father always makes absently at table. He presses little pieces of the pumpernickel rye bread that he pulls from the leftover loaf on the table. He uses a fork tine to mark in the dots. They are talking of FDR, of the latest dog fight, of his lecture trip, of Margaret, of Paula's ideas for the place, which he accepts with admiration. And he reads aloud and she attends.

I am called in. "What in the world? And at this hour!" Although they admire my passion, I am commanded back to my room. Never mind. Soon they will ascend the stairs to lie together in their room. It is when he works late in his attic quarters that he sleeps alone up there. I am wide awake and listening. When sounds cease, I am off on tiptoe, letting myself out to the crisp stars which bloom like little moons at this marvelous hour.

Nubile, Helga is filled with tender feelings. The dolls are long since gone (though still missed). But they did not depend on me. I am on the path to the barn. The wind rises. I am restless. There is a need for caring that overflows toward what awaits me. Into the air comes a low call from the Tom Thumb Dairy stable. Helga is wanted!

All the while that Paula's handsome barn is being completed, Carl is finishing a long poem that has grasped him by the roots and shaken him so that the Lincoln is put aside for a while. It is his sixth book of poetry. Current events have stirred him. The whole book is one poem.

The world is in turmoil. War drums are sounding and maps are changing. *Der Führer* is in control and his troops are reoccupying the Rhineland. Himmler has taken over the Gestapo. *Fascisti* are provoking the Spanish Civil War. Mussolini has seized and annexed Ethiopia. FDR came to power in the last days of 1932 and now, 1935, Carl praises the president, ". . . you are the best light of democracy that has occupied the White House since Lincoln. . . . may the cunning of your right hand increase. More power to you." And Roosevelt responds, "Your letter has at last reached my desk and I am indeed grateful to you. I have long wanted to talk with you about Lincoln . . . so if at any time you are coming to Washington I hope you will let me know beforehand and come in to see me. . . ."

The new book is *The People, Yes.* As my father says, it takes four hours to read aloud. He defends himself against certain of the Horseshoe Tournament companions who are Republicans, "If I had a purpose to rouse and inflame the masses of people against the small fraction of the population who own control of the large industries, I would employ the methods of an agitator and frame appeals and shape issues and coin slogans. Only time will tell whether what I have put down has the element of true history and valid memoranda. . . . True democracy is as difficult and as mystic in its operations as true religion or true art. . . . I belong to no political party and have not for 24 years. . . ."

Carl likes to stand alone. The Academy of American Poets at this time asks to use his name as a sponsor. And, "You may be sure that it is wise to keep my name off the list of sponsors of the Academy. When you see my next book of verse . . ." And, "My books bother some people, and in my staying out of organizations and committees, life is made more convenient for some people." So there.

It is February of 1936. And while Carl is defending his lone position, his wife and daughters are at the barn, seeing to the delivering of the first baby goats. Not one of the daughters of the house has ever seen a birthing. We have very vague ideas about intercourse between animals or humans. The same goes for the birthing process. Even our kittens are born by the cats in secret. This is an event. One of the family is having a baby and we are determined that it shall not happen unattended! Paula writes Carl, who is visiting Uncle Ed, and he responds, "Went to a German restaurant with Ed and Dana before train. We read your letter out loud and the time and the moon and all had a miracle touch as to the new arrivals. Ed . . . gets all the big main slants of the new adventuring, sees Helga and Janet and Margaret joined in something they were lucky to happen on. Deep love to you."

By mid-March Helga has acquired a horse. In the journal kept at the time it seems like the proclamation of a wedding day. "She is a Buckskin Mare! Her color is lovely. Her hair is soft. Her name is Nancy." They are a little like profound ecstasy, Helga's feelings now. She plans, when high school is over shortly, never to leave this small farm. The future is tomorrow and spring and summer.

In the mornings I bring a book to the barn under my arm. With Nancy watching over the door of her box stall, with the wondrous scent of hay and animals about, I go through the milking of the does. A book is propped before me on the milking stand. The foam rises in the pail. I am memorizing poetry without being instructed. I want something to recite as I dash about on foot or horse. Tennyson, Blake, Shakespeare, Keats, Pascal. Not Sandburg.

The letters are there, Carl writing a friend, "We are witnessing a rather lovely thing here in the way our girl Helga is developing something with her horse. . . . Helga rode her out beyond the second sandbar of Lake Michigan this Sabbath morning and they had a swim together . . . and I will get you an original of Helga on a nice mare we have all come to love."

I have asked for a horse for years. The key is the goats. When they arrived there was a reason (besides eternal and continual pleading from the girl). The beast will eat the hay the goats leave. And she did. Noble Nancy. Now I am committed to the barns and the work there. It seems to be in the blood.

And now something is happening with the dairy goats that stirs my mother. There is a program called Advanced Registry Testing that she has been looking into. If the requirements are filled we will be issued a certificate of Advanced Milk Production. The doe must produce a minimum of ten pounds of milk (about five quarts) a day for three days straight and must do this for three consecutive months to earn the certificate. Paula is hoping that from a small beginning she may, in time, make high milk production records on our flock. She reviews pedigrees and letters from breeders around the country and selects bucklings to be our future herd sires. She sees the program on paper. Her daughter? Helga is wild to handle the animals themselves. When the first smelly shaggy male Toggenburg beauty arrives from the famous "Mile High" Colorado herd, he is named Chief Pokagon and has curls on his forehead and a tiny beard and rears on his hind legs and plunges down in a way that enchants Helga.

There is a new pattern to the days for the family. There is the "milking hour" in the evening now. Carl likes it. The family does. He comes by and milks one now and then (Helga checks after to be sure the job is correctly done). The "March of Time" is on the radio in the milking parlor. And the testing for the new Advanced Registry program is underway. It is the thirteenth of May of 1936, a day to remember. Janet and Margaret and Carl and Paula are there. And two neighbors to witness and sign that it is indeed Felicia of Chikaming (we now have a "herd name" of our own, registered with the American Milk Goat Record Association!) and Meggi of Chikaming who produce the amount of milk exhibited in the pail that is hung on the scale. Felicia passes with flying colors—13.2 pounds. Meggi squeaks through with 10.2. After the three months are over, these two will receive their Advanced Registry certificates. The journal proclaims, "This is a great night on the Chikaming Goat Farm!"

The happenings of the household and the barnyard. Helga, followed by Sophie and Leona and Meggi, takes a walk and goes into Martha's kitchen for a visit. Another day, she rides the buckskin up the steps and into the dining room and hall where the family approves. She has wrist-tamed a crow and a hawk and, wearing a cloak (D'Artagnan), goes dashing about the dunes with one or the other on her wrist.

Carl's brother, our Uncle Mart, arrives. The two men sing songs out of their past.

Vie ska spela,
Via, via vo!
Boom, scalalalalala,
Boom, scalalalalala,
Via, via vo!

Carl takes out his pocket knife and cuts a two-inch length from a cigar. He lights it and stashes the other piece in his vest pocket. The men tell tales. They pour wine into the tiny glasses Paula sets out. She might have a bit. The daughters do not share or expect to. "I'll have another ration about midnight," says Carl.

They talk of Grandfather Sandburg, who called our father "Sharlie." Of Uncle Mart, when he was a night agent in the Galesburg railway express depot, pawning his gold watch to send money to "Sharlie" when he got a hungry letter. Of how as children, a treat was bread spread with lard and sprinkled with salt. Of Grandfather Sandburg eating white bread only at Easter and Christmas. Of how, as a blacksmith in the shops of the Chicago, Burlington and Quincy Railroad, he signed his checks with an *X* and how he had a deforming hump on his back from slinging the hammer. Before leaving in the morning, Carl hands Uncle Mart one of the cards his Horseshoe Tournament Chicago friends have printed up for him, so he won't be embarrassed when folks in the seat next to him on trains ask his occupation.

NORTH AMERICAN

Association of Paw-Paw Growers

CARL SANDBURG

Chairman of the Board of Directors

And then Mart is gone. More happenings. Bells are ordered from Sears so the dairy goat flock is now a musical one. Uncle Ed and Dana arrive for a visit. He writes in Janet's autograph book:

Some likes coffee
Some likes tea
But by golly
I certainly love you!

And Helga leaves them all. She is galloping her mare bareback to the beach to swim far out, while the city folk, the neighboring vacationers, lie sunburning near their umbrellas and canoes. In half an hour she is back at the barn. She knows as a farmer where duty lies, picking baskets of cucumbers, squash, strawberries, green beans, cherries, peaches, root crops along with Paula and Martha. And she is dickering for another horse, a paint called Nelly, who is rejected at once as too slow in the saddle. Nelly is turned in for Nip (she does just that when being saddled), a shiny dark bay of about twelve years. Now Janet rides with Helga at times.

Janet is at home with animals and fearless, saddles, bridles and manages the large beasts very well.

The People, Yes is off the press. Carl has bet with Martha that the book will not sell ten thousand copies by the end of the year. If it does, she will get $100 (a century, he says). When Stephen Vincent Benet reviews it for the New York *Herald Tribune,* he says, "The Liberty League won't like it, and I doubt if it receives the official imprimatur of the Communist party. . . . This voice does not come from Moscow or Union Square. It comes out of Western America, soil of that soil and wheat of that wheat, and it is the voice of somebody who knows the faces, the folkwords and the tall tales of the people . . . And there is warning in it as well as hope."

Paula has a new contentment in her life. She has control and absorption in the new style of her days. She has accepted her daughters and loves them as they are. Carl is managing also, writing a friend, "The eldest daughter is an invalid, the second is still below normal from being struck and run over by a careless motorist, the youngest is as good as God ever bestowed on a house; she is as nice as anything in a Russian Ballet when she rides her horse out into Lake Michigan for a swim together. . . . fresh milk from the gentle and allwise Felicia is ready and waiting, if you should ever be this way."

And he is placing the century in Martha's hand. Peers and reviewers cheer. ". . . What a show-up of the Lewises, Spenders, Fearings, Rukeysers et al! . . . Have you seen MacLeish's review of it in the New Masses! Swell! At last Mencken is hit where he lives. And Red Lewis, too. And all the superior people, the literary Nietzscheans of the nineteen twenties. Your book sh'd be the bible of the new Farmer-Labor Party . . ."

That book is now on its own and he is back laboring on finishing the Lincoln work. He writes an emotional letter about the progress of it to his publisher that he never does send, "Dear Alf. . . . It now runs over 7,000 words. . . . It has lamentations and beatitudes enough to make an American Bible, has enough political wisdom to guide this country thru several crises and depressions. . . . What is darkly great and subtly beautiful in it was made entirely by other men who are faded and gone. They lived the book before it could be written."

In the evenings the family gathers on the terrace (the great vault is below us, stashed with manuscripts, books, treasures) to watch the sun settle into Lake Michigan in a pool of glory. We do not tire of the scene. It is never the same. The processional of sunsets. The great ball dropping into the water in a bath of gold and vermilion. The twilight starting, luminous and soft. The only sound our breathing. Again, we assemble in an ozone-smelling gloom to wait the coming fury. Thunder calls and lightning replies. My father's voice hangs like a bell in the turbid air. We do not fear lightning and Helga swims the buckskin mare in the waters in sun or storm.

In the night all of them stand there, the girls about and Martha. Paula in Carl's arm. Later he writes that "we watched tonight, for the first time in our lives, old blue silver Arcturus slowly drop into the lake. I thought it was the last star in the Dipper handle but Paula knew better. Every piece I've written about this old Lake is woefully inadequate, it is mysterious with more parades and changes than when I first tried to fraternize with it . . ."

Has Carl any idea of how far Helga's dream of a kindly sweet-breathed Jersey cow, which he'd translated into a goat, will carry us? There is the vast barn loft, now set with shelves alongside the hay in one area. Stacks of books weeded from the house collection by Margaret on his orders, are sent out there. As he says, "I know where to go now when I need material." And he sends newspapers and magazines, just in case sometime he might want to look up an issue.

And me, I have finished high school now (our class motto, "Build for character, not for fame") and have set my typewriter up on a crate in a corner near the shelves by the fragrant bales and have begun work for him that will continue for some years. He calls me his secretary and sends telegrams, "HOMEBOUND TOMORROW ARRIVING CHICAGO FRIDAY LOVE AND KISSES PAPPY." I drive one of our cars now (a second-hand $100 Hudson) and will pick him up.

He looks worn and has a temperature. Paula puts him to bed. She writes Uncle Ed and Dana that "all the trouble of the World had been in his thoughts night and day—Spain—the Floods—the strikes. . . . Tears filled his eyes when General Motors yielded and began negotiating with Lewis' men. Again when Steel capitulated. . . . Things are all coming better now for the CIO. . . . He had 80 dates this year—and you may be sure at all of them he managed to refer to our coming industrial unions. . . . for which he battled years ago. . . . Margaret somewhat better than when you left and will surely be much better soon. . . . etc."

At home, surrounded by attention, he heals fast. He is impressed with Janet's involvement with the farm. Her special duties involve regular three-time-a-day feeding of the kids. She likes the task and the young ones follow her about. And Paula. Official milk testers come down monthly now from Michigan State College to supervise the twenty-four-hour milk weigh-ins. We are the first to test for goat milk production in our state and we relish the status. Paula's name begins to appear in "research bulletins." ("The bulk of the excellent growth and milk production data was furnished by Mrs. Carl Sandburg and Miss Helga Sandburg, Chikaming Goat Farm.") Many in the goat business have no idea who Mrs. Sandburg's husband is.

Not only do we have a barnful of high producing Advanced Registry milking does and young milkers being tested, but there is an Advanced Registry sire in our buck barn. The requirement for this honor is to have three daughters who have given enough milk to qualify for Advanced Registry certificates. One of our Nubian bucks, Park Holme Caesar, sleek and black with white belly and long elegant ears, is the first of his breed to qualify in the United States, having four Advanced Registry daughters, one more than needed to receive his certificate. Caesar is docile and enormous and when he rears up before me to hold hoofs-and-hands, a favorite trick of his, he towers a head above. Mother is not only standing Caesar at stud for visiting does, but is selling his sons at high prices to breeders who hope to improve their stock and challenge our records.

Mother is into the politics of the industry too by now. I go along with her to meetings. Carl sends wires from his travels. He is in New York. "MRS. CARL SANDBURG, AMERICAN GOAT SOCIETY CONVENTION COLUMBIA MO DEEP LOVE TO YOU AND HELGA UNCLE ED JOINING CARL." We have a wonderful time, "SAFE HOME TRIP HIGHLY INFORMATIVE EXCEEDING EXPECTATIONS BUSHELS LOVE PAULA."

Mother is elected to the Board of Directors of the American Milk Goat Record Association and begins publishing articles on care and feeding of goats for high milk production, on standards for the breeds, on how to make "Nut Neufchatel Cheese" and others properly. There she is at her desk in the many-windowed sunporch room. Far into the nights. The light burns. Her feet are tucked on the rungs of the chair. Her hair curls about her face. She frowns in concentration. She is happy.

Helga is long asleep. She rises before the crack of dawn. And she is enlisted also as secretary for her mother. Paula's files are building and her notebooks filling with records and calculations and decisions. She plans which doe is to be bred to which buck and why and when. Helga, the "barn boss," carries out her orders. In the Farm Office, pedigrees are laid out to be typed for prospective customers to consider. Folks are wanting Chikaming Herd bucklings for their herd sires nowadays.

1937. Horrors take place outside our nation. Carl goes to a Spanish Loyalist Medical Aid meeting. Barcelona is being bombed daily. The Basque town of Guernica is annihilated by *Der Führer*'s bombers and strafers. Carl says if he were younger and free of responsibilities, he'd go over and fight with the Loyalists of Madrid, although they "are no set of angels." And he is standing for the third-term draft of FDR in 1940, too. Writes the president that he may arrive at the White House door at some point, guitar in hand "for an evening of songs and of stories . . . which may rest you on one hell of a job." Roosevelt says any day will suit him.

There are honors in addition to letters from our leader. His Majesty the King of Sweden sends on the Royal Order of the North Star. And for good measure, along with the elegantly boxed gold-and-blue-and-white decoration, there are three golden pins surmounted by crowns for the daughters of the family. Carl is not sure of a pat on the head from royalty, "Considering what I've written about the upper and ruling classes as such I can stand this if the King of Sweden can. No conditions attach. They know I am a Social Democrat, a laborite."

February 1938. Henry Luce puts him on the cover of *Life*

Magazine. He wears his old plaid shirt and wool vest. A scarf about the neck, cigar in hand. He stands at the living-room window that looks to the lake with Paula at his side. Helga is there (in braids and jodhpurs) kneeling by Felicia and Carlotta and a couple of Nubians. He holds his lute-shaped guitar and Luce is praising him for the new Musicraft record album just out. He is singing *Songbag* songs.

Old Bill Jones had two daughters and a song,
One went to Denver and the other went wrong.

And

Mama, mama, mama have you heard the news?
Daddy got killed on the C-B-and Q's.
Shut your eyes and hold your breath,
We'll all draw a pension upon papa's death.

Uncle Ed and Dana write that they see the issue all over the newsstands in Mexico. He is taking off from work for a couple of months. He says he's in a new phase of his life. At fifty-nine, he quits smoking. And fashion photography is out too. Of it, he says, "too much repetition and practically no experimentation." He wants to spend time at Umpawaug with his plant-breeding program. His articles are in the current American Delphinium Society Yearbook.

Feelings of mortality and the desire to finish their work while holding on to their health are always there with the "blood brothers". Carl is losing friends. They've been going since back in 1931, when Vachel Lindsay, as my father said, "crossed to the afterworld." Helga never forgot it. She was thirteen. Sitting in her nightgown at the top of the stairs listening to Carl and Paula speak of their friend's death. Suicide. Discouraged and depressed.

Now Harriet Monroe, stricken at the Inca ruins 8,500 feet up in the Andes near Arequipa in Peru. Carl speaks for her at the Fortnightly Club in Chicago. Elinor Frost. She and Robert married forty years. It is March 28 of 1938, "Dear Robert—Sorrow here too. Always she was infinitely gracious to me in a way I can never forget. Your grief is deep and beyond any others knowing. Now it is past any of the other sharp griefs you have sung. As ever, Carl." Frost is sixty-four, four years older than Carl. He receives the Gold Medal for Poetry of the National Institute of Arts and Letters and has three Pulitzers already.

Will the wartime Lincoln that Carl is laboring on now ever make a Pulitzer? The book moves on. Surrounded by materials in his attic rooms. Engulfed by references and papers and pencils. Occupied with rewrites. Burning out in the sunlight of the deck where the trumpet vine has reached up from the land three stories below. He is approaching the murder scene, writes Lloyd Lewis, ". . . the Old Eagle has five days to live. Then the blackout." And Lewis, ". . . You are the only living man who can make Lincoln's biography rise up at the end in full chorus . . . So think of it as the Trojan Wars and yourself as Homer. As always, Lloyd."

Now while the Master of the House labors in his vineyard, where are Paula and Helga? Not satisfied with being farmers, we want Glory. State Fairs. There are two close by—in Illinois and Ohio. We study catalogs. The Illinois State Fair offers a "Governor Horner Trophy" for "Best Eight Head" of the different breeds. We hope to snatch it. (Best Eight Head consists of two kids, two yearlings, two milkers under three years and two milkers over three.) The pictured trophy is gloriously golden and stands nearly a foot high.

Paula locates a used house trailer for a hundred dollars. Our carpenter is called and outfits it with removable stalls imposed on the sleeping area and table. Straw is put down.

We depart at dawn, me at the wheel. Dew sparkles in the cornfields and lights are on in the barns of the countryside. Truckers honk at us, comrades. We are a part of the scene. Paula wears a white seersucker suit and a wide-brimmed hat and low-heeled shoes. I am in a tan boy's shirt from a Sears catalog (sleeves rolled up) and tan jodhpurs (white ones are packed for evenings and the show ring). My hair, as usual, is in two braids. I have no knowledge of the Art of Flirtation and use no lipstick or other cosmetic. The same applies to Paula (perhaps a puff of powder?).

Our hearts beat fast as the ring fills for the various classes. I have schooled the does and they are sheared and beardless and groomed. A blue ribbon. And then, in a Radiance of Light, Paula receives the Governor Horner Trophy. She sends a wire at once to Carl in care of the "Zephyr leaving Denver at 4 P.M." He can't make a visit to our scene of triumph, "Dearest, Too much that has to be done, too wide a swing down around to Springfield, so many chores. . . . A ten minute talk with New York yesterday and they insist on five minutes of guitar and song. Blessings on you. Maybe next year you'll let pass so that others can have a shot at the ribbons. . . ." Not a chance. We are off for the Ohio State Fair.

Note that Helga is observing the daughters of other dairy goat breeders. They wear long gingham dresses. Bobby socks. They fluff their hair. She makes friends. She holds hands (out of sight of Paula) in the evenings with a herdsman of a reputable competitor of ours. He is ancient, at least forty. But he is male and as skittery as Helga of his employer seeing us together. She begins to sense the danger and excitement of sex. The problems.

In Ohio we come off with the Toggenburg Grand Champion Banner—royal purple with gold lettering and corded fringe and rod. Detailed telegrams go home as to who captures what. Paula is photographed in wide white hat and smile. Her arms are about our Grand Champion, Sonia, and our Junior Champion, Shasta of Chikaming. The trophies and banners and ribbons are placed and hung about the dining room. Conquest. We can't wait till next year.

Helga, with her new knowledge, gets kissed by another male not long after. He is immortalized in a poem that ends

Nothing has changed, with the same hollow thunder
The waves die in their everlasting snow.
Only the place we sat is drifted over,
Lost in the blowing sand, long long ago.

And then, of course, there are the milk testers who come and go (and will through my life in the next years as I go in and out of marriage). Martha advises me to catch one. It is he who calls forth Paula's demand of her daughter, "Were you out walking with him!" "Not at all." "Yes, I know. And you are not to do it again!" But she does. Helga has bitten of the apple and finds it bittersweet. She immerses herself in Edna St. Vincent Millay and Dorothy Parker. The poem for Martha's favorite ends,

You are the songs I sing, love,
You are the stars in the sky,
And if you should cease to love me,
I think that I should die.

And Carl. He stops me one winter day when I am about to leave his attic work room. It is the War Years, he dictating, Helga typing. Is he more worldly than Paula? "Remember, Swipes. If you should happen to be having a baby ever, stay home. It would be a wanted child."

I love him. I appreciate his concern. I wonder too, descending the steep attic stairs two at a time, if he knows how virginal and unworldly I am.

Come. See the household of the Poet. Take a look through the window at their world. Lesley Frost has compared her family to the Brontës, unworldly, introverted. Compare her father and Carl. Robert is a stocky man and wears an old suit and scuffed shoes, a fresh-laundered soft shirt open at the throat. He makes wonderful pronouncements, "Poetry is a way of taking life by the throat!" Carl? He is taller but as casual in dress. As prone to statements that make headlines. No wonder they avoid each other. Pay no attention to Robert's testiness. That is his way.

An odd household, Carl's. A mystery to the neighbors, who whisper that the man of the family sometimes does not rise until noon. Shocking. Rumors. He writes naked on his deck. Not a stitch to cover his parts. Well.

Margaret. A devotee of the piano. She has a grand and practices every Bach exercise known to the civilized world. Reads the *Encyclopedia Britannica* through page by page (that may be stretching it a bit, however . . .). It will be many years before the dragon is really tamed.

Janet. Milk pails in hand. Busy. Cheerful. A clatter of pans in the dairy and the baby kids are in a state of excitement. Back at the house, one of her chores when he is home is to make up her father's breakfast tray, setting it on the floor outside his door, a thermos of coffee, a glass of goat milk, a pot of honey, pumpernickel bread, goat butter, a bit of cheese, fruit. Janet is not easily ruffled, but if she is, stand aside. Peace then follows.

Helga. She has a new mare, Silver, who has the build of a circus horse and is dazzling white and swiftly learns to kneel or lie down or rear spectacularly when asked, just as

Nancy does. The neighbors sigh, "There goes Brünhilde," as she gallops by, braids flying.

Paula. Engrossed in her work now with the Chikaming Herd, she is content. Does she look to the future? I doubt it. Unless as a challenge to what she can bring to the dairy goat industry and her hope for a world champion. Her faith in Carl is serene and untouchable. She stands with total firmness as to his genius and his destiny. Her love is composed of a quiet temper (not shared by her daughters), an optimistic nature (shared by all of us), a generous belief in her own capabilities. It is impossible not to agree with her when she is bent on that. And, of course, she is beautiful.

How wonderful, with Carl engrossed in the final throes of *The War Years,* dashing to New York and back, reading page proofs, checking half-tones, working at a preface, that she is off again to a state fair. This is her business. And it is a success. Soon she and Helga are again sending wires home with listings of triumphs. Is there a wistful tone in the telegram he wires back to us? "WE ARE ALL PROUD OF YOU I AM DEEPLY PROUD OF YOU AND PRAYING YOUR BURDENS NOT TOO HEAVY CARL."

Heavy? They are feathers! We capture another Governor Horner Trophy. And we are wiser now as to better grooming and show techniques. We've been alert. We shoot a telegram back, relating cups and banners and ending, "LEAVING AT DAYBREAK TOMORROW FOR COLUMBUS LOVE TO YOU ALL HELGA AND PAULA."

At the fairgrounds, I wear my hair loose now. And curl it at night as my new friends do. And a peasant-skirted dress in the evenings to walk about the grounds. A respectful heated man from the Sheep Barn teaches me a lot I need to know in the cab of his truck.

I have decided not to be a farmer the rest of my life and

Paula agrees. College. Why not? What has motivated Helga to aspire to higher education? Is it the look at the outside world she got at the fairs? Is it the pleasure of the rendezvous by the Ferris wheel or the Sheep Barn? Perhaps I will meet men while my brain is being stirred by foreign and mathematical terms. My mother is delighted at the sudden interest in study (She is fluent in French and German and Luxembourg and Latin is a snap to her), and at once sees to it that I am enrolled in Michigan State College where her dairy husbandry friends are.

Carl, meanwhile, is at Uncle Ed's for a short visit. It is the day after the last proofs of *Abraham Lincoln: The War Years* have been corrected. My uncle says, "Carl sat at the breakfast table that morning with a serene and relaxed look, a look that brought to mind Gardner's beautiful photographs of Lincoln made the day after the Civil War surrender. This is the only picture of Lincoln in existence which shows a real smile, a tired smile of relief, a smile of infinite warmth and tenderness." And Edward Steichen's six-head montage print made in that September visit is published later in *Vanity Fair* and becomes famous.

I am in Lansing at my new dormitory quarters. Carl has not forgotten me. He cares. "Dear Helga honey—Swipes—How is you? how am yuh? And is your English improving already so much yet as the franch? I tink I shall like yore franch. The big book is done, washed up, finish. If you don't show here soon I will be there—Your loving fadder. PS—Uncle Ed wished me to bring you his deep respect and a terrible hug."

Fall 1939. Helga has never been away from home and parents at the same time before. She is twenty-one. She spends time composing love poems. Parts go:

I wish I was at home again
Riding my little mare across the plains
Delight in my veins and never a single care
But I must stay and wait awhile
Though my soul is sick to go and hide my heart
Though with sorrow it start
Till I may go home with the snow

Carl answers, ". . . the poem you send is the registration of a mood and a deep feeling it is intensely personal and you can't be sure about an intensely personal piece of that kind until you have had it by you for a year or two go ahead and feel free to let yourself go at any time like that in response to a deep feeling or a mood homesick is a queer word as we use it sometimes when what we really mean is that we would like to be in two places at the same time and so we are trying to live more of life than can be lived in one place at a certain time . . . I would like to stay home and go to east lansing next week when the orders are that I must go to Chicago on a dozen errands and on october 27 be in New York to receive a medal of the Roosevelt Memorial Association I would like next week to be in four places at once 1) here at home 2) there at east lansing with you 3) in chicago 4) in new york so you would like to ride a horse recite french study english and do several other things all at once just like your mother and uncle ed they can never be in enough places at one time to get done and see and hear the things moving them and calling them many bushels of love much luv Dad."

And he keeps me informed of his commitments. ". . . on the afternoon of the 23rd will broadcast ten minutes on the NY Herald-Trib national annual forum your ears will not catch anything about Creative American Art which you haven't already heard across the dinner table but it may be fun for you to see whether Pop slips." And arranges for

Helga to come to Chicago or nearby Detroit when he is there. Sees that she notes the comments on *The War Years.* She's been watching and writes, "Did you see all the grand reviews? Not only Time and Newsweek, but the New Yorker and the New York Times is having one Sunday . . ."

Carl has never really understood this daughter's avoidance of second-hand notice. Margaret and Janet are not shy. They have no desire, as I have, for anonymity, to be "ordinary." Hadn't I squirmed in my seat in the auditorium at grade school when our father came to lecture? Janet listened (not too attentively—we had heard it all before at the supper table), while I attempted invisibility. Here at Michigan State, I am still really in adolescence, trying to shed home connections, wanting my own power and identity. Not a daughter of someone! Someone herself with opinions not derived from a parent! At Lansing, the taunts come now and then, "Something there is that doesn't love a wall. Right? Yeah! What's it like to have a Daddy be a poet! Hah!" And so on. Lowering her head, she plows down the way.

The violence of the hurting of homesickness! Lots of Helga's dreams when asleep and daydreams when awake are of the ways of her family and the beauties of her life with them. The sunsets! Her father has read Whistler's comment to the family when someone said they never had seen sunsets like the ones he painted, "Don't you wish you had!" Swimming the buckskin while the sun blazes in great round wheels of color like a Van Gogh oil. The shrieks of Canada geese in the falltime, following the lake shore, their voices lost in the wind and wave noise. The loons' shrill halloo in the hour before dawn. The fireplace in the living room, the wind snuffing about the windows, her dogs snoring in the flame's heat.

Walks. Visiting neighbors with Carl. Out on a winter night, the blasts from the lake swirling about the two, being welcomed at another fireside a mile from our house. Treading home in the sparkle of the silent whitened woods and ravines, our breath steaming on the frosted air. Valuing stillness. Listening for country sounds.

The close-knit family. Margaret practicing her infinite Bach preludes and sonatas, and continual Chopin, Mozart, Beethoven. Janet bringing another newborn kid to the house to place in Paula's arms. (In the cold seasons the baby goats do not remain in the barns. They are taken quickly from the mothers at birth, before a bond can be formed. Their tiny cries are not unlike a baby's when the caul is removed and they breathe air.) Paula places the kid among the others in the special box she has designed, with a screen false floor so their droppings fall through and they stay clean. When Carl is at the table, viewing his mail and finishing his lunch, she comes to join him and lifts the tiny newborn sweet-smelling lanky warm creatures out to prance and gambol on the rugs. Helga is not present any more in the homey scene. But she dwells on it. And on Carl's light which is washing out into the nights from his windows above Helga's old room. (Hired hands come in nowadays to work at the barns.)

Carl's funny letters that he takes the time to type keep coming to her.

"Dear Swipes, The letters from you are lovely to have and each one is passed around and sometimes it is like the light of your face and voice are in the room. The time when I am most homesick for you to be here is when I look at the horses the hosses the fellows that know your language like nobody else that talks to them. Take care of yourself take keer uv yussef. Loads of love colossal cargoes of affection Swipes you divvil dovel deevil baby kiddo keeddo hows about a teeny weeny kiss? good-a-bye and dont take anything that's nailed down around the state capitol much luv Dad."

If it fits in with his travels, he arrives at the dormitory. He is unexpected. Helga is at class. He lights his pipe or cigar and settles in a chair. The "housemother" is aghast. Smoking is definitely prohibited! He requests that his daughter be sent to him outside on the steps in the open air. There he sits, a newspaper in his hand, busy, burly, familiar-smelling, adored.

He's on the cover of *Time*'s December third issue, in a proper shirt and tie this time, with "That son-of-a-gun Lincoln grows on you," for the caption. And Henry Luce (He likes Luce and writes him, "Dear Harry, . . . With all your faults, . . . you are holding pretty nicely to so difficult a course. . . . Health and many strengths be yours—as always.") gives him a four-page review along with two of Uncle Ed's photographs of Carl with Leona and Meggi and Felicia and Sophie on the sand dunes and then working in the attic at the Underwood. And

> Each of the first three volumes of *The War Years* is over 650 pages long, the fourth volume 413 pages. By rough computation that makes about 1,175,000 words. Other word totals, as given in Sandburg's foreword:
>
> The Bible, including the
> Apocrypha 926,877
> Shakespeare, complete works 1,025,000
> Lincoln's printed speeches
> & writings 1,078,365
>
> *The War Years* is therefore no weekend biography. . . .

Carl loves it. "Dear Harry, A buckram and all-rag copy of the limited edition of the War Years has been sent to you, for various reasons, and partly because of sentiment ranging around your great performance in the field of recording the changing tumultuous world scene of the past ten years. As always."

Paula even goes to Chicago where he is autographing the four-volume sets at Marshall Field's and where the Tavern Club is hosting an affair. She's been shopping. A bright blue crepe evening dress. Blue and aqua sensible daytime ones. (She's going on from Chicago to a meeting of the American Milk Goat Record Association.) And a new hat and low shoes.

Franklin Delano Roosevelt writes that he is delighted with his "four grand volumes" and sends congratulations and, "I do hope you will come to see me the next time you are in Washington." My father has stopped in once or twice. In *The War Years'* Foreword he thanks FDR, "for personally conducting me in 1937 to Lincoln corners of special interest in the White House." And Harcourts are putting out a six-volume boxed set of the whole works that includes *The Prairie Years.* And then there is a $50 deluxe boxed first edition, limited to 525 numbered copies all signed by the author. (500 are for sale.) Carl sends Helga #1.

And how is she doing? She has located a stables and is riding. She enters a cow milking contest in the Rodeo (a Red Ribbon) and meets a cowboy. And writes her poem, hopefully derivative of Edna St. Vincent Millay.

Let me forget, my love, the way you touch your hat
Or walk or start to laugh. Let me forget.
You have my heart within your hand,
But you shall never know.
I'll keep the secret in my heart and never let it show.

Does Carl worry about how it goes with her? He sends advice, ". . . in a biog sketch of John Steinbeck I notice: 'At intervals from 1919 to 1925 he attended Stanford University but was not entirely happy there until it was understood that he wasn't anxious for a degree but wanted to study only what interested him.' so you can do the same if you like don't let any but very special responsibilities chosen by yourself ever weigh you down as ever and ever Dad."

The school year is ending, "My darling Dad, Life is very wonderful and rushed and exciting for me all the time. Last night I went canoeing. It was the loveliest of nights. The moon was only a half, but it was radiant and magical. There wasn't a ripple on the river. How've you been keeping yourself? Been thinking about you. Be good to yourself. Took a walk in the rain today. The sun was shining. Like to get my hands in some garden dirt. All the love in the world from your daughter, Helga. And I do mean love, bushels of it."

"Swipes me lassie reading your letters lately after having been away from them so long is almost like hearing your voice and seeing your face for you do put your speech tones in those letters into your letters goes dese dose dem shall be hoping to be here when you come we have a faith in our hearts about your flowering so many ways this year and there are always prayers for you here that time and all the fates may be good to you and that your wise love heart may go on growing Dad."

Ah, if one could look ahead! Pilgrims all on our way. What will the years hold? What will love do? Ah, love.

Part Three

THE WAR WIDOW

JULY 1940. "This is London," reports CBS correspondent Edward R. Murrow as the news unravels. Nazis have invaded Norway and Denmark. The blitzkrieg rains upon the Netherlands and Belgium and Luxembourg. Paula mourns the last, our grandparents' homeland. Uncle Ed burns the blue, white and red and gold birthland flag, now the property of *Der Führer.* The retreat from Dunkirk is over. Britain, France and Italy are at war. The bombing of London has begun.

Where is Helga? Dancing. The cowboy has come to visit. She reports to Carl, "We went to the Blackhawk, Old Heidelberg and the Bismarck Hotel among sundry others. . . . Unlimited bushels of love to the Best of Fathers from the most devoted of daughters."

And Carl? He is elected to the American Academy of Arts and Letters. The four-volume *Abraham Lincoln: The War Years* has its Pulitzer in the category of History. Doctor of Letters diplomas come from Lafayette College, New York University, Lincoln Memorial, Wesleyan, Yale, Harvard. Soon Rollins and Dartmouth. When he goes to Yale and Harvard, Paula and Helga come along. It is the start of summer vacation and Helga photographs the glories of the campuses as well as the sons of professors given to her as guides. At the dinner at Harvard, Carl says, "When your invitation came I said to myself, as I did twelve years ago when asked to read a Phi Beta Kappa poem: 'Harvard has more of a reputation to lose than I have, so I'll go.' "

Paula? Why the state fairs, of course, with Helga, who has thrown herself into the farm again with abandon and enthusiasm to Paula's delight. The cream of the dairy herd is selected by the two of them and Helga shears the animals so they are sleek and elegant. The beards are the first to go. She practices handling them for the show ring so that they stand to their best advantage for the judges. Then Paula and Helga are off in the small crisp hours of morning. See them speeding through the dusty countryside, the old reconverted trailer behind, loaded with the precious cargo. Helga is singing while Paula dozes. Helga is knowledgable at last in the areas of the Snake and the Apple and the Garden. There is no nonsense about Sears jodhpurs or boy's shirts. I have a Panama hat, rayon dresses, gloves and confidence.

When the does are settled in their pens and Paula is away discussing the world of dairy goats with other breeders, Helga is busy. The cowboy has come to the fair and he is left standing at the curb, while Helga whirls about in a red roadster with two young men. One of them is seventeen, handsome and with curly auburn hair. Joe. He's come to the fair on a lark and to help goat-breeder friends with their stock. Paula likes him and makes no remarks when Helga and Joe go off hand in hand to get an ice cream rainbow dip.

We leave again with "Best Eight Head, 1940" trophies for both Toggenburgs and Nubians as well as the Grand Champion Toggenburg Silver Cup and the Grand Champion Nubian Golden one. I send wires home, ending, "LOVE AND STUFF HELGA." After coming home from a similar triumph at the Ohio State Fair, Paula has another acquisition—Joe. Since I am bent on higher education, she has been looking about for a herdsman. Joe is it.

Restless and avoiding my cowboy, I decide, with my mother's blessing, not to return to Michigan State, but to try out the University of Chicago. I enroll in late August, take housing at International House, know not a soul, have a room of my own. Second thoughts about deserting the amorous cowboy result in what but a poem, the last stanza going

That sends a shiver through me
And I feel that I have known

All that I need ever know,
I love you and you alone.

However, I do like the university. I meet poets and politicians, attend lectures, take French again and go to foreign movies for the first time. I meet a friend of Amy Lowell's, who tells me that Carl once said talking to Amy was like talking to a "great blue wave," she did so like to have her way in conversation.

Chicago is close to home, an hour by car, and I go there often. Not only are my mares there but companions to ride with. There are always the milk testers, some dashing ones. And then Joe. We pack picnics and travel over to "Pikes Peak." At home we build a fire in the front room and talk. Joe goes dancing with me. We know all the local orchestras and when they see us coming through the door, they break into the "Saint Louis Blues." I am wildly content.

Helga sends reports about all this to "My very dearest father . . ." And how I have memorized (at last) one of his poems, "Tawny."

These are the tawny days: your face comes back.

The grapes take on purple: the sunsets redden
early on the trellis.

The bashful mornings hurl gray mist on the stripes
of sunrise. . . .

Tawny days: and your face again.

How "I've never been so happy in my life." How "The war is sad and terrible, but I don't think life's important enough to split a gut about it. Right?"

Does Carl, receiving these lengthy euphoric letters, read in danger? Were the milk testers and Joe having too good a time with this daughter? Does he discuss this with Paula? Who knows? Not Helga. But into her idyllic life, into the Garden, creeps the Snake.

Joe arrives one evening at International House in the family car. Helga is astonished. He reports that Mother is about to send him away! Does she feel we are getting too close? What other reason? His work at the barn and with the animals is without fault. As for the attachment between them, for Helga it has been that of dancing partners. We have been having a wonderful time! I couldn't wait for the weekends home where we were welcomed at the dance spots with the "Saint Louis Blues." But Helga has felt no more passion in the kisses with Joe than for any of the rest of her male companions. What she felt for the Sheep Barn man at her first State Fair (in her jodhpurs and naiveté) aroused greater sensuality than much she has experienced since. The two need to talk.

They drive to a spaghetti house. Joe despairs. Not Helga. She will come home on the weekend, say she has a dental appointment. They will slip about and get married. And they do. It is said that it takes three days to tie the knot. It cannot be done in one Saturday. But an appealing Romeo with bright auburn hair and a dark-haired firm Juliet do.

And at dusk they return home with the thunderous news. Carl has been out for a walk and has stopped in at the milk house. He raises his eyebrows, keeps his cool, remarks about the possibility of grandchildren and accompanies the couple to the next scene—my mother. She does not keep her cool. She departs weeping to the attic for a private time with Carl. She puts her head on his shoulder and will lie in his arms awhile. They talk. They may not have chosen Joe, but their daughter has. It is her life. And she is back in the home again, a part of the family. They have missed her.

Meantime Joe and Helga have broken the delicious news

"Her name is Helga. I see her there as through a glass darkly."

"There is a cadence to that voice which lingers in memory."

“Remembering is a dream that comes in waves.”

“‘Remember me to Mrs. Sandburg and my friends, Margaret, Janet, and Helmar.’”

"By the flagstones of Mother's gardens are heliotrope, nasturtiums, larkspur, bachelor buttons, marigolds, cosmos, asters, poppies."

"And it suits Carl."

"She has located another summer resort that she fancies . . . Its wildness suits her."

"Helga feels her luck at seven years."

"And there are swim suits
. . . and 'a big hardwood
Liar's Log where you are
invited to tell tall ones.'"

"There are a multitude of windows (Carl has written, 'I was foolish about windows . . .')."

"Helen Keller had a handicap of sorts. Does Janet? Our sunny girl who in time will become a sunny woman?"

" . . . Helga, bless her, will remain with the same teacher and a new set of faces in the Fourth." (Second row, third from right)

"There they are—Helga, Uncle Ed, Bosco, Carl, Janet—tongues out panting and our paws, along with Bosco's, before us in the warm sand."

"Kneeling against him, seeing to it that I am the one next to him in the picture."

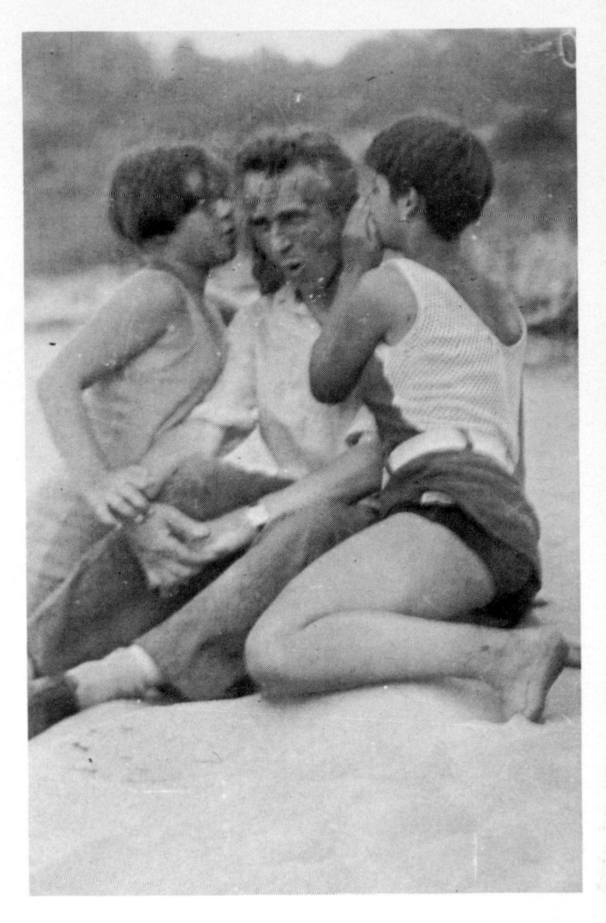

"She will join a circus and all the dogs now shake hands, roll over, jump through hoops, sit on pedestals or stand on tree branches."

"Into the air comes a low call from Tom Thumb Dairy stable. Helga is wanted."

"All the while that Paula's long handsome barn is being completed, . . ."
(Mother's handwriting)

"'She is a Buckskin Mare! Her color is lovely. Her hair is soft. Her name is Nancy.'"

"Caesar is docile and enormous and when he rears up before me to hold hoofs-and-hands, a favorite trick of his, he towers a head above."

"Mother is elected to the Board of Directors of The American Milk Goat Record Association . . . There she is at her desk in the many-windowed sunporch room."

"I am in a tan boy's shirt from a Sears catalog (sleeves rolled up) and tan jodhpurs . . ." (The Illinois State Fair)

"Henry Luce puts him on the cover of *Life* Magazine." (Photograph credit: Bernard Hoffman, *Life* Magazine ©1958 Time, Inc.)

"Helga . . . has a new mare, Silver, who has the build of a circus horse and is dazzling white and swiftly learns to kneel or lie down or rear spectacularly when asked, just as Nancy does."

"My father has a grandson. He gives the news to the papers, 'CARL SANDBURG IS GRANDDAD!'" (Joe, Joseph Carl, Helga)

"Helga is twenty-four now and feels she is near heaven . . . Joe too is near heaven."

"Ah, that Christmas! It is a dazzling one, the man child again the center, . . . And when he reaches up to hold his grandfather's nose, all gasp . . ."

"Carl comes by every day to go walking and talking, enchanted with the boy child. They are close. My father is wonderfully humorous and curious and protective . . ."

"'The poet is sitting on an obstacle course he made for the boy, out of pieces of driftwood from the beach.'"

"And now Paula is off to a goat meeting . . . Her white hair is waved and shining . . . and the family stays impressed."

"My father likes my little house, Orchard Cottage." (Karlen Paula, Helga, Carl, Joe Carl)

to Margaret, Janet and Martha and it is marveled on. After the two have returned from the attic and supper is over, Paula takes her daughter aside. With old-fashioned directness she gives her a jar of Vaseline which she says may be needed. Also Joe and she are to give up their single-bed rooms and hereafter "The Lincoln Room" will be theirs.

The newlyweds are virgins both. Kisses have been the extent of their explorations of the Garden. (This does not apply to all of Helga's adventures in Eden, including the respectful Sheep Barn man.) The two are a little dazed still by the family's acceptance of their new roles. The Vaseline stays untouched, not because it is not needed, but they are unsure of its exact use and have had no explicit directions. Helga (although she does not say this to the new husband) is a bit dismayed that this is what all of her reading, from King Solomon's *Songs* to Dorothy Parker and Edna St. Vincent Millay, from *Sister Carrie* to *Gone With the Wind,* is about. However (the Vaseline still untouched), as another night passes and another, and passion is spent in the Lincoln Room, as well as the hayloft and a variety of other spots in house, barn and dune, she begins truly to fall in love and then has.

Higher education is abandoned. Helga will resume secretarial work for Carl and help Joe at the barns. Paula proceeds to get out blueprints again and calls her carpenter and will put up a little house on the place for her daughter. She feels that the herd now will prosper under Helga's vigilant eye.

Gazing back into the sunlit days of that time, I wonder at the ease with which Carl and Paula accepted the elopement. Joe is seventeen. Helga almost twenty-two. And mingled with my puzzlement, is adoration and a blessing for their stance. They are busy at their affairs, each of them. He is writing Dorothy Parker about a cause he is interested in, "I tried to get you by phone today. . . . I wanted to make sure that my telegram had reached you saying I could not help joining you and Helen Keller in sponsoring your work for Spanish refugees. The check enclosed I would like to make larger. . . ."

There is Helga's little house. We call it "Orchard Cottage," just below the hillside where Paula set out the tiny trees six years ago. The perfume of flowers sweeps through the windows. Apples and cherries and peaches and plums and nectarines and pears and apricots blossoming in pink and white. Helga is alert for evidence of pregnancy. Her cycles, however, stay uninterrupted although love and sensuality are in their full now. She is aware that many in the countryside are waiting for her apron to be worn high, having placed bets that "she had to get married to that boy."

She saddles Nancy or Silver and rides at a canter, seeing to it that, when she picks up the mail at the post office a mile away, the mares rear as if out of control before they light out for the farm. It is April when she begins to hope and May when she is sure. A small Joe will arrive before Christmas.

Germany is invading Yugoslavia, Greece, Crete, and by June, Soviet Russia. In August, while we are at the state fairs again, our president and Prime Minister Churchill meet secretly off the coast of Newfoundland and come up with the Atlantic Charter. War is at hand. *Der Führer* may some day set foot on our land.

Meantime Carl has been asked to speak his mind on politics. In June (he is sixty-two now) there he is at the Chicago Stadium one evening, doing his best to bring about Franklin Delano Roosevelt's unprecedented third term and the defeat of Wendell Wilkie. As the summer moves into fall, he appears at a "Fight for Freedom" rally with an audience of ten thousand.

November fourth. He arrives at the White House for an hour with FDR on the Sunday afternoon before Election

Day. That night is the final third-term rally in Madison Square Garden with a two-hour nationwide radio broadcast to end at midnight. Carl has the final five minutes. He compares Lincoln and Roosevelt, " '. . . Such an epoch of perplexity, transition, change, is not often witnessed. . . . Misunderstood and misrepresented at the time; attacked from both sides. . . . The explanation of his every act is this: He executes the will of the people . . . He stands before you. . . . a not perfect man and yet more precious than fine gold.' And for some of us, that goes in the main in the present hour of national fate, for Franklin Delano Roosevelt."

What magic does Carl sense in FDR? Their beginnings are as far apart as riches and poverty—upper and lower classes—can be. Their correspondence goes back and forth with Lincoln the spark. Carl sends a message to the White House after the Madison Square Garden broadcast, ". . . I am glad you are cunning—as Lincoln and Jackson were cunning. I am glad you have had suffering and exquisite pain such as few men have known. I am glad you have had preparations for the awful role you now fill. . . . With all good wishes—and deep prayers. . . ." At this time in early 1941 Roosevelt, now safely into his third term, has the same problem Lincoln had eighty years earlier. He and his counselors are puzzling out how to arouse the people to want to get into an all-out conflict. They consult *The War Years.*

The draft is on. The country is divided. My father tells his publisher, ". . . Have resigned from Council for Democracy directors board, tho shall cooperate with them. . . ." The Isolationists in Congress stand against any measure proposed by the president. They are committed to neutrality. Fascist Bund groups spring up (one just down the Michigan shoreline from our dune holds regular meetings). The Bohemian village of Lidice in Czechoslovakia is in holocaust, entirely destroyed. The methodical elimination of all European and other Jews within the Gestapo's grasp is begun. The world looks sidewise. Carl writes a scary poem he calls "Secret History of the War, Slightly Bowdlerized."

Hobwig through the horf came the nation
while wibblehoots woofed in the holm
while ever the hoolweeves brangled over
and we saw the country impooshed besloam.

Yet now again the doombratches dordle
and hornches are heard from fleebwoots
and the dibwags snooker their mibbles.

Hist came the hoogles and haggles
when the borsches swarmswoggled
and the hongdorms of the solvoklosnogs
brought frimsies of faddledeewrangs
and we saw hoodledeehorngs on hoostips.

Take it from rangdoo whangpoo to spitz
the bemaddle will get hoarse and horse
and God only knows who will wimble or woof
when those sons of hoobwitches climper
and the clamp of their hodags splutterblit.

and czekoslovakia who blims its bloocher?
Who can foresay its floort in the flimming
  where the bennesh bedangles so brimmsy
  and a mashrick rides a homeward hodag?

Rinse thyself of the shambles, dibwag.
Go take a spit for yourself, doombratch.

There are his patriotic poems published in newspapers and magazines all the time. He reads "The Man With the Broken Fingers" on a Treasury Hour Show and it is translated and short-waved about Europe and published in Scandinavia and Russia.

And there are those like you and me and many many others
Who can never forget the Man with the Broken Fingers.
His will, his pride as a free man, shall go on. . . .
Better to die one by one than to say yes yes yes . . .

As for Helga, the year moves with contrasts of love and fear. The old dog Jack is hit by a car, suffers, is shot. The Companion of the Girl of My Childhood, Nancy, contracts lockjaw. What had she been, my beauty, but first love in its wildest of thrills—a pure easy lavishment on a silky perfumed responsive great beast? Nancy! That love has nothing to do with the Garden of Eden! And the vet comes and she too must go. While I speak to her, Joe shoots her carefully through the temple. She sighs and drops. It is the end of Girlhood, the great golden beast there at Helga's feet.

The year goes its way and the little one within me kicks and rolls and True Love is not something to read of or pine for—it is present and encompassing. Carl tells a friend, ". . . if God is kind and willing this coming November I shall be a grandfather." Helga wants to do it alone when her time comes. She and Joe. The event will be a casual one. She had helped so many does at birthings. And then the moment. And it goes wrong. Carl and Paula are hastily called in. They phone Dr. Jake Buchbinder at Chicago's Passavant Memorial Hospital. Helga is whisked there by ambulance. Dr. James Bloomfield brings forth my son by Caesarean section at six-thirty on the morning of 4 December 1941. Joseph Carl. Exquisitely beautiful.

My father has a grandson. He gives the news to the papers, "CARL SANDBURG IS GRANDDAD!" And he sends me a note, "Everybody is smiling and so happy about the little feller and YOU. We love you much and deep. We couldn't keep back tears when you were making your grand fight last night. We love you more than ever. And we love JOE and the couple of you more than ever. Dad. P.S. I'll be seeing you soon after you get this—you and our John Carl."

Why does he call Helga's son John Carl? It is many years before I learn that when Paula was seven months pregnant with Helga and Carl was going to Stockholm as a reporter for the NEA, he had anticipated a son they would name John Edward. My mother had already borne three daughters, losing one at birth. Why not hope for a son next? Carl wrote her then, "The day John comes, cable me . . . Whether it's John or another little sissenfrass . . . Take care of John: he may see great days never known to our eyes. . . . Maybe we will sit under our own cherry tree someday with John plucking our shoe strings. . . ." Soon now he writes me, "Dear Swipes, You and I know well enough that JOSEPH CARL is a dandy name and is perfect. Then why does it happen that about half the time I speak of him as JOHN? I dont understand this. So you are warned now and should know that when I speak of JOHN I mean none other than JOSEPH CARL. Also I am sure he will collect several nicknames before he turns the different corners of the next few years. Just now he seems to be an important person while nevertheless he is just a smidgeon . . . Joe tells us about the clean scar on you, a thin thread of a memorandum of what happened. We like it. We love it. It is you. Daddy."

Helga is lucky. In 1935, sulfa drug chemotherapy had been introduced, revolutionizing the treatment of infection and reducing the danger of peritonitis in abdominal surgery. Baskets of fruit and bundles of flowers flood the room. Visitors. Uncle Ed's wire: "HALLELUJAH FOR THE BOY WE ARE GETTING DRUNK TO CELEBRATE LOVE AND CONGRATULATIONS TO ALL AND MAW AND GRANPA AND GRANDMA AND TO THE AUNTS FROM US ALL BRUDDER." Janet's special delivery letter,

"I'm so happy to find out it was a bouncing baby BOY. Auntie Janet." My life is complete.

Three days later, on a late Sunday morning, the nurses begin calling out to each other. The news comes on the radio. Helga is still drained and content. To her it is of little import. Her son has survived and is alive and well.

2,344 men are not. Many are at the bottom of Pearl Harbor on the island of Oahu. Five battleships have gone down and three are hurt of the eight anchored in tandem. Three cruisers and three destroyers are lost. Two hundred planes were shot out of the air as 360 Japanese carrier-based ones swarmed in. We are at war.

Franklin Delano Roosevelt, wearing a black armband, signs the declaration passed by Congress in special session at 4:10 the next day. Great Britain and De Gaulle's "Free France" follow. By the next day, we take on Germany and Italy.

Uncle Ed wants to get into the thick of it. He telephones the War Department. Can he be accepted in the army as a specialist or advisor in photography? He is sixty-two. Born in 1879. No! Isn't he ancient? He has put on an exhibition for the Museum of Modern Art in New York, called "The Arsenal of Democracy." Carl wrote the captions. And then Pearl Harbor. The title is changed to "Road to Victory."

The Navy Department hears of it. Calls him in. How about doing some photographing for them? Uncle Ed is commissioned lieutenant commander. He phones the news to us. The delphinium experiments are put on hold. The "Glass House" he and Dana have just moved in to overlooking the new lake (and the Irish wolfhounds) are to go into a caretaker's hands. He's going to war. Dana is finding an apartment in Washington. Uncle Ed is on fire.

And Carl? He is being pushed to go into politics. The president himself writes that ". . . it would be grand to have your kind of Lincoln liberal in the Congress." But my father will stick to areas in which he feels at home. The Chicago *Times* syndicate contracts him for a piece every weekend. That suits him.

A little wrangle with Robert Frost. It seems that Carl has done a preface at this time for a collection of three-books-in-one for Harcourts. *Smoke and Steel, Slabs of the Sunburnt West, Good Morning, America.* The *Atlantic* prints it. Some of it goes, ". . . Recently a poet was quoted as saying he would as soon play tennis without a net as to write free verse. . . ." And Robert? "I am challenged to single combat by Carl Sandburg in an article in the *Atlantic* for March. His works prove you can play tennis more imaginatively with the net down, or so he maintains."

The two like the fray. Only in January, Robert had written Carl, "It's a long time since I said your name to you in speech or writing. But you won't have forgotten me. I'm the fellow you talked revolution with in an old fashioned saloon in Chicago before the Volstead Act. I hear you're high up helping run the government now. I am only too jealous. Nevertheless all the neighbors know I read you with swelling patriotism in The Boston *Globe*. . . . You and I have come to differ slightly in politics. You have found (or formed?) the party whose boast it is that it has appeased the proletariat. I am still a revolutionary. I want to see the Russians come right up to the English Channel and bring their typhus with them. But we are still true friends." And he had added that he "should like nothing better than to entertain you any time. Ever yours, Robert." In 1874 a birth happened in a fancy estate called Sevenels in Brookline, Massachusetts, Amy Lowell. Next year, in the raw frontier town of San Francisco, Robert Frost. Three years later, in a shack in Galesburg, Illinois, Carl. As the two youths and the girl matured and began to write, the New Manner came into being. They all got published in Harriet Monroe's *Poetry: A Magazine of Verse.* The world was to be made anew and all the country felt the magic. Amy Lowell went long ago in 1925 and here are the two survivors. Robert saying, "The poet must have something large it would break his heart not to have come true." And Carl? *The People, Yes.*

Changes. Lives continually rearranged. Martha has gone back to Indiana to be with her family and in her place vibrant eighteen-year-old Adaline, blonde and blue-eyed and calling Paula "Mom." Joe and Helga are restless and soon will be gone. Adaline asks her brother Stanley to come and help out. We get ready to go. There are more reasons for the flight. The draft. Joe is not yet eligible (he's under twenty-one), but if the war continues, there's one area fairly safe from conscription—a farm, a real one growing wheat, corn, soybeans, priority crops. That's Joe's specialty. We will go down into the St. Louis countryside where he comes from and where his people are. He'll find a farm to sharecrop.

And so Paula and Carl stand at the Chikaming Goat Farm gate and "have tears" (so my mother relates long years later) watching their daughter and husband and grandson, along with a young goat-breeder friend (it's his pickup loaded with our household goods) drive off in the early spring. Down the hill and around the bend.

As Helga slips away between the two young men, her lovely child in her arms, she is walking into a book. I have read all the farm novels from Willa Cather's *O Pioneers!* to Elizabeth Madox Roberts' *The Time of Man,* from Ole Rölvaag's *Giants In the Earth* to Tolstoy. Neither of the men beside her know these writers or their books. They live the latter. She cannot wait for the New Life before her. She does not look back at her folks standing there.

The first habitation is a tiny two-room cottage on a bit of land. There is a WPA outhouse and no plumbing. There is a sweet-water well and electricity and a small porch where I can set a washing machine if I wish. Joe is hunting a farm. Me, I'm setting out a garden.

By fall Joe finds a fifty-acre place that suits him. The widow who owns it will take half of any crops sold off it. We are welcome to any eggs the hens in the barn lay. Any money from the milk we sell from any cows we have is ours. Joe takes on a few other pieces of land to work. Soon there is a sow and a litter of piglets. Paula ships down a couple of goats for her grandson's benefit. The new home has high ceilings, bare floors, a long screened porch, no electricity. The wash machine is gone. There is a coal furnace, and water for washing is heated on the boiler beside it. Helga has a scrub board and purchases a hand wringer and is in business. They use kerosene lamps and have a three-burner stove.

Helga is twenty-four now and feels she is near heaven. When Joe and his brother-in-law run the great combine in the ripe field, they urge her to take it around a few times. The men call to her. The combine clatters. The golden grain shimmers. Helga is in the book.

She goes with pails after dewberries to put up, settling her son nearby in the shade. Tomatoes go into mason jars along with green beans and pickles and chickens and whatever is set in her kitchen in peck or bushel basket or pail or bucket. Joe now has his own second-hand pickup with his name on the door. And he's got a tractor too, supplied with orange tools, an orange oil can, orange nuts and bolts and an orange hard hat.

The sun blazes in the hot blue sky. The tractor roars in the dust of the field. Joe too is near heaven. He's got six cows now and the five-gallon cans are set out mornings for the dairy truck to pick up. The weekly "milk check" goes a long way to pay expenses.

Friends, relatives, milk testers back in Michigan, one by one are going into uniform, drafted or enlisting. War mobilization is in progress. New Deal ways are being employed. A no-strike policy goes into effect. The War Labor Board is set up. And an Office of Price Administration and Civilian Supply. Posters urge induction, "UNCLE SAM NEEDS YOU! JOIN THE WAAC." Helga's schoolgirl friends are Waacs or Waves. War ration books are issued to obtain sugar and soon coffee, canned goods, shoes, meat, cheese. Gas rationing. Three gallons a week per family.

Paula and Margaret come to visit in September. We meet their train in St. Louis. In a couple of days Carl joins us. The beautiful boy is the center of the universe. There is a picnic, an old flowered tablecloth spread on the grass. My mother takes her camera out. She has bought a baby swing in town and will use one of the pictures of the child in it for their Christmas card. She photographs Helga and Joe too before their rambling house, strutting in their overalls.

My father speaks about patriotism and approves of Joe and what he is doing for the "war effort." Carl and Margaret sing new songs for me to pick up.

God damn Republicans, scum of the earth,
We will meet them and beat them,
We will show them what we are worth.
Out of Wall Street came a Willkie, etc . . .

And

Oh, won't it be wonderful after the war!
There won't be no rich and there won't be no poor. . . .
The beer will be quicker and better and more,

And there's only one avenue I'd like to explore.
Oh, why didn't we have this old war before?

I am content. My family have come to look and approve and then are off in a hurry.

By falltime they have news and so have I. Theirs is that my father now has a new secretary—a Nisei. The country has been advised to start victory gardens in their backyards or communal plots as vegetables get scarce. Two-thirds of California's produce has been grown by Japanese-Americans out there. After Pearl Harbor, FDR issued an Executive Order causing some 117,000 of these people, along with alien Japanese, to be placed in concentration camps. Japanese-Americans elsewhere in the country are not molested. The only way to release a Nisei from the situation is for a non-Japanese citizen to vouch for one and guarantee employment and keep. My folks are happy with the skills and personality of Miss Sunao. A request is put in for a man to help at the barns too. He's expected soon.

And Helga is sick at breakfast and loses her lunch and this time wants a girl child. She and Joe talk about the "old days" (two years past) when they went dancing and bands played their "St. Louis Blues." The waltzing nowadays is to a battery radio and rarely. Joe is putting in fifteen- and sixteen-hour days and as Helga says, ". . . looks like a coal miner when he gets home. He's happy with the work though, even if he sometimes swears that only a damn fool is a farmer!"

The letters go back and forth. "Dearest Dad, . . . Joe got his classification paper and if they classify him 1–A, why I expect he'll be saluting Lieutenant Commander Steichen in a little while." "Dear Swipes, Every one of your letters I read first for the facts and the fun—and then a second time to see how the red inside heart of you is ticking. I feel mighty good about how you are now and where you are and the way things are going. To love the good old earth and to make a little piece of it behave under your hands, that is to have riches if along with it you have health and strength. Jiminy, those is nice photographs of Joe Carl: he is giving a good account of himself. And the one showing you with a laugh from every last rib of you, that for me is a song. Love to your Joe, to your Joe Carl, and to your blessed self—Daddy."

The Nazi army has advanced upon the Soviet Union over the past months. The 1941 winter was Russia's worst in thirty years. By the summer of 1942, the Germans reached the Black Sea. Leningrad is in ruins. The Luftwaffe destroyed the stores of food and all pet birds and dogs and cats were long since consumed. Now they are boiling leather belts and wallets and eating cold cream. Thousands are dead of starvation. The world waits to see what will happen. By November, the Russias recoup and counterattack and the Germans, now in Leningrad, are encircled.

My father and Charlie Chaplin admire the Soviets. "A SALUTE TO OUR RUSSIAN ALLY" takes place on the twenty-fifth of November in Orchestra Hall "sponsored by 300 leading Chicagoans." Sandburg speaks and the star of *The Great Dictator* throws a kiss at the ending. My father has written a poem to one of the Russian heroes, "Take a letter to Dmitri Shostakovich." He sends it to Moscow (The composer was airlifted out of Leningrad when the situation became too dangerous).

All over America last Sunday afternoon goes your Symphony No. 7, millions listening to your music portrait of Russia in blood and shadows.

You sit there in Moscow last summer a year ago writing music—and into the time of the falling leaves and the blowing snow writing music.

Sometimes as a fire warden you run to the streets and help put out a fire set by Nazi Luftwaffe bombs—then you walk home and write more music. . . .
Summer comes and you, Dmitri Shostakovich, see your music writing, your script, put on microfilm, a symphony held in a tomato can.
From Moscow across old Persia to still older Egypt, from Cairo round and roundabout to New York goes this little can of film. Then what? Then a Maestro Toscanini tells the NBC ninety-two-piece orchestra what to do with it and they put it on the air for the listening millions. . . .
Your song tells us of a great singing people beyond defeat or conquest who across years to come shall pay their share and contribution to the meanings of human freedom and discipline.

A reply comes from Moscow and the State Department translates it, "Dear Mr. Sandburg! I read your letter to me. It gave me much pleasure. Am sending you very best wishes and warmly grip your hand. D. Shostakovich."

It is a time of danger in the nation. A New Age is under way. The first controlled, self-sustaining nuclear chain reaction has just been achieved at the University of Chicago's Stagg Field. And Helga is boarding the train in St. Louis for Christmas in Michigan with her son.

Ah, that Christmas! It is a dazzling one, the man child again the center, the tree heavy with old and new baubles and lights and tinsel. There is a small red wood horse and a toy to pull. Everyone has his picture taken by the tree with the child. And when he reaches up to hold his grandfather's nose, all gasp and the photograph will be reprinted for the Public now and then over the years to come.

Carl is a monologist. Face it. Hasn't he always dominated the table conversations of family and friends? Isn't he courted by the world, listened to by the president, applauded by his audiences? Helga is changed. In her new life she (in a very small way, of course) has been courted, listened to and applauded by husband and friends. And that is why she is happy to return to her share-cropped farm place. She adores her father, her family. By now she is aware that the Household of her Childhood is not a customary one. She has thrown herself into the new scene. A farmer's wife. The wondrous incognito aspect. When I go into the nearby town, my boy child is admired as a farmer's son. Not some famous poet's grandson. Ah.

My father is coming down our way. "DAD WILL LEAVE TWO TICKETS IN JOES NAME AT ST LOUIS SYMPHONY BOX OFFICE IN CASE YOU WANT TO COME AND CAN MAKE IT MOM." We can and place Joey with a nearby state fair goat breeder girlfriend of mine, and are off for the Municipal Auditorium's Opera House where André Kostelanetz is conducting "A Lincoln Portrait" by Aaron Copland.

Carl performs the obligato. He and Kostelanetz worked together on the "Portrait" last August during its radio premiere on a Sunday afternoon for CBS's "The Pause That Refreshes On the Air" (Coca-Cola in the family icebox). My father speaks Lincoln's words and the explanations that precede them. At the conclusion of the performance, he bows and opens his arms wide to his audience. They give him an ovation. Kostelanetz claps his hands and smiles. Carl is called back a few times.

There is a party for the performers afterwards. We are introduced. And while the ladies crowd about the leads, they also flock about curly-auburn-headed Joe in his gray tweed (once dancing) suit, looking quite unlike the worker Helga knows daily. Of course, there is no question that the "lion" of the evening, my brilliant father, will return to our home.

The subject is not brought up. Does that seem odd? Consider that we have no electricity and use coal-oil lamps. We have arrived in Joe's truck with his name proudly painted on the door. Why in the world would my father, courted by the beauties of St. Louis, spending time with Copland and handsome André Kostelanetz and his wife, ever dream of coming home with us? It never occurs to my father or us to bring it up. We return in the small morning hours to our farm, our friend and the baby asleep by lamplight. We will be up at dawn for chores.

Now our plans, along with those of the nation, are changing again. The draft board people have offered to defer Joe two more years. He does not accept. All of his friends are in the army, navy, merchant marines. We talk but the decision is his. There is a thrill to it. For him, the unexpected, new faces, new lands, new work. For Helga, a patriot in the service, a star in the window (obviously no man in her bed). There is excitement in the prospects.

The time for my girl child's arrival is close at hand and I trust no one but Dr. Bloomfield at Passavant to bring a baby of mine into the world. She will be a Caesarean as advised. Joe will close up affairs in the south and Mother will clear Orchard Cottage for our return. Helga and Joey are boarding the train north. Paula loves having her grandson about, his toys under everyone's feet. She reports to Carl, "Helga's big day is only four days off—and she is more than ready—is counting off each day . . . I know that she feels as full of courage as her talk. . . . Joe Carl spends most of his waking hours in the barns & goat yard & vegetable garden with whoever is at work. Of course he 'helps'! Love from *all* here, big and little—your Paula."

When the beautiful girl child is handed to me in the hospital bed, she has a dimple in her chin and fair hair and Helga thinks she will have Paula's way, firm-natured. This will prove to be so. She is "Karlen Paula." My father phones to say that he will be arriving with his friend, Oliver Barrett, to celebrate the granddaughter's arrival. They plan many toasts and will come during visiting hours—seven to nine. At 7:30, Carl calls. They are getting a bite to eat and will be right over.

This second Caesarean has not been comfortable—the birth contractions are continuing. Helga, bless her, is cross. At 9:30 Oliver and Carl are at the door, beaming and with an enormous basket of fruit. A nervous floor nurse is behind them, having pointed out the baby among the crowd. The nursing of Karlen Paula has gone beautifully, but it brings on the pains. This, Helga feels, is something delicate which one does not explain to a glowing grandfather and friend. Sighs of pleasure as the two depart at ten for a night of walking and lifting a stein or two and discussing the State of the Nation.

Carl's life has a new dimension. There is an enchanting little boy just under two years of age who is a part of his life now. During Helga's absence, a long magazine article is being prepared, "Sandburg enjoys playing with his grandson, Joe Carl. The poet is sitting on an obstacle course he made for the boy, out of pieces of driftwood from the beach. He spends hours with the child . . . The poet's house is littered with his grandson's toys, but the household runs beautifully. The life the Sandburgs live is the kind of life everyone wants for himself, quiet, peaceful, hardworking. All are very happy. . . ." And sure enough, there in the photo is my curly-auburn-haired son in his rompers, confident beside his grandfather, a bowl of food between them. Again he stands erect and waves his arms, making a speech on the brick wall along the edge of the terrace (below us is the great vault, get the picture?). There is a ten-foot drop two inches behind the child which seems not to bother my father or the photographer or the reporter. The magazine piece is not because of the child. It is concerned with Carl's new book to be published in August by Harcourts and called *Home Front Memo,* a collection of his writings over the past three years—essays, poems, his newspaper columns, platform speeches and radio broadcasts, more.

The brand-new child is not neglected, Carl writing a friend that there is now a "little figment of a pigment designated as a granddaughter. . . . When she yawns the whole face yawns and there are tremors at the toes sort of saying they too are joining in on the yawn."

He tells of his days there on top of the house in the burning sun, of moments (he is sixty-five now), ". . . often when I work on an outdoor desk here, hummingbirds flutter stationary before trumpet-vine blossoms, sending their long bills into the tube of the flower, enjoying these meals only three or four feet from my chair. It sounds trite and of course is only a commonplace action of getting a living for them. But it always stops me in whatever I am doing and always has a little of a miracle about it."

July and August go along and every day when his grandfather is at home, the boy is dressed and sent up to the Big House after lunch. The "obstacle course" of sun-and-water bleached planks and boards retrieved from beach walks, remain their object of attention.

On a sultry afternoon, Helga feels a storm stirring far away. Thunder mutters and the air is wet and heated. Karlen wakes from a nap and Helga picks her up, slams the door and they are off for the Big House. The family has gathered on the terrace. Thunder crashes over the dune and lightning darts. The lake is white-flecked and brooding.

Time stands still. The wind gathers. The boy is watching beside my father. Here is a "son" now. Here a "John" of his own blood "plucks at his shoe laces" as Carl had written to Paula back in 1918 as a war was ending and another daughter came into the world. Then he had said too, "Take care of John. He may see great days never known to our eyes." What will come to pass between the two? And all of us here?

Helga will be a war widow soon. And we are not seeing much of Uncle Ed. His "Road to Victory" show is going on the road and an edition is being sent to England. He writes that "We are adding a few new pictures . . . we have a couple of good shots for the Merchant Marines. One shot of a torpedoed tanker on fire and a couple of shots of oil-covered sea men that have been rescued."

Our family will have a merchant marine pretty soon. By now Joe is living at Orchard Cottage with a wife and son and daughter. He is twenty and has enlisted in the "Seabees," the construction battalion of the merchant marines. While waiting to be called up, he's gone to work at a defense plant twenty miles away and is assigned to the graveyard shift. Sometimes he ferries Carl about. Wires come addressed to Joe Carl from Uncle Ed (My father is in New York doing last-minute captions for "The Road to Victory"), "YOU ARE HEREWITH ADVISED YOUR GRANDFATHER SUCCESSFULLY DEPOSITED ON WOLVERINE STOP PLEASE INSTRUCT YOUR FATHER TO MEET TRAIN MICHIGAN CITY TUESDAY MORNING 10:40 LOVE AND KISSES YOUR GRANDUNCLE."

While Helga is fastened to her house with a new baby, her young husband sometimes has a wonderful time in the afternoons, out on beach walks and games with Janet, twenty-year-old Adaline and Adaline's brother Stanley. Sometimes Margaret and Miss Sunao go along too. When Joe returns from a long walk in high spirits, Helga feels the hamperings of maternity and her age. While glorying in her beautiful "jewels," her babies, she wishes for some freedom.

The world wishes for freedom. The U.S. Fifth Army has landed at Salerno and taken heavy losses. Bombings continually devastate occupied France and Germany. Allied forces have dug in on the shores of the Solomons. FDR, Stalin and Churchill have their Teheran Conference in late November. Bill Mauldin is shipped overseas to cover the Italian, French and German fronts for the army's *Stars and Stripes.*

Uncle Ed gets his true heart's desire. He is reporting for duty on an aircraft carrier, the USS *Lexington.* It sails with him on the tenth of November 1943 from Pearl Harbor. Dana closes up the Washington apartment and will stay at Umpawaug with the Irish wolfhounds until he is back. The Japanese call the *Lexington* "The Blue Ghost." Their torpedoes sink her time and again, they claim, and yet there she comes slipping into their waters once more. And here she is now, moving toward Tarawa and the Marshall Islands. A torpedo hits her late in the night of 4 December. For five hours she is under constant attack by Japanese aircraft.

When my uncle comes to see us on the way back to Washington, he talks late into the night, waving his hands and describing the quality of the moonlight on the night of the torpedo hit. Our family has a hero. He is towering and his blue eyes are direct. When he arrived wearing an overcoat with twelve gold buttons and with eagles on his cap and stripes on his shoulders and sleeves, everyone cheered. His arms are strong and embracing. His voice is dramatic (it was his hour of glory).

Waving his arms, telling how it was! His sister, Paula, is in the chair, following. Carl? This is his brother! Margaret and Janet adore. Me? Enraptured. A famous hero. Lieutenant Commander Edward Steichen. There is an article on the table over here, "STEICHEN ENTERS NAVAL AVIA-

TION. One of the greatest photographers in history, Steichen is an even greater American. A Colonel in the Army, in charge of all aerial photography in the last war, the Navy gladly accepted his services in this one, etc . . ." And he is ours. Ah.

We are there on the carrier with him. Danger. "The moon is a blaze of brightness. Its broad glittering moonpath brings memories of a procession of other moon-nights . . . beginning far back in my teens . . . then in my twenties, when to me the moon and the moonlit scene were nature's supreme evocation of beauty, and the nocturne theme became the subject for many of my paintings. . . . this very night's moon also bathes the hills and home in Connecticut . . . bathes them with a vast soft stillness. BOOM-BOOM-BOOM . . . BOP . . . ABULMP. . . . All hell is let loose around us. This moon is no neutral bystander, starkly it points out our ships to the enemy." And he calls out (the audience will never forget), "I would have reached up and plucked that moon from the sky with my fingers if I could have!"

Uncle Ed was swept with two others into a safety net by the edge of a plane he'd been filming as it came in for landing. The plane was lost with the pilot. He claims that the time on the USS *Lexington* was the most exciting of his life.

Before leaving for Washington to make his report, he writes in my sister's autograph book.

Janet
Round is the Ring
That has no end
So is the love
For you my Friend
Your
Uncle Ed

Now Helga has put her star in the Orchard Cottage window and Joe Carl has a sailor suit and a coat of navy blue. Joe sends a merchant marine pin for my lapel. For his twenty-first birthday present, I mail to "Daddy bye bye" an 8-by-10 sepia enlargement of myself wearing the pin (dark hair long, smile glowing) with little Joe beside (in the new outfit, confident) and Karlen on my lap (in a lace-collared dress, blonde, laughing).

Joe has a three-day furlough before being shipped out. I send a wire, "ARRIVING GRAND CENTRAL STATION FRIDAY NIGHT MEET ME ENTRANCE USO AT 8 OCLOCK HELGA." And I am off to New York on the Wolverine. On the way I hold hands with a navy man returning from leave. He is sad. There seems no harm in it. Carl has given Helga the key to the penthouse apartment of a cartoonist friend of his who leaves the city on long weekends. It overlooks the Hudson River. A buddy of Joe's and his date are here and daring farewell pictures are taken of each other kissing. The girls are in flowered frocks and the novice Seabees in navy blues and little round white caps.

The four go dancing nightly. And once attempt to get into the Stork Club, where they know Carl's name but flatly refuse to let in anyone but a full-fledged officer! Daughter or no daughter. So there. At home, sleepy and almost content, Helga reports the Stork Club incident to Carl, who says we should have called his night-life New York friends, Walter Winchell and Leonard Lyons. In Helga's letter to Joe she explains that Carl can't get to the base to see Joe before he's shipped out because he's involved in some work. And, "Dad said don't mind getting ordered around. You're only one in a million."

Carl sends a letter. By now it is the end of May of 1944, "Dear Joe, It was good to hear your voice today coming all the way from the Atlantic Coast to the shores of Lake Michigan. We talk about you all the time. We are proud of you. Maybe you know your name is going on the plaque at Harbert along with the other fellows who are out taking their chances. Little Joey makes his face like yours, enough so that we can't forget your smile and the crinkle of your eyes. Good health and luck, Joe, and our prayers go with you. Dad."

A few days later. The sixth of June. The early morning radio crackles the news. "D-Day" is under way. Helga dresses the children and is off to the Big House. Leaving Karlen with the family, she brings little Joe up the steps to Carl's attic bed. They wake him and put on the radio as the news unravels. Before dawn, a thousand planes and gliders began dropping parachuters. A thousand of Britain's Royal Air Force and over a thousand of our bombers have been striking railroad yards, junctions, repair stations between the Rhine and Normandy. The first assault troops are sloshing through the water and dying and surviving along a sixty-mile beachhead. Fog and storm prevail.

Joe Carl sits on the bed and plays with a paperweight, impressed by the unusual visit. Helga is on the chair beside. Carl is delighted to be wakened, rubs his eyes, settles the pillows so his head is raised. The scent of a sleeping man. A secure scent. Familiar.

Carl and Helga whisper and listen and wonder. The world is watching and hanging upon radios and newspapers. Can the allies' combined forces pull it off? *Der Führer's* Field Marshal von Rundstedt refuses to accept the report that an invasion is happening. He is confident that Ike would not make the move. Hitler is out of town and doesn't want to be bothered. And so, helped by Allied knowledge of the secret German code and the 156,000 soldiers either plummeting down or wading in during the first two days of the attack, success.

Helga has no address for Joe. Wait. The unsatisfied females all over the nation are working it out. We sing with Marlene, "They're either too young or too old, they're either too gray or too grassy green." And wait.

Paula has negotiated and got her Nisei man to help at the barns. After some attempts he is now accepted as a private in the army. He leaves in May and Helga takes his place. Up at five, with Joey along while Karlen sleeps. My hands are cramped at night and swell. Here are more goats to milk than I've had for a long time. It is lonely. The garden helps. Hands in the dirt, hoeing, weeding, transplanting. Bringing in flowers to fill the vases at Orchard Cottage and the Big House. When the night milking is finished, dropping into sleep early.

FDR is nominated at the Democratic National Convention in July to run for a fourth term. Carl likes that. Hitler is almost assassinated. General Patton's Third Army shatters *Der Führer's* defenses at St. Lo and begins the sweep across France. Helga gets a letter! Joe is in England, likes the countryside and expects to be home in November for a thirty-day furlough. His ship is the SS *John W. Powell.* I send him long letters, ending or beginning (or in the middle) saying, "All my love always and always and always." No replies.

Carl comes by every day to go walking and talking, enchanted with the boy child. They are close. My father is wonderfully humorous and curious and protective of Joe Carl. And of course, he observes the girl child and is kindly, but she is a baby. Joey has a mind of his own. And now Paula is off to a goat meeting in Columbus, Ohio. Her white hair is waved and shining and she wears a new sweater and the family stays impressed. Carl feels her enthusiasm and makes no attempt at understanding the politics of that industry.

My father likes my little house, Orchard Cottage. And while my mother is away, he brings some visiting poet friends over. He has his guitar under his arm. The songs we sing fit the war. Some are about a past one.

A Spanish cavalier stood in his retreat
And on his guitar played a tune, dear,
The music so sweet would oft times repeat
The blessings of my country and you, dear.

I'm off to the war, to the war I must go
To fight for my country and you, dear.
And if I be slain, you may seek me in vain,
Upon the battlefield you will find me!

And (for the sake of Joe)

My Bonnie lies over the ocean,
Oh, bring back my Bonnie to me!

And

Sailing, sailing, over the bounding main,
There's many a stormy wind shall blow
Till Joe comes home again!

When Paula is back, she speaks again of an idea she has. She'd like to move whenever the war is over. She'd like a grand farm to put the goats out on where they could pasture on alfalfa and clover for much of the year. Not just on hay. She repeats her notion. Carl says anywhere will suit him as long as he can take walks with Joey every day. And the boy? He puts his finger up like a preacher in front of his nose and says in a low voice, "Daddy on a big ship!" He does no wrong. Helga's hero.

Joey has a name for his grandfather. Rather, the grandfather picks out the name from the various ones the child attempts. *Buppong.* And so it will stay. He writes the boy's father, "Well, son, we go on day after day wondering where you are and talking about this or that you might be doing. It's the biggest war there ever was and we're glad you're throwing in on it . . . Always good wishes and prayers from Grandma and Buppong."

We are pressing shirts and packing sandwiches of goat butter and cheese and pumpernickel bread and containers of goat milk (he does not mind if it curdles) for my father. He is leaving for Hollywood and will be gone a few weeks. For the first time in his life he has been asked to write a novel, a piece of fiction. He hopes to return with "some odd news out of movie land" for Paula. Metro-Goldwyn-Mayer has put Sidney Franklin and Voldemar Vetluguin in charge of the project. They are to work with Carl.

It is the concept of a pair of lovers who are reincarnated again and again as crises in the history of our country unfold. If they like the novel when Carl finishes it, and a movie results, he will get $20,000. Meantime, Harcourt will publish it. Now, a studio limousine is at his disposal and transports him elegantly to and from conferences. He returns home on fire. How my father enjoys the idea of another field before him! Poet, troubador, historian, newspaperman. "The Great American Novel," he cries at the supper table. Seven days a week he works at it. Miss Sunao is there. Sundays and Labor Day too. "Being Labor Day, we shall labor," he states.

Helga informs her fighting Seabee of all these happenings and perhaps not too tactfully. Is he impressed with the conquests of his father-in-law? And with the reports of Uncle Ed's triumphs? And how my uncle calls our daughter his

"Little Ballerina?" I wait in vain for news of the promised furlough.

The lights are on again in London. The war race moves forward. The Allied troops cross the Loire. Paris is liberated after four years of occupation. And Antwerp and Brussels. And Luxembourg! Uncle Ed writes Paula, "Now that we are cleaning the heinies out of Luxembourg so that country can smell sweet again . . . everything else seems easy. . . . I'm working harder than ever. . . . I may be heading out to the Pacific again before winter and if so will try to stop over for a day. Love to all . . . Brudder (that's me)."

No letters for Helga. It is mid-October and we are putting up Christmas boxes. At Orchard Cottage. And at the Big House. For Joe. Packing and fussing over what to put in. Margaret is taking care of the children while Helga puts in more time at the barns. And the sisters stay for supper. And sometimes Adaline and Miss Sunao. We play bridge in the evenings now and then. Helga is working on not being lonesome. Her life is turning in different ways. She is reading books again.

Paula writes a letter, "Dear Son Joe—we are all listening—hoping you will telephone one of these days from Brooklyn telling us you are again in America and coming home for a visit. It seems a long time since you left home for Merchant Marine training and we all thought you would have a furlough soon. We miss you so much. Helga lives thinking of the days to come when you will be home and the little family together again. Dad has just returned from his California trip and was he surprised how Karlen developed in the short time that he was away. M.G.M. is going to use a book that Dad is writing for a movie 'American Cavalcade.' So that is a big wind-fall! We just have the news that MacArthur has landed in the Philippines with a big army. So the war is going well ahead of schedule. Our thoughts are with you, dear son, in your service for your country and for us all who stay at home, waiting for (and praying for) your safe return. Love from us all here always—and 'God keep you safe!' Lovingly, Mother."

Three letters from overseas! Helga is in love again. The Christmas packages arrived. She bursts into tears in Carl's arms. He pats her shoulder while her sobs continue. "Dad! I hate this war!" The family is impressed (Joey too). She promises in her next letter out, that she will not write to Joe in a wandering way about her feelings, and "I'll always be your woman as long as you want me and I hope that will be always," etc.

Isn't Helga one of many who think secretly of how it would be if she wrote a "Dear John" letter and told Joe not to return to her, but because of "love," "devotion," "morality," puts it off? Helga has forgotten Joe's ways and mourns in a long letter to him, ". . . Yesterday was Sunday and I was alone and so blue, so we put Karlen to bed and Joey and I went to the Big House . . ." And a new note, "It doesn't make me feel good when you say you stayed home to be a good boy while everyone else went out—that's crazy. Get your mind off your work. . . . Just getting out a little doesn't mean you're unfaithful to me. . . . You're going to forget how to dance and everything, so remember you're doing what I *want* when you go out. . . ." And so on.

And then, "You'll find me changed a great deal, Joe. I might as well tell you. The only thing that's the same is the way I love you and that is more and more. . . ." Is that put in for reassurance—love, devotion, morality? She continues, "but I'm not a bit bashful any more and like lots of company and going places. I don't mean with men but Ad and I go out once in a while and I dance when I get a chance. But I'm not doing anything but enjoying myself and I'm only afraid that you aren't. . . . just figure someone else is me (when you first knew me—not married!) and have a good time. I'm serious, Joe, and please don't get bully and stubborn. . . ."

Is she preparing the way to leave? And how is that taken when the young man on board his ship reads it? Some four-letter words are included in his few missives back to his restless wife. And she is. Her life is changing. Feeling freedom. Someone to leave her children with—the family. No reports on how the day went. Going to the movies with Adaline and perhaps a cafe with a jukebox.

Uncle Ed comes by, heading west. Does Helga muddy the water more while writing her husband of her uncle's visit, of champagne and then, "I mentioned to mother how nice it was that Ed and Dad were both famous and so there was no jealousy between them and they both respected each other. And I said that was where it was hard with you because you were so young and had not yet done anything, and Mom said yes, if you and Ed and Dad were on a desert island, who would they turn to, or if their car broke down who would they turn to. I guess she is right, Joe, and every man has his own special field and you can stand on your own feet with any man. . . ."

How did all this sit with the young fighter for his country? Her letters coming in small parcels now and then and loaded like little novels with information over which he has no control. His letters declare not only affection but faithfulness and staying aboard ship while mates head for whores and adventure. Her letters contain her working it out. I know what mold I wish my husband to fit into. And he has a head like a rock in the deep blue sea.

Already Helga's missives suggest that perhaps a farm is

too far away from culture and civilization and that Joe might consider investing his income and talents in a garage upon his return. And then the good times, ". . . you should see your daughter. Ed and Dad have decided to quit working and enjoy their old age on her money. They're going to start 'Karlen, Inc.' and put her in pictures and when she gets bigger they'll run her against Clare Booth Luce for Congress. . . . Dad said he's seen children, but never any so remarkable as these. We didn't even compare to them. And Ed says, 'Or any so intelligent. Other kids are so dumb.' It was really very funny, those two . . ." Does Joe know who Clare Booth Luce is? Helga, bless her. How does that go down with our faraway Seabee on his ship, handling the long restless letters that arrive in bundles from another world?

Joe is saving his money to bring home. Obviously I am being taken care of on my parents' place. But I want independence. And tell him so, ". . . People keep asking how much you make and I haven't the slightest idea. . . . You know I get $40 the first of every month from Mother. . . . You do what you like because I signed over all claims, but couldn't you fix it so I get an allotment some way? How do the other men do that have wives? . . . Anyway, I'm just letting you know how it is and you do what you want. . . ."

Another note creeps quietly in, "I've been typing for Dad lately to help him out. . . ." And the lonesome Christmas comes and goes and no furlough and time moves and the year is almost through. ". . . I've been very busy. Dad just left on another trip and left me a pile of typing so I'd better get started. I've taken up typing for Dad & Mom for some extra cash and I enjoy it. . . . I've been taking up my French again. . . . I believe I've been getting into a rut lately. . . . Uncle Ed has been promoted. . . . He is a captain. . . ." And on and on.

Then sending a poem that surely falls on an unaccepting heart, "I was reading last night and there's one I liked especially because it sort of suits me. It's by Bryant." (Could straightforward Joe ever know who William Cullen Bryant was or what the lines were about?)

"I broke the spell that held me long,
The dear dear witchery of song.
I said, the poet's idle lore
Shall waste my prime of years no more,
For Poetry, though heavenly born,
Consorts with poverty & scorn.

"I broke the spell—nor deemed its power
Could fetter me another hour.
Ah, thoughtless! how could I forget
Its causes were around me yet?
For wheresoe'er I looked, the while,
Was Nature's everlasting smile.

"Still came and lingered on my sight
Of flowers and streams the bloom & light,
And glory of the stars & seen;—
And these & poetry are one.
They, ere the world had held me long,
Recalled me to the love of song!"

Helga is back in the old pattern of her days. The camaraderie, the gaiety, the ease, the understanding, the acceptance. No arguments. Margaret reads to her nephew of three, beginning his education, and stays at Orchard Cottage in the early nights while Helga is typing at the Big House. Janet is always available to entertain the little ones or hang around while naps are underway. All the pain and all the mourning and weeping and wanting are over for Helga. I am healed.

Do you understand Helga at all at this time in her life? How can I convey the power of Carl? He is exciting! His ideas are ones I understand. I am again surrounded by the weight of books and papers. Creation. Helga feels it. And then he always admires me, always praises. Not like my marriage where the man often wants to fight in what I consider are the wrong arenas! The bed? That is all this father-daughter relationship lacks. But aren't there men always somewhere about. Surely.

I discuss this turning of mine with my parents. Divorce. And they accept my decision with the same completeness as the elopement. Their support is total. Helga writes no more letters. When Joe does come before long, bearing gifts and cash for his wife, my father stands beside me. Joe goes with him to sleep solitary at the Big House and then take the bus away. (It's all right. Two years later, he and Adaline will fall in love and wed. Babies. A happy ending.)

There is Helga, hurling herself at the typing load Carl has given her. His novel starts:

> The boy not yet two years old tried to say "Grandpa" and it came out "Bowbong." That, anyhow, was the one they picked from bowbong, buppong, boohbong, bahbong, babbong, pahpong and still other variations. The older ones took to saying and writing it Bowbong and it was really nobody's business except Bowbong the grandfather's and Raymond the grandson's.
>
> More than twenty years ago, that was. And now

from the South Pacific letters had come that began with "Dear Bowbong." And from India, Egypt, Italy, England, Pearl Harbor, Los Angeles, had come letters or postal cards that began with "Dear Bowbong," these from Raymond, a pilot, "on a mission" here, "on a mission" there, leading a global life that neither he nor Bowbong had expected in the years just before 1944. . . .

Part Four

THE GOLDEN PLACE

BY NOW I have kissed a 4–F and a married man or two. And I am surprised and also enchanted when my uncle kisses me. Honored and curious. It is, as he says, Biblical. A war is on. Does he sense his fragility, his mortality? Whether interesting or inconsequential, it is history. Helga loves it.

It is March. He is on his way to the Pacific, to Guam and Iwo Jima. Dana is with him. Paula has her camera out. The three-year-old in sailor suit and round cap stands on the steps beside the sixty-six-year-old in full dress uniform with commander stripes. They salute. And stand at rigid attention. Karlen is there too with pink coat and bonnet. A toddler.

Uncle Ed captivates the children, down on his knees growling and barking and shaking hands on command. In the evening, the young ones are put to bed at Orchard Cottage and there is a feast at the Big House with Yorkshire pudding and roast beef. My uncle is electric and there are frequent toasts to freedom at last in Luxembourg. He has brought along a record of "Die Wacht Am Rhein" and plays it to his antics like Chaplin.

The Battle of Iwo Jima is on. Our troops have taken Manila and Mindanao. Uncle Ed wants to get into the thick of it. Secretary Forrestal signs an order placing him in direct command of all naval combat photography. And he is made director of the U.S. Navy Photographic Institute and awarded the Distinguished Service Medal. He also receives the Art Directors Club Medal for his work on a navy film that, through Twentieth Century–Fox, becomes a popular movie—*The Fighting Lady,* most of the footage shot by cameramen of his unit on the USS *Lexington.* His exhibit on now at the Museum of Modern Art follows the pattern of "Road to Victory" and is called "Power In the Pacific." The critics like it.

He tells us about all of this. Our hero. Helga has baked

and frosted a three-layer Lord Baltimore cake for the occasion. Macaroons and pecans and almonds and maraschino cherries are in the filling. A heavy thick white frosting. When ready and presented to the table, the layers have fallen and the moist filling is revealed. The triumph is clearly lopsided. Uncle Ed nods approval. To the family's delight, he makes sounds of greed. "Any cake that has a perfect shape is cardboardy," he declares. And, "Not worth the time!" He cuts and serves it himself, "A gem."

At the evening's end, he walks Helga home to Orchard Cottage. There is forty years difference in our ages. This has nothing to do with incest. This is tribute. I am not about to reject this man we all adore. And also I may learn something. As time goes on and the war reaches an end and "the boys" come home, Helga hopes to garner more kisses, more honors.

When Uncle Ed arrives at Iwo Jima, it is the day after it is declared secure. Close to 500 ships were used in the invasion, including 17 aircraft carriers and over a thousand planes. U.S. troop losses are 4,590 men. Japanese dead are over twenty thousand. Okinawa is next on April Fool's Day in the war's final land campaign. The sky fills with kamikazes.

Another casualty. On April twelfth. My father's friend. The radios stop their scheduled programs and play dark solemn music with occasional breaks to speak of the loss of our leader, aged sixty-three, of a cerebral hemorrhage in Warm Springs, Georgia. Carl is sixty-seven. The *Woman's Home Companion* asks for a poem. $1,000. The fee is to be divided, he says, "among several anti-Franco organizations."

Can a bell ring in the heart
telling the time, telling a moment,
telling off a stillness come,

in the afternoon a stillness come
and now never come morning? . . .

Can a bell ring in the heart
in time with the tall headlines,
the high fidelity transmitters,
the somber consoles rolling sorrow,
the choirs in ancient laments—chanting
"Dreamer, sleep deep,
Toiler, sleep long,
Fighter, be rested now.
Commander, sweet good-night."

V-E Day is approaching. Out in Hollywood, Norman Corwin wires that he wants Carl on a live broadcast from his home. He has one minute and fifteen seconds exactly. Can he do it? He can. CBS radio network hookup crews arrive in Harbert on the twenty-fourth of April. Local excitement is keen. The workers make demands and get their way. And so (from the script):

> WE SWITCH TO SANDBURG'S HOME IN HARBERT MICHIGAN FROM FRISCO AT APPROXIMATELY 10.48.30 PM EWT ON FOLLOWING WORD CUE: WE TAKE YOU EASTWARD IN A STRAIGHT LINE ACROSS ONE OF THE GREAT LAKES TO THE HOME OF CARL SANDBURG IN THE TOWN OF HARBERT MICHIGAN WHERE THE EMINENT POET AND BIOGRAPHER OF ABRAHAM LINCOLN WILL SPEAK TO YOU FROM HIS STUDY. . . .

The words are Lincoln's and my father will use them over and over in the rest of his days. His voice is clear and deep.

The family listens in the kitchen, confident. The statements are noble.

> We can succeed only by concert. The dogmas of the quiet past are inadequate to the stormy present. The occasion is piled high with difficulty and we must rise with the occasion. As our case is new, so we must think anew and act anew. Fellow citizens, we cannot escape history. We of this congress and this administration will be remembered in spite of ourselves. No personal significance or insignificance can spare one or another of us. The fiery trial through which we pass will light us down in honor or dishonor, to the latest generation. We shall nobly save or meanly lose the last best hope of earth.

V-E Day. The eighth of May 1945. *Il Duce* and his officers are executed by partisans. *Der Führer* and Eva Braun commit suicide. And Goebbels and his family. The country looks toward V-J Day. On the sixth of August, "Little Boy" gets pitched into Hiroshima's 343,969 people and 100,000 go instantly. August ninth and another atomic bomb goes into Nagasaki's 252,630 and 75,000 are finished. So is the Second World War after six terrifying years. Over fifty million perished, in the main civilians. One third of the world's Jews went, perhaps four million, by cyanide gas in southern Poland at the Auschwitz-Birkenau death camp. A lot of Japanese generals commit ritual suicide and even though Emperor Hirohito attempts hara-kiri, he fails and signs the peace treaty on board the USS *Missouri* in Tokyo Bay on the second of September.

By now Helga has her divorce (July 31. Cost: $124.15, the small change due to postage and filing fees). I have custody and control of Joey and Karlen with visitation rights. I renounce all claims on support. I am on a regular salary from Carl besides daily chores at the barns.

Joe? He does not come by. He too is busy putting his life together, back with his family for the time down in Illinois. Isn't he as aware as Helga that their deep interests are at variance? Hasn't he felt the power of Carl? The headstrong nature of Helga? It will not happen yet. Two years will go by and then Joe will seek Adaline out. Those two are natural companions. Her love will come through his persuasions. What will time bring to all of these?

My family is about to fulfil Paula's dream. (Helga's too.) We will desert our home on its sandy bluff where the winds arrive at the door straight from the North Pole. We will find a place with black soil, green fields, barns, a farmhouse. Carl? He says that since his wife and daughter are aware of his needs, he will let them look and make reports. So the children are put in the care of one of Adaline's sisters. Helga is at the wheel of the family car. Paula holds the road map and directs. We whirr through back roads and past fields and barns. We inquire of agents and reject with ease. Until one seems right. After a couple of weeks we have found our heart's desire. Carl is summoned for approval and gives it.

On a rainy morning in November, Paula, Janet and Adaline head away to our new home in Flat Rock, North Carolina, where workmen are busy altering and repairing and following the instructions my mother left with them as to changes. Adaline drives the station wagon and the old trailer is hitched behind, loaded with some of our best does. Helga, Margaret and the children hold the fort and see to the shipping of the rest of the animals as well as the packing of the household goods. The thousands of books. Even bookshelves (wartime restrictions are still on) are torn down and will go. Helga keeps hammer and tools at the ready.

Carl? There he sits (with an occasional child visitor) wearing his visor, pecking away. He works at the last typewriter not yet packed, a portable set on an orange crate, the immediate materials on boxes nearby. The plan is that at the last moment, he will leave the spot and the set-up will be whisked off to the top floor of the new home where he can continue when he arrives. He hopes to finish his novel in a year and will never make it. The press arrives for interviews.

It is an exhilarating time. The house is like a camp with improvised chairs and tables. With packing cases everywhere. My father and his small companions take continual pleasure in each others' company. He reads to them in the evenings. The guitar stays with us (he will carry that to the new home himself). They go walking, scuffing through the autumn leaves that cascade about us. They bring in bouquets of colorful maple and oak and sassafras and pawpaw. We have talked and Joey is now firmly renamed John Carl. I am content and like it (I love my father). As for Karlen, she has a nickname that he has come upon. It is just between the two of them—"Snick." It will stay with her.

Carl has started a poem for the two-year-old.

First Sonata For Karlen Paula

At an autumn evening bonfire
came rose-candle co-ordinations.
Burning and burnt
came a slow song of fire leaves. . . .

Make like before, sweet child.
Be you like five new oranges in a wicker basket.
Step out like
a summer evening fireworks over black waters.
Be dizzy in a haze of yellow silk bandannas.

Then in a change of costume
sit silent in a chair of tarnished bronze
Having spoken with a grave mouth:
"Now I will be
a clavichord melody
in October brown.
You will see me in
deep-sea contemplation
on a yellow horse in a white wind." . . .

It is mid-December and the shipping vans arrive. Some trouble arises when there is talk of breaking into the sealed boxcar. The guards are suspicious. A considerable weight for "Household Goods." They are appeased when they learn that the load is mostly books belonging to some author.

The last day of December. Helga and the children drive Carl to the station and put him on the train to Los Angeles and consultation with the Hollywood people. A snow storm is building. We telegraph the time of our arrival at our new home. It is called "Connemara" (the last owner was a homesick Irishman) and is set in the Appalachian Mountains between the Blue Ridge and the Great Smokey ranges.

Spring. The mountains are in bloom. The dairy goats are in the near pasture. Watch Paula's face as for the first time they are turned in. Satisfaction. Glory. Helga too. She has horses to ride again. Beauties. Five-gaited easygoing Storm. Pretty buckskin Blueberry. For the children stolid black-and-white Patches. There is a big gray work team too, Pearl and Major. A herdsman worker and his family are in the little house on the place. Mr. Mintz (and Helga now and then) drives the team, hitched to the manure spreader and later the hay rake. The dream come true.

Uncle Ed and Dana are arriving on the noon train. Carl greets them on the white-pillared porch. At his side, in military salute, are John Carl and Karlen, along with the new Doberman, Leif, and the children's cocker spaniel, Hannah. We walk the boundaries and the wonders are told. Here are hundred-year-old remnants of boxwood formal gardens. Ginkgo trees, towering magnolias, hollies, bamboo, Chinese elms. All placed by old-time planters.

Here are 240 acres to explore. A small mountain named "Little Glassy" (sheer granite rock slabs on the sides) and a big steep and rugged one behind, "Big Glassy." Connemara's first owner was Christopher Gustavus Memminger, secretary of the treasury of the Confederate States of America, picked as one of his cabinet by fifty-two-year-old Jefferson Davis of Mississippi. John and Snick sing readily with Buppong:

We'll hang Jeff Davis to a sour apple tree
As we go marching on. . . .

Memminger's main problem with his job was that there was no money in the treasury. He levied taxes. The currency gradually collapsed. He resigned. He came here to remain until the war's end. His home was Charleston. This was a summer place, a haven from the heat of South Carolina. The house was built of nearby timber, the beams and sills and sidings hand-hewn. Every May his slaves went ahead in wagons to prepare for the family following in carriages and by horseback, a ten-day trip.

There are loopholes in the ground floor so that when marauding bushwackers came up the hill, their fire could be returned. Memminger tried to persuade his president to move the southern capitol from Richmond to this place. We hear stories from our new neighbors of how the Great Provisional Seal of the Confederate States was sent by cavalry officer from Davis to Memminger for safekeeping. It may be buried on Connemara! Union boys were hidden by local people in garrets and cellars until underground guides could get them through the lines and north. Neighbors sheltered a Gray boy one month and a Blue the next.

Carl is at home here. He tells how when he came to look it over first, the patriarchal caretaker, Ulysses Ballard, came to fetch Paula and himself at the front gate because there was a snow-and-ice storm and the drive was slippery. Carl arrived at his front porch riding in a wagon pulled by Ballard's brindled and horned team of oxen, their cloven hooves sure-footed. And he tells how the Cherokee nation once held this land. Then came Memminger in the 1830s when the mountain laurel was in bloom, as it is now.

The children and the dogs circle us, clambering up and down the rock faces, as we climb Big Glassy. My mother names the trees. Oaks, tulips, hickories, maples, horse chestnuts, gums, yellow poplars, white pines. At their feet huckleberry, winterberry, rhododendron, azaleas, laurel, dogwood. My father talks about Lincoln and Reconstruction and the history of those days. How the President of the North had not wanted Jeff Davis made a martyr and how after he'd been captured and held awhile, he was allowed to slip off to Canada. Then he was pardoned when general amnesty was proclaimed on Christmas Day of 1868. Memminger got his pardon too and his citizenship restored.

Carl gives names to places and trees about his new domain. The way around Little Glassy is Memminger Path. The front pasture oaks are Abraham Lincoln and Robert E. Lee. There is a Jefferson Davis Slab and for his wife, the Varina Davis Bridge across the dam of Memminger Lake. The big white pines in the goat pasture are The Four Brothers. The children help him. The Dragon is a torn giant oak. The

Sleeping Tree is a reclining hickory. The Confluence is where the two pasture lake overflows come together. Big Igneous is a great rock slab. Little Igneous is smaller. The Precipitous Declivity is just that.

The grandfather has a song too and they sing it together (tune: "Sweet Betsy from Pike" from *The American Songbag*) for the granduncle and Dana as we traipse down the mountain:

Do you remember sweet Snick from Connemara,
Who crossed the Confluence with her brother, John?
With Lief and with Hannah and two guinea pigs
They made the trip in an old yellow rig.

When they got down as far as the store
They were so tired they couldn't go any more,
So they turned around and to home they did go
With the dogs and the pigs and the rig going slow.

Memminger died in 1888 and the Irishman ("Captain" Ellison Adger Smythe also from Charleston) arrived soon and took over. He dammed pasture streams and excavated for the lake and dug for an ice house and put in more shrubbery and ornamental trees and built tenant houses and set out an orchard and rock-walled a trout pond and planted a rose garden and built an underground greenhouse to winter delicate plantings and kept the mountain trails open for horseback riders. He died at ninety-four, three years before our arrival. There had been a coachman here, a butler, cook, maids, gardeners. Now what? Helga counts her lucky stars here on the mountain with Uncle Ed and Dana and the children singing with Carl, while the three examine the ground under a horse chestnut tree to collect buckeyes, the glossy mahogany nuts broken from the tree's burrs over the winter.

John Carl's wagon's painted blue. . . .
Snick is pretty as a redbird and a bluebird too. . . .
Buppong's hat got torn in two,
Skip to my Lou, my darling.

When we return to the porch of the house, the three salute "Mister Magillicuddy." He is a three-legged stick wearing an old twelve-dollar hat that Carl rescued from the wastebasket of one of his Chicago lawyer horseshoe-pitching friends. He likes the hat because it is handy to fold and stick in his belt. "Mr. Magillicuddy" is very like a Rootabaga character. He is recognizable by the hat which sometimes perches, not on the stick, but on my father's sweater thrown over a porch chair and with a pair of his weatherbeaten shoes beneath.

It is night. The dishes are cleared. The family and the dogs move into the living room. The moon is high outside. The spring wind comes through the open door. Janet brings a bowl of walnuts and pecans and nutcrackers and picks. And another of apples and fruit knives. Uncle Ed tells John Carl that the next day they will slip out the bolts of at least one door's hinges and take it down, inspect it and replace it. He takes down the dish from the mantel where the buckeyes were piled. He offers everyone "a chocolate." Carl puts his aside for later. Dana is on a diet and refuses even one. My uncle is a natural mime. He makes noises of appreciation of the flavor. With difficulty, he extracts a piece of nut stuck in a back tooth. His audience share his anxiety and then his relief when, successful, he smiles sweetly. "More like Charlie Chaplin every year, Buddy," Carl tells Paula.

The children are led off to be read to and to fall asleep in their bunk beds. My father watches them go. "Those two," he says, "are almost too good to be true and a fellow wonders what time will bring. They have loveliness and rare lights and shake the house with their promises."

What will Connemara hold for us all?

There Helga stands in the center as the Golden Time wheels about her. Riding chestnut sorrel Storm who never tires of climbing the mountains, sliding down the steep ravines, a two-hour jaunt to Jumpoff Mountain or the long miles to Five Point Mountain. He is glossy and gentle and fiery and quickly learns to rear as Nancy and Silver had. She writes Buppong, "I'm sorry I missed your voice the other night. We have been putting up quantities of strawberry jam, cherry jam and Connemara peas. The garden is beautiful. No incidents of tragedy or note occurring beyond that of Sophie the rabbit drowning one child in her water basin. Paula sold two guinea pigs for two dollars and has become a downright Capitalist. I am cleaning your room thoroughly today myself in hopes that I shall hear you are returning to the Ancestral Halls shortly. Your daughter who loves you, Helga."

My mother and I are busy with projects. I am making goat cheeses, thinking perhaps of a market some day. The cover of *The Goat World* has my picture again with a champion doe and "The New Partner at Chikaming." Paula signs over the goat herd to Helga and gives her a paper, "I have also leased the pastures and barns . . . in return for supplying the family with milk and butter, etc . . ." Helga handles the paperwork for the farm and does Carl's correspondence. Yearly salary: $3,600. (A secretary from the nearby mountains helps in the afternoons as Carl wrestles with the finishing of his novel.)

By now there are three "books" within Carl's opus: "The First Comers" (Plymouth Rock and Roger Williams), "The

Arch Begins" (Valley Forge and Washington), "The Arch Holds" (what Carl calls "the terrific Now"). He writes Archie MacLeish at the Library of Congress, "I have laid an egg in the shape of another long chaotic book." He puts MacLeish into the Epilog. In a chapter called "Wherein the Lonely Speak," MacLeish becomes the Librarian of Congress and is reading one of his poems over the radio to some of the characters in the book:

The young dead soldiers do not speak.
Nevertheless, they are heard in the still houses:
Who has not heard them?
They have a silence that speaks for them at night
and when the clock counts
They say: "We were young. We have died. Remember us. . . ."

Carl puts other friends in his book. There is our Eric Sevareid. One of the book's characters has met him and is now listening as "Across the Atlantic now came his voice, 'The soldier knows the real story of the war; he feels it sharply, but he couldn't tell it to you himself. . . . War happens inside a man . . .'" And after the Sevareid piece, Carl slips in one of his own war poems done back in June of 1943.

Freedom is a habit
and a coat worn
some born to wear it
some never to know it.
Freedom is cheap
or again as a garment
is so costly
men pay their lives
rather than not have it. . . .

There are long excerpts from letters that a new friend, Lt. Kenneth MacKenzie Dodson, wrote home during the war, describing the aftermath of battle on Pacific beaches where he'd been from Guadalcanal to Okinawa, from Saipan to Kwajalein to Palau. Carl writes to Dodson as spring ends and summer comes on, "Dear Kennie: On this anniversary of D-Day I have finished reading about a dozen of your letters. I find them now as at first deeply moving. . . . Your letters have given me a lift to go on in the final shapings of this long book that curiously and inevitably has gone so much longer than originally planned. . . . As always. . . ."

Look back at the strange unconventional family. What do the new neighbors think of them? Here at Flat Rock we are in the remains of a summer settlement created during the peak of the antebellum years in Charleston, where fortunes were built on the slave system and the social customs on the gentry of Old England. (Sandburg is not a Red, but he has been close.) None of us have heard English spoken as our new neighbors use it. The children pick up the accent quickly, spending time with the herdsman's small daughters, listening to our mountain household helper, who explains why the War Between the States lasted so long, "Because South Carolina fit North Carolina and that was practically The War."

Among others, we meet Mrs. Robert E. Lee III. Her ancestor, Henry I. Middleton, was the first president of the Continental Congress. Another, Arthur Middleton, signed the Declaration of Independence. She is the widow of the grandson of our Gen. Robert E. Lee and comes to call wearing a fox stole and a flowered hat. Paula meets her in a print dress, a newborn kid in her arms.

And there is Helga. She is twenty-seven as the Golden Summer enfolds. By now there are Lochinvars about, young friends of Carl's friends traveling through and not averse to a canter about the mountains, a painter of some repute. The latter sheds a bottle of Chanel No. 5 over me, in love, and an armful of roses. Uncle Ed is a sort of Lochinvar, remaining impressed with my self-confidence. He likes the new field I am exploring, stretching canvases and preparing panels and acquiring pastels and oils and boxes of water colors and palettes and easels. Uncle Ed says my work has feelings a little like Modigliani. He presents me with a large brilliant Ben Shahn tempera.

Margaret and I go now and then to the nearby Lake Summit Playhouse to see *Arsenic and Old Lace* or whatever. There a dashing young actor, Art, enchants me. He is twenty-three. It is the Snake in the Garden again. The Apple and the Tree and Enraptured Eve.

See this odd family. Look back through the glass. The house is a stately one from the outside. Paula has altered the inside. The tall ceilings are brought down and hundreds of shelves for books are put in. There are no curtains in the windows. They look out on heaven. Here is Paula, seated in her "Farm Office," her feet tucked in the rung of her chair. The bookshelves filled with data and information and references. Pedigrees and forms and letters scattered about. Photographs of family and champion dairy goats and herd sires thumbtacked to the bulletin boards on the walls. Cups and blue ribbons are on a high shelf along with a bust of her husband done by somebody. Or she is at the barns, a thoughtful look on her as she studies the does and considers future plans. Or she is in the kitchen at the preparation of some utterly simple food. Yogurt. Soups. Plain fare when she is responsible. My mother's enthusiasm glistens in her blue-gray eyes. Her laugh is easy and quick.

Carl. Up at noon or thereabouts. His nights, like the old times in Michigan, are spent in the attic, the lamplight now pouring out onto surrounding forest trees, out into the dark or the moonlight, his reconditioned Remington clucking away as the book moves. Having lunch at the dining table, the children at his side asking questions. He writes down their sayings in a little notebook or handy paper. His blue shirt is open and his sleeves rolled. He is casual about laundry. His pants are old and shabby and comfortable. The belt is ancient. He carries a pocket knife and a pocket watch. His laugh is deep. His resonant unusual voice is part of the air of Connemara.

Margaret. Her etudes and exercises and arpeggios ring through the house from the living room in the afternoons and late in the night. (The children are starting piano lessons and will give recitals soon.) Sometimes the dragon is about. My sister is in her mid-thirties. Her hair is dark. Her laugh is sweet. There she is on Blueberry, in slacks and shirt. John Carl is on Patches at her side. They are grinning!

Janet. Confident and easygoing. The one of us with handsome Steichen features. Energetic. Up at early light to feed her kids at the barns. Janet, too, is seen on Blueberry now and then. She is capable and surely if our family had not had a famous man at its head, or if we had lived in olden times when marriages were arranged, guileless Janet would have made a good man's wife. The baby goats suit her maternal feelings. And she always has a kitten or cat in her arms.

Helga. Locking her room doors (to keep the friendly family, including Carl, at bay) after supper to try her hand not only at painting, but at poetry, filling her notebooks. When Carl looks over her efforts, he speaks of Emily Dickinson and the advisability of not rushing headlong into print. Rejections from publications do not daunt her. And now, there she is—dizzy in the Garden again. Ah, love.

The beautiful son and daughter, who do no wrong. Their father, Joe? He comes by, on his way somewhere, and takes a look and returns to his own life, satisfied. The boy, John Carl, sturdy and comely. Freckles and curly red hair. The girl blonde and winsome, her hair in braids or curls. She is strong-willed and very like her grandmother, Paula, whose name she has. The family has decided to give up her surname Karlen. From now on she is Little Paula and Big Paula likes that. The children look upon their grandfather as a sort of playmate. He never gives orders. He observes and promotes conversation and sport.

The household of the poet.

Helga (the Garden and all that) begins what will be yearly trips to New York, leaving for a couple of weeks in February or March when farm work is light. Restless. Meeting the actor, Art, there, or her painter, someone. Lunching with Carl's friends. Leonard Lyons gets her tickets for *Death of a Salesman* and *The Big Knife* and so on. Uncle Ed, elegant, dashing, sixty-eight, now director of the Museum of Modern Art's Department of Photography, leads Helga through new and old exhibits, takes her to the Museum lunchroom, "They wonder who is with me now," he smiles, like some old-time Pan.

She meets Pete Seeger and hears him sing and has dinner with Alan Lomax and his wife Elizabeth. Sits on Louis Untermeyer's knee. Meets e.e. cummings at his house in the Village (his beautiful wife has modeled for my uncle). Stays at the quarters of Carl's cartoonist friend, Pulitzer Prize-winner C.D. Batchelor of the New York *Daily News.*

She eats things she has only read of, never tasted. Napoleons at Longchamps. Lobster at the Palm. Veal Scaloppine at Nino Nello's. Russian, Hindu, Japanese foods. Sees ballets, movies, plays (up to then the only Shakespeare I had experienced was from reading it and finding it heady), symphonies, whatever. Walking the streets night and day. Hungry for any experience.

And then home where Mother is setting out fig trees, Scotch broom shrubs, scuppernong grapes, content. My father makes notes on the children. He wants to look into their minds. He types these up and shows them to me, ". . . It is near their bedtime and I tell them, 'Soon you will be down in your beds, but still you will be here at my desk with me.' John took Paula's hand, 'Let's go. I think he's going to write a poem.' " His notes are endless. He carries them in his pocket. The three of them are coming from the Memminger Path that circles Little Glassy. They have been collecting mosses and lichen for miniature gardens they have started somewhere. Their voices come like the murmuring of bees or the rushing of waves or the sounds of faraway contented fabulous creatures in their own world away from mine.

I am right back there in the Garden again. My parents like Art. He worships my father. During the war he'd been on Tinian, an island in the Pacific. He gives me snapshots of himself taken there beside a great silver bomber. He wears khaki shorts. Leather jacket. Tall and bronzed. Curly blond hair sun-bleached. In working jumper by the shining machine. Wearing dark glasses. An ammunition belt over his shoulder. As an actor, he has publicity glossies, holding a script or a cigarette. Dashing. Handsome. Irresistible. A graduate student at Chapel Hill, North Carolina, not too far a drive from Connemara. A producer, director of plays, he plans somehow to take the cultural world by storm.

When Art comes to visit, we ride (I bargain for new horses all the time—beauties—Gray Boy, Daniel) over the mountains and through valleys under Connemara's golden sun and misted rain. Art plans to complete a play or novel, some piece of writing and will come to Connemara for a while and do some work for Carl also. Near at hand all the time with only walls and and floors between us! I explain in detail why others have fallen short and have been dismissed by my father. Carl wants everything done when said. At midnight. At the supper table. Not later. He can spot the most mosquito-small error and will build it into a mountain.

Carl asks Helga carefully whether she surely wants the man to come. He says, after the lover leaves, gently, "You've got a big empty place now, haven't you?" Paula does not have conversations of this sort with her daughter. My mother, determined, loyal, shy, brilliant. Her gray-blue eyes are steady, a classic Grecian nose, small broad strong hands. She will not meet a group of women for lunch, tea, coffee or a drink. She does not play cards, tennis, pool, or swim very well. She takes moonlight walks throughout her life. She knows the names of the stars and the constellations. At the age of seventeen, she knelt before a cross through a night on the stone floor of the chapel of the Catholic boarding school she attended for a year.

Paula's feeling for Margaret mingles love and concern. For Janet it is permissive and protective. Helga is a problem as she goes her many ways. Paula tries molding Helga now and then with commands from a doorway. "You must not see that man any more!" "Stop sitting at that easel painting. There's work to be done outside!" "This is not the time of day to be reading a book!" I turn her wrath easily by giving in, by agreeing. Can't I see him when she does not know? Or find another? Can't I paint or read at midnight?

What should a mother be to a daughter? A daughter to a mother? Don't I have downright respect for the small figure hurrying along a path, telling the hired man who carries the sapling, "Walk a little faster." Isn't there pure admiration for her serenity at the supper table while my father roars? Isn't there simple adoration for the frowning person swinging the door to and demanding that brushes and pencils and lovers be put aside?

What is the feeling for this one's ability to catch fire at the same time as myself in relation to the care of some creature of ours? Or for this one's way of explaining some piece of family history and why she felt as she did about my father at some time (all of which Helga needs passionately to know)? Wasn't there security in her instant answer to any childhood question regarding menstruation or sexual intercourse or parturition? (Mysteries I have never really unraveled.) Doesn't this sweet woman move always through my dreams, although she is gone now and ashes?

My father. He never worries about Helga in her ways. He never stops to study out what I am doing. He likes my company. When I work at the typewriter in the Farm Office, he comes to sit reading in a nearby chair. At night when I write or read in my locked room, the children asleep in theirs, he taps on the door to be let in. To smile and sit awhile. We may share a loving cup of wine.

He finds me reading Balzac, "That Tory! But go ahead." I do. He leaves materials for me to read with imperative notes attached. He talks of the desires and satisfactions of work. "Write until you are ashamed of yourself, Swipes!" He gives me a quote from Blaise Pascal to memorize, "The miseries of men come from not being able to sit alone in a quiet room." He does not believe in waiting for inspiration. "If when writing the Lincoln work, I had said, 'Now this morning I feel inspirational. I will write,' and wrote, and another morning said 'I don't feel so good today. Not so inspirational. Today I will not write,' the books wouldn't stand today." He is immersed in finishing the novel. He declares he will not make concessions to the reader or the publisher or Metro-Goldwyn-Mayer! He is in the midst of the rewrite and has a deadline.

Carl is keyed up and exhausted. He doesn't sleep until daylight and he wants company and talk all the time. When he asks Helga to help with correspondence, he puts it darkly, "Let's get going on this thing. It's something in the nature of my will." He becomes stiff and angry, "Well, it is good to know that help is offered." And puts his hand on his chest, "There is either something wrong with my heart or my pen and pencil here in this pocket have pressed in and made me sore." (In other words neglect and indolence on my part may be responsible for his demise.)

Does he fear an ending? "Swipes, I called three old friends last week. One was dead as of last winter. The others a week ago." He continues with calculations of odds, "One to five, I die at seventy-seven. One to ten, I die at eighty. One to twenty, I live to be eighty-four." He sits at his mail. Brooding. When the soup is brought, he frowns, "It's a bundle of tricks. The soup is always cold!" It is sent back to the kitchen, rewarmed again and brought steaming.

There he is with spilled milk about the chair and himself. Helga mops it up. She has warned the children, stay out of their playmate-grandfather's way! All know the irritation is due to the time press and his frustration. The household will be relieved to see him go. Harcourts are asking for the book. It has not been accepted yet. Helga thinks they will snap it up. Paula is not so sure. And I am still working on the Book Three rewrite, going through the secretary's copying for errors.

At last he is ready to be driven to the station. He comes to my room with a tall stack which he dumps on my chair. I am to have all transfers made and up to date for the publishers and as soon as possible. Next week I will have a secretary for two nights for copying. "Swipes," my father says clearly, pontifical (glad to be leaving), "It will do you good to see what revisions I have made and how I did it."

And that is that.

The Iron Curtain falls on Europe. The United Nations is born. The Nuremberg trials take place. The Truman Doctrine and the Marshall Plan are under way. The Central Intelligence Agency is authorized by Congress. Sugar rationing ends and we throw out our OPA Ration Checks. The term "cold war" is understood. Carl, nearly seventy now, broods about it all. He fears "warmongers," he says at the supper table, frowning. At his lunch, he reads the newspapers and praises Secretary of State George Marshall's pleas for patience. In the mail is a letter from Archie MacLeish who says that "some citizens in Chicago" want my father to run for the Senate and is he interested? Carl writes back that "they'll have to work a snatch racket and transfer my corpus to Illinois before I say I run for any office in the good old Sucker State." And that he has "no slightest hestitation at declaring that as a people and a nation we have before this hour of time hung on the rim of the moon with greasy fingers."

And Carl is fussing with his book. Harcourts is trying to get more money out of MGM. The title goes here and there. *American Cavalcade* became *Storm and Dream* and is now *The Angel of the Backward Look.* In the writing of this book, he has given the same attention to research and detail as with the Lincoln work. William Bradford and others of the time of the Puritans, believed in an apparition that stood at one's side before the last breath and took a backward look over the span of that life. Immersed in all of this lore, does Carl feel the "apparition" beside him? Perhaps he feels he is making a final statement of sorts.

Helga, due to her lonely early life (and aided by Margaret), is an avid reader of novels. During the typing of her father's manuscript, she is appalled by the characters and their unreality, by the heavy load of historical detail. Her problem is not to hurt the writer's feelings. She goes to her mother and voices her protests. Paula shares lots of the opinions but not the passion and advises Helga to do what she will. My father is happy to hear the objections. He loves the subject. He says, "You sweet critics of mine speak softly!" But what happens after the airing? He puts off from day to day the reviewing of even the technical slip-ups that are pointed out. He will never get to them.

The family are involved. Margaret, the researcher, hunting out "lost" quotes he wants found. Paula backing her up, leafing through the hefty volumes. Helga fired up and missing jaunts on the mountain with her steeds. And then he is gone to New York, vigorous, happy, shedding the load of the daily routine from him, portmanteau in hand (not forgetting the goat milk and the sandwiches home-prepared). The rest of us breathe freely now. Order is made in the rooms. After all it is his book and almost finished. A new name will come. *Remembrance Rock.* He is at his publishers where nobody argues with him. He is working on introductions and acknowledgements. "Library and research labors of my wife and daughters should be mentioned, with a rose pinned on Helga for sustained industry and enterprise as a troubleshooter." I like that and feel I've earned it. I also get #3 of Harcourts special six-pound two-volume boxed first edition that ran a thousand copies.

The book never makes it to the movies for some reason known only to Hollywood. Problems with the contract? Producers quailing before the work of *War and Peace* scale? My father is emotional about it all. Hasn't he every time won acclaim after the long trial of a book! This one took close to five years. It is 1948. What do the reviewers say? The powerful critics? Lloyd Lewis calls it "Carl Sandburg's ride to an American Canterbury" and likes it. Someone says it's "the long-sought-after Great American Novel." (He keeps that clipping in his pocket with Lloyd's.) Others that it is long, theatrical, repetitive. The New York *Times, "Remembrance Rock* is not really a novel; it is the chant of an antique Bard who fills out the beat with stereotypes and repetitions. Or rather, it is four novels for the price of one. . . . etc."

Carl is upset, hurt, unused to the ferocity. He broods from fury to sorrow to disbelief. He goes to autographing parties at bookstores. He sends messages home, "Dearest Swipes, Tell Snick on even days I love her the same as odd numbers. Dad." And to the boy:

Dear John

you are my grandson but I can tell by your letter you are my dear old friend and Christopher is my friend and next week when I get home we are going on a walk together: tell all ALL in the house I love them a million bushels & see you soon

Buffong, Esq.

And then he is back with us and the children are surcease. He teaches Little Paula to speak clearly, using Spartacus to the gladiators, "Ye call me chief and ye do well to call me chief!" Her blue believing eyes are upon him. Continually he makes his notes, typing them in his attic room later and holding on to them like talismans, taking them with him on his travels to show to friends.

As he walks with the two about the Golden Place or sits on the pillared porch or reads his mail in the dining room, the three communicate. He writes nonsense notes on discarded letters and envelopes and signs himself in various ways, "Poobah, Heathcliffe Moskowitz, T.S. Eliot." The small girl child has a great wish to see her grandfather play checkers with the man who runs the little store across from the post office half a mile away (she has heard Carl was a champion in his faraway school days). So the two trudge over there and afterwards mail some letters and walk back, their voices, high and low, lingering on the air.

And then in the night up in his room, with a rag doll in his file box, he works upon two new poems.

Poem for Karlen Paula

sweet child
what I said was
sweet child
and now I say it again
sugar molasses honey
and once more
which will be enough
potatoes carrots onions
    and I love you for the way
    you can eat while you talk
    and talk while you eat and
    I like it when you spill on
    your chin and once in a big
    long while I like to hear
    you slurrpp slurrpp your
    soup

why do you sweep me
with your eyes?
can you see how I am swept
when you sweep me
with your blue eyes
ever so blue
ever so deep blue
have I even once asked you a question
and you didn't have an answer?
no—NO NO.
each and every time you had an answer
maybe not the right answer
but a fresh quick fast one
and this is proper right
when it happens
between you and me
for you and I have a book
together we have a book
it is our own personal book
and it says on page one
on page five and fifty-five
I Buppong ask any question
you Snick make any answer
and if anybody says
my question is wrong
or your answer is wrong
we bring out the book
your book my book
our personal book together
each by each us by us
we can show where it says
we do what we do
when we do what we do
and it is proper it is right

the law says we can
if we love each other a bushel
and it is a big enough bushel

Poem for John Carl

Music is made of sound.
When you measure sound it is music.
It may be good music or bad
but if it is measured sound
then it is music.
I tell you this because you have
become a musician.
I have seen you and heard you at the piano
measuring sound
making music
and I thank you and I am proud of your music
and I am proud of your teacher the blessed Marne
and the way you go along with her in learning

and I have heard you hammering fixing
putting things together
taking things apart
and I am going to make a prediction
here and now a prediction:
you will go on hammering and fixing
putting things together
taking things apart
SO LONG AS YOU LIVE

you have angels in you
little bright sweet angels
and sometimes when you do what you do
it is the little angels telling you
to do what you do

you have devils in you
funny slipperly little devils
and sometimes when you do what you do
it is the little devils telling you
to do what you do
Buppong too has angels in him
and one devil for every angel
and when he do what he do
it is sometimes an angel
sometimes a devil
telling Buppong
to do what he do
so now maybe you will let
ole Buppong make one more prediction
like this
exactly like this:
so long as you live John Carl
you will keep your angels
you will keep your devils
and you will listen to your angels
more often than you listen to your devils
telling you
to do what you do

He is seventy, the children five and seven. Are his poems typed out in the night in his way, using the two forefingers of his hands at the old Remington, are they a comfort to Carl, my father, the grandfather, a little hurt there by the world and studying out what he would write next?

1949. Seventy-one is not so old. But mortality is there. All about Carl is the life of the farm. A lamb is born. A duck hatches out eleven young. The cow, Rosemary, has her calf, Milky. The children come by on their horses, Storm and

Remember (Paula's frisky new gelding, long-flaxen-maned and named for the book). Red roses from Paula's garden are in their bridles. Carl is on the Rock out in back, in the old cedar chair, his writing on his lap. In the afternoon the children are planting pansies, dirty and dynamic, hacking weeds where Paula points them out. Margaret is nearby starting a flower garden, serene. The fields are being plowed. Radishes are in. Lettuce. Peas. Spinach. It is spring!

Lloyd Lewis dies. Heart attack. Oliver Barrett, Carl's old horseshoe-pitching companion, a Lincoln collector, goes. Oliver had seen it coming. The sunset call, he named it. Carl and he had just finished a book together on Oliver's collection. Did my father, losing old and true friends who had laughed and lighted his life, wonder about his own sunset call? He will look backward soon.

October. He is on a lecture trip on the West Coast. He sends a letter home, "Swipes my sweet Andalusia gal, please send 5 shirts, collars attached. Audience 9,000 of which 400 standing at Men's Gym U of Calif. First I told 'em, then Ah turned on duh forces. . . . I head down to LA and Mary about October 25. Hug the little fellers for me."

Carl wants a talk with his sister Mary, who lives in Los Angeles. Aunt Mary is seventy-four. He is going to look back into his life. Mary says, "They took me out of the cradle and put Charlie in!" The little three-room shack where they'd been born, down by the C.B. & Q. Railroad tracks in Galesburg. And he may start the autobiography, "I was born on a cornhusk mattress."

At home he pins up a large plain note on his wall with plans

After Barrett Book:
1- Revise poems and shape book
2- Revise Onk and shape book

3- Write Spider-and-mole novel of less than 100,000 words
4- Write Killer novel 60,000 words
5- One-volume Lincoln
6- One–act plays for high school

The poems are new ones that will fit into a collection of his lifetime to be called *Complete Poems.* (Are his publishers also having thoughts of mortality?) The Onk are nonsense "Onkadonk" stories that somehow never get anywhere any more than the two novels. The one-volume Lincoln will come to pass (Harcourts has it in mind). No "one-act plays" although he hopes always to break into more fields, "Swipes! I'll surprise them yet." He speaks with me of a personal "Poetry Anthology" that he'd like to do, composed of verses he's lived with and new ones that come along.

There is one of the latter that he fit into *Remembrance Rock* (he does the same thing when he lectures—gets in what he wants). It is part of a letter of Roger Williams of Pilgrim days. Carl set up the prose like a poem and he reads it over and over to us. The children know it. I memorize parts and go about the farm and housework reciting it.

Alas! Sir, in calm midnight thoughts,
what are these leaves and flowers
and smoke and shadows,
and dreams of early nothings,
about which we poor fools and children,
as David saith, disquiet ourselves in vain?
Alas! what is all this scuffling of this world for,
but, "come, will you smoke it?" . . .
And as to myself, in endeavoring
after your temporal and spiritual peace,
I humbly desire to say,
if I perish, I perish.
It is but a shadow vanished,

a bubble broke, a dream finished.
Eternity will pay for all. . . .
My study is to be swift to hear,
And slow to speak. . . .
Well beloved friends and neighbors,
I am, like a man in a great fog.
I know not well how to steer . . .
I fear to run quite backward,
as men in a mist do, and undo all.

Like the early pieces of Blaise Pascal that he used to hand me. Brilliant and quiet and advising loneliness. I am true kin to my father, although the Garden of Eden is shining not far away.

The Garden of Eden and all that. Snakes and Apples. Helga is always trying to get away from home and then dashing back. Will she ever find one to rival her father? She looks. At this time there is a plan. Before the lover escapes. Does this sound like fiction? It is fact.

Art—the actor, the dramatist, the would-be writer. He comes to stay awhile at Connemara, helping file and copy and type and arrange papers as Carl plans for what will come from him next. Then Art moves into a cabin a quarter-mile off, which he rents for a few months, working on road gangs, a steam-drill in his hands, for ready cash. In early mornings and late nights and spare hours, he looks for direction in his writing.

Helga meets him at his cabin sometimes. Candlelight. Thoughts of giving up other Lochinvars. He returns to Brooklyn and his family's home, trying to work out where he will go and what he will do for our living. He feels his talent lies in writing, but he is not averse to teaching.

Sometimes he meets Carl in New York as time goes on, seeing plays, sharing bock beer, walking the streets at night. They talk. Carl reports to his daughter that he thinks Art will make a good teacher. And then I write a letter, "Dear Bup-pong, No special news except all here are in top shape. The maid is gone and the girls and the kids and myself are keeping things running. Art is in Chapel Hill trying to wangle something, not knowing if he will land in Florida, Charlotte, or back here with a steam-drill in his hands again, waiting for something to break. Well, well. Take care of your good sweet self. You have no idea how you are missed by all of us. Come home while the mountains are so beautiful. With great bushels of love, daughter #3."

And other letters, swearing, "I will love you always and way out into the trees and into the air and forever and ever with no limits or boundaries, etc."

Spring 1950. The cold war gets colder. Trouble brews hot in Korea. China is now the People's Republic and gigantic posters of Chairman Mao appear throughout the land. Art has found a job. He will be teaching drama at a high school in Charlotte and is busy with rehearsals for plays. On Friday nights he comes to Connemara for weekends, returning late Sundays. I figure he will be here for the summer recess. And my father approves. He has filing, sorting, copying, work.

Moments with Carl. I am his driver back and forth to trains or planes. He is never hurried. He likes to be put on at the last moment. He will not wait in any station. We break speed limits and he approves of my skill at the wheel. He fights with agents. At the airport, one tells him his baggage is ten pounds overweight. Danger of throttling! A roar. Eight pounds, not counting the sandwiches and goat milk in the bag! Helga gives the agent a ten-dollar bill and both men stop talking. The author collects the change and off he goes.

Another moment. Carl is in a storm about typewriters

clacking in the nights from Helga's room and the Farm Office where Paula spends delicious hours. He sends his entire family (not bold carefree Janet) up to his room to listen while he demonstrates. He beats out his passion upon the keys! "Now is the time for all men to come to the aid of the party we are making a test here as to how this sounds up on the floor above and whether it disturbs sleepers who wish to sleep and get their proper rest. See what I mean? How many times has it been that good people requiring their sleep have been kept awake by a god-dam lowlived sonofagun who didn't know any better than to go on pegging away at his high-power typewriter." There is much scurrying about. Peace at last. Soft voices. The lion smiles.

The Korean War begins on the twenty-fifth of June. Truman orders our air and sea forces over to give "cover and support" and before long our ground forces are entering as a "police action." September. *Complete Poems* is out and Carl is busy again at autographing parties (3,000 signed earlier at Harcourts). Sales are booming. An atom bomb scare in New York and Harcourts mails the original Lincoln photos to Connemara. Microfilm and duplicating companies are busy as all records are being sent out of the city. As for Helga, the Walk about the Garden continues. We are getting married.

Actually it is a plan. Eve. For Art has said that the rushing over to Connemara weekly is cutting into his schedule. Almost wrecked as he was falling asleep at the wheel. Danger for Helga. And so the plan. She knows inside herself that it can not work. Two Bears together in a house? One her father, famous for roars and sulks and demands (as well as love). But get the man. No one else has been sighted (like the Baroness Blixen, Isak Dinesen). Helga is thirty-two. Art is five years younger (so was Joe).

They will put the farm on a business basis, make it into a dairy, as well as a breeding venture. Paula will lease the land, the barns, the tractors, milking machines, animals, in return for "supplying the family with milk and vegetables and maintaining the private drives." We get the final word on expenses. She decides the pedigrees. Art can write in his spare time. Obviously I will still type for my father whenever he needs me. I don't have to leave. I get my cake and eat it too. My mother is pleased. I am off for the airport to pick up Carl, whose reaction has nothing to do with the business of the dairy. He speaks of adjustments he's seen couples trying to make and not succeeding. And then, "So you want to get hitched legally?" He's been aware over the years of our sleeping together and tells me plainly that if we hadn't been there would be something wrong with us. We were clearly in Batchelor's bed in New York (an unexpected visit) and nearly spotted at Connemara various times.

December. Carl asks his daughter (at the work bench, hammering away, making order), "Are you going to have a preacher or a justice or haven't you made plans?" We had thought of a justice and having him come to Connemara so the children would be there. Carl says, "I want to have some people in and have a celebration! And I want my old-time friend from Galesburg boyhood days to do the honors, Reverend Frank Bishop. I'll write him." So there.

Christmas Day. Uncle Ed lands at Pearl Harbor. He is busy! Commander-in-Chief of the Pacific Fleet Admiral Radford asked him to resume his uniform when the present war began. My uncle is getting an exhibition ready at the Museum of Modern Art of Korean War photographs. He comes through on his way back to New York. Art is stretched out on my father's favorite chair. My uncle raises his eyebrows at me and makes a face. Helga does not speak about the Bears. She shrugs and laughs. Time will have its way.

And so there I am, leaving the Garden of Enchantment and Desire and Euphoria and starting the climb up the

Mountain of Marriage. Isn't it sometimes so? Not always. The romance will be over when the words are spoken. Marriage is tending and fostering and making peace. The Garden is wanting and never knowing for sure and that is romance.

There is the husband. Handsome, curly-golden-haired. Little Paula wears a hoop skirt and is all in pink and white. John Carl in gray tweeds and new tie. They are beautiful, my jewels, with pink bouquet and white boutonniere. The newspapers report, "The couple will reside at 'Connemara.'"

"Dear Carl, I throw up my hat in the air and I holler out with delight! The Big Day I've been waiting for came—today. As you damned well know, I'm hollering about the Pulitzer award you received for your Complete Poems. I'm so glad about it, Carl. I've been waiting for this so long—too damned long . . . Faithfully . . ." It is the eighth of May in 1951 and Lew Sarett, poet (poetry prize-winner), Indian guide, and my father's old-time friend, is writing on hearing the news on the radio. Carl, "Dear Old Lew of the Strong Young Heart—Your letter comes along and is good to read twice. . . . Carl Older than the Pyramids." Friends everywhere write and wire and phone.

It is his second Pulitzer. And where is the winner? Why, out on the Rock, working at his autobiography, a pencil in hand, sometimes dozing in the sun. Here there is stillness. Except for the sounds of birds. Bees. Insects droning. The children, whispering, tending the moss gardens they share with him.

The book is coming along. Aunt Mary had a stroke. She gives him a bulging box of photographs, letters, clippings, collected during her life and mostly about her brother. When the press, complimenting him on his prize, ask about the new work he says, "In an autobiography, you are supposed to tell all, and I will never tell all." The press loves it.

When he visited Mary, he also saw Kenneth Dodson again. Carl had used long sections of his war letters in *Remembrance Rock.* In that book he gave Dodson the name Kenneth MacKenzie MacDougall. Now Dodson has a novel of his own on the way (stirred by Carl) and his lead character has the same surname—MacDougall. Carl likes Dodson and will "go the limit" to urge Harcourts to publish the book.

But now my father is at home, the children whispering in the underbrush nearby. Helga is not at ease. The house, large enough before her marriage, is becoming smaller, holding two families. The quarters are somewhat close for arguments, for discussions that need space for shouts, door-slammings. The air is electric with two Bears where there was one.

Years later, in my father's papers, I have come on a long notation he made at the Time of the Two Bears. I understand him. It is my life. Helga is not the first nor the last daughter in this situation!

> He worked in the fields and at repairing this and that. He was a willing worker and it seemed to be a pleasure for him to be joining us in the work—until after the wedding . . . He would keep asking me if he could help with my correspondence or copying from books or manuscripts. After the wedding he turned all of this over to Helga. And instead of writing his own letters he would dictate them to Helga. Before the marriage, when he came nearly every week and we often ate in the kitchen, there was fellowship, laughter and songs. . . . As the months went by over his first summer at Connemara he came for a longer and longer

> time at noon to lie down in their room. . . . Meantime from month to month a fellowship that there had been between him and me began shading away into something else. . . . Often he would come in from the barn and take a chair at his desk next to Helga's where she was working on records and accounts and letters connected with the business. There he would sit for an hour and two hours thumbing around in a Sears catalog. . . . etc.

I adore my father. Doesn't everything I want seem right to him? How can he look upon a Young untried Bear with approval? My husband sends out feelers for a teaching position. The Tried Bear is seventy-four and is getting a lot of attention from his country. He is awarded the Gold Medal of the American Academy and the National Institute of Arts and Letters. He is on television, doing five minutes on Ed Murrow's Friday night show. He was on the last "Robert Montgomery's New Year's Eve program." Dave Garroway's "Today" is inaugurated, working live out of an NBC street-floor studio in Rockefeller Center and helped by J. Fred Muggs. Garroway writes, "When we ran the film this morning of your interview for my show, there were sensations running up and down my spine that haven't been there for years. . . . from general good feeling about the things you said. . . . Peace, Dave."

Art accepts a position teaching in Arlington, Virginia, across the Potomac from Washington. We can't wait to go. Carl, doing correspondence with Helga, is cross to begin with. It is his way. As the work progresses, he becomes benevolent. As it is finished, and he is being driven to the train station, he likes the idea of his daughter and family in Washington. He says "Take the encyclopedia set. The old one. Go see my friend, Dave Mearns, at the Manuscripts

Division of the Library of Congress." And what books does Helga plan on taking? Only my own and I have a lot. Hoping to leave him slightly anxious. On the way, we stop so he can buy some Jack Daniels to take along in his satchel. He hands me a bottle at the station and hugs me goodbye.

Part Five

THE MOUNTAIN

DON'T THINK Helga's ties to home are broken. While she is heady with independence, setting up in a new house, looking for a job (David Mearns will surely find an opening), Paula sends on the typing work for Carl's autobiography, which is nearing its end (50¢ a typed sheet). He wants some research done at the Library of Congress ($2 an hour). Carl is interested in the Welsh poet, Taliesin, for help in his new long poem, "The Head One."

The rhythms and themes of the Welshman's are like those in Carl's old poem from *Cornhuskers* back in 1918 (before me) and called "Wilderness."

There is a wolf in me . . . fangs pointed for tearing gashes . . .

There is a fox in me . . . a silver-gray fox . . . I sniff . . .

There is a hog in me . . . a snout and a belly . . .

There is a fish in me . . . I know I came from salt-blue water-gates . . . I scurried with shoals of herring . . . I blew waterspouts with porpoises . . . before land was . . . before the water went down . . . before Noah . . . before the first chapter of Genesis.

And Taliesin's lines copied for him:

I was a kingfisher; I was a young salmon;
I was a hound, and I was a hind:
I was a buck on the mountain. . . .
I was a grain in the furrow's womb;
I grew up on a hill;
He who sowed, reaped me: . . .
I am Taliesin . . .

And now Carl's "The Head One" that he has been working with off and on for some time. Helga types it:

I was born in the morning of the world, . . .

I am a grasshopper taking in one jump
a hundred grasshopper lengths.

I buzz with earnest bees
in the lingering sun of apple orchards. . . .

I am the chameleon taking the tint of what I live on,
the water frog green as the scum he sits on,
the tree frog gray as the tree-bark-gray.
The duck, the swan, the goose, met me as sisters,
the beaver, the porcupine, the chinchilla, as brothers.

In the mail comes his letter, "Dear Swipes, on Taliesen you worked to perfection, got precisely what I wanted, what I suspected but didnt quite dare to expect to be there. Could you now go on and do another piece covering further ground about what is known or conjectured about Taliesen—and along with that a further lot of the poems? . . . There might be a book in it, no telling. Dad." And he sends an old piece from his files with a note on it for me.

Tiller of the mountain, who is that man? — A man.

What tongue does he speak? -- All.

What things does he know? -- All.

What is his country? -- None and all.

Who is his God? -- God.

What do you call him? -- The Madman.

What do you say you call him? -- The wise man.

In your band what is he? -- He is what he is.

The chief? — No.

Then what is he? -- The soul

---Thalisen
old Welsh poet of the 6th Century.

Helga dear one — this I met some 40 years ago. I haven't seen quite the like of it in all our diggings so far. It wears well = Buppong

The grandfather comes to visit. The white-haired and the curly-blond-haired Bears are relaxed on neutral territory. Carl lights his cigar and observes the horseless children. He buys them bikes. Paula calls hers "Uthyr Pendragon" (the Book of Taliesin XLVIII contains Uthyr's "Death Song"). Carl makes reports. The book is finished. No more batches for me to copy. It is to be called *Always the Young Strangers* from a poem in *Smoke and Steel,* ending ". . . and looking two ways to the ends of the street for the new people, the young strangers, coming, coming, always coming. . . ." Carl states that he has autographed 3,000 of the regular edition and 700 of the limited! Harcourt is going all the way and "plunging on a first printing of 50,000 copies," he cries. Uncle Ed designed the end papers, using early photographs.

My uncle is on fire. It is fall of 1952. He flies to Europe and sends love to all, including the "little angels." He is smitten with a concept and is carrying it through. Edward Steichen will not again put on exhibitions of war photographs. Never. Instead, he says, ". . . what was needed was a positive statement on what a wonderful thing life was, how marvelous people were, and, above all, how alike people were in all parts of the world." In leafing through his "blood brother's" Lincoln volumes, Uncle Ed came on a speech of Lincoln's in which he saw the phrase "The Family of Man." That was the spark. It is the title and theme for his new exhibition. He is visiting twenty-nine cities in eleven countries to make a survey of European photographers to be featured in the show.

He is not the only one in the family on fire. Helga has a job with the government (due to David Mearns). She is a clerk-typist, GS–3 at $2,950 a year in the Manuscripts Division of the Library of Congress and she is in heaven. "Graduation from high school" is the minimum qualification, as well as "Ability to type at the rate of 40 words per minute" and

"One year of general office experience is desirable." She does 65 a minute for long midnight stretches. It does not count that she has several years experience in a special Farm Office.

As the days go along, Helga, bless her, learns the insidious, delicious pleasures of the Working Woman, who owes none of her income to father, mother, husband. John Carl and Paula are "latchkey children" and do household chores now. See Helga sailing off to work in her car, crossing the bridge from Virginia to Washington, singing. I am in my thirty-fourth year and feel the power of secret time away from all bent on owning me.

As for the country, Carl is on television from Madison Square Garden again. It is the Democratic rally and he has two minutes to speak for Adlai Stevenson for President. We all wear our "Madly For Adlai" buttons that Margaret sends. And then General Ike sweeps in with 442 electoral votes to 89. My father writes, "Dear Adlai: It was all worth the time and toil. Yours is a high name now & for a long time. You are cherished and remembered in multitudes of deep prayers. . . ."

The sixth of January. A Birthday Party for the new book and for Carl (in a black double-breasted new suit). In the Crystal Ballroom of the Blackstone Hotel in Chicago. Paula is there (decked with an orchid corsage!) and Uncle Ed, elegant, Dana on his arm. Not my family. We were asked, but do not come, busy with our lives. On the program for the event are the last lines of "The Head One," with its overtones of Taliesin:

There is only one horse on the earth
and his name is All Horses.
There is only one bird in the air
and his name is All Wings.

There is only one fish in the sea
and his name is All Fins.
There is only one man in the world
and his name is All Men.
There is only one woman in the world
and her name is All Women.
There is only one child in the world
and the child's name is All Children.
There is only one Maker in the world
and His children cover the earth
and they are named All God's Children.

Adlai, as governor, proclaims "Carl Sandburg Day in Illinois." Frost, our whimsical poet? "Dear Carl: Congratulations old man—congratulations *old* man. Seventy-five years is quite an achievement though nothing of course compared with what you have done for us in prose and verse. . . . At three you were half my age. Now you are better than twelve thirteenths. A little more and I shall have you for a contemporary. And proud of it. Keep grandly on. Ever yours, Robert." The Swedish ambassador hangs a decoration about Carl's neck and makes him a Commander in the Order of the North Star. Paula cuts the cake.

My father tells the press, "Robert Frost is a fine poet most of the time. His work is read by strong men, farmers, thieves and deacons—and not by little cliques. I say to hell with the new poetry. They don't want poetry to say what it means. They have symbols and abstractions and a code amongst themselves—sometimes I think it's a series of ear wigglings. . . . this new bunch—if you write a line that means what it says you are in bad, you don't belong. . . ." He has a wonderful time.

There is a special boxed first edition and he brings us a copy for our new house, ". . . to read & soil & throw around—and read again. C.S. Fathers Day 1953." Doesn't Helga feel a little edgy when he comes by? I am at home with Carl as the children are. We know him. Will the peace in my house last?

Time moves. Carl stays a part of our lives. In June he comes through Washington and stops over for a night. I drive him in from the Manuscripts Division, where he is visiting with Dave Mearns and where I have a new position—secretary to the assistant chief. We collect the children and go to the local supermarket, where my father picks up strange foods that I am to prepare and all will taste. Some to be set aside for future meals. Also an assortment of fireworks for a backyard pre-Fourth personal display.

His cigar smoke is in the air. The lamps are lit. Art is there, jovial, my Bear. All is well. Carl demonstrates his new way of exercising, lifting the armchair over his head slowly and returning it to its place. He writes the children's and our names and some remarks with his broad-tipped pen on paper he has taken from the Library. He folds the sheet in half. The black ink is still wet and he gives us the impressions. Some read "remember me," "John & Paula," "Art and Helga," "Hell is Hot" and "Connemara."

The guitar is brought from its case. Later he reads at the supper table a new fanciful piece that Helga is to type up.

> Bo had a face like a bun in a box. When he laughed the bun popped out of the box, saying, "Why not be a bun in a box?"
>
> Buff had a face like a fish in a frying pan ready to flip out and when he laughed his face said, "Fish for me, fresh fish from the pan every day."

Bong had a face like two mittens telling each other, "Mittens, yessir yessir, why not be mittens?"

Now if you could wish for a face and have the face you wished, which one would you rather have? Would it be Bo, or Buff, or Bong?

Or would you rather have the face you have?

Or would you rather have five or six faces and each morning pick the one you like best?

There is my father, in the lamplight, papers strewn before him. The table is long past time for clearing and we are waiting on him. His daughter is alert that his coffee cup stays filled. Is he comfortable? Does she concern herself with Art, who, pleased, leans back in his chair? The children are singing with my father. They have known him all their young lives. The three make up a new song to go with the new home, adapting the Connemara songs. He asks us to come to the farm in the summer. We three will go, the two small ones for a couple of weeks before me. Art will visit his parents and friends in New York. He is getting restless with his teaching job. We stay away from the subject.

Back at Connemara, Buppong, stirred by the visit, begins a "Second Sonata for Karlen Paula" and dates it on her tenth birthday, June 28, some of it going:

Could the calm of the sea today
or the storm of the sea tomorrow
be held in one drop of water—
peace today, anger tomorrow,
in one drop of water?

Could you be calm today
and tomorrow be a storm
and so yourself be

maybe the sea yesterday
maybe one drop of water today? . . .

Be jungle dark in your heart
and then find the black moonlight
of a silence holding your soft voice:
"Sleep and peace always wash my heart."

Study the wingbone of a dry dead bird—
how light it was for flying!
Look easy at the knee-joint of a goat skeleton—
how it could summon a leap from rock to rock!
Contemplate a rose gone to ashes—
and the perfect dignity of ashes! . . .

Looking at a tall elm swaying in a storm-wind
you may find yourself saying: "I honor, Oh Tree,
I honor the deep roots unseen underground
holding you seen overground."

The children precede me to the farm, sending back notes, "I am taking the beehive apart . . . I have made a large moss garden beside the rock. I have also made a Tom Thumb golf course on the front lawn. Buppong, Paula and I have been sleeping in the crows nest. I have caught six salamanders. I mowed the lawn and was paid two dollars. Be seeing you." Helga hones for a glimpse of the Lost Golden Place.

The three meet me on the pillared porch, all slightly disheveled. Little Paula bears a bouquet of just-picked zinnias. Their eyes shine. Her hair is tangled. John Carl's jeans are unwashed. An army rucksack is on his shoulder from which he seemingly never parts. There are living creatures in it, most of them on purpose. My father's news is regarding the golf course. "No question my grandson has a feel for the clubs." Paula, "I have a new moss garden now." Buppong,

"In a secret place. Known to a selected few. Gramma among them."

Helga roams old trails on foot, the lovely steeds now departed. With the family, she takes walks over pastures and lanes in the warm nights, Carl's voice rising and falling, the children wandering, the old moon dying in its last quarter. Then the endless voice of the mockingbird outside the dark windows. In the days, Carl dictates letters. Between it all is talk of the world.

Stalin is dead. The Korean War is over. The Department of Justice is exiling our Charlie Chaplin, black-listed ("a dangerous and unwholesome character"). *Playboy* Magazine begins to publish, its first calendar featuring Marilyn Monroe. Hillary and Norkay get to the summit of Mount Everest. And Uncle Ed at seventy-four is in Tokyo doing an exhibition of contemporary photographs. One show is called "Always the Young Strangers."

We talk to him over the phone now and then. He, like Carl, has had what the family calls "spells of dizziness." "The Family of Man" is progressing and a million pictures have come in. "And how are the little hellions?" My father reports that he goes to bed along with the "little hellions" every night at nine-thirty. With John at the helm of the machine, the three have made tape recordings and at my uncle's next visit, he will hear how their voices still keep their sweetness. As for the one-volume Lincoln, Carl is putting in no more than four hours of work a day on it.

The six volumes are to be condensed. His publishers have urged it and Carl likes the idea. He wants Helga to type up the manuscript and she can't wait, the pay to be the same as before or whatever she asks. Mother will see that it is sent piecemeal in the mail. Harcourt is lit up about the packaging of the best seller into one volume. *The Prairie*

Years will take a lot of revising. Not so much for *The War Years.*

How easy to sit there with the beloved ones, knowing each's ways and honored by all. Arguments do not exist or are easily skirted after years of practice. Of course, Helga cannot wait to return to home and husband, the latter having rescued her from these so that she is now a Free and Independent Woman. But there is the nervous aspect in my own home, due to the coming into my life of this Lochinvar, Art, who does not always see eye-to-eye with me and sometimes vehemently and unreasonably stands for a totally different point of view! Helga has had a reputation in her family for firmness and a bit of temper which her parents have not only not tried to alter or break, but have admired. Now she is living in close quarters with one who does not agree always on politics, character readings of friends, the school system, you name it, but most particularly on the raising of her two children, who are perfection and in whom there is no fault. This is the stuff of arguments!

And now my father is reading a new poem. Hear his voice, made for recitation, wooing the words.

Zinnia Sonata

For Karlen Paula and John Carl

I have seen zinnias give out
with little songs and begging pardon
for the songs being short.
I have seen zinnias claim their rights
to speak promises saying to beholders,
"Whatever may be your wish, sir or madam,
I promise you shall have it—today, tomorrow,
somewhere over the blue hills and bright valleys,

it shall be yours to keep—whatever you wish—
we so promise—we zinnias God made for promising."

I have heard zinnias counseling together:
"Ever the summer is kind to us,
summer belonging to us as we belong to summer.
When God said, 'Let there be summer'
He also said, 'And let there be zinnias
bathed in colors called from sunsets and early stars.'
And God having so spoken
how can we be either proud or humble?
how can we be aught else than quiet blooming zinnias?"

Thus having heard the zinnias
I shall go again and again to hear the zinnias.

I am hurting from the pain of nostalgia. My days here are up. In my travel bag, as we board the train, are varied kinds of work I have been handed as the week progressed. At home again, we speak of the zinnias and read over the Sonata and remember that my mother's stunning flower beds were true after all.

She writes me, her letter ending, "Dad says tell John the flags are still doing duty on his golf course! 'Not to be disturbed!' Tell Paula we keep watch over her moss garden—it's lovely and refreshed with rains this week. . . ."

Helga tries to get her family onto her land, "Dear Buppong, it was lovely that you called the other night. I had been thinking of you so often lately. I am glad the book goes good. . . . I am taking a day off the Friday after Thanksgiving—which means that we will all be home November 26 to 30. Wonder if you and Mother could come then? What do you think? Before, on, around, about, that date? Maybe and/or/besides the girls? Here is a kiss for you, Buppong, and love for all. . . ."

Helga does not ever get both her parents simultaneously at her home. Margaret once and Janet never at all. The family is not a casual visiting one. Paula is continually off to dairy goat association meetings that engross her. All are busy. Chores need doing. And perhaps they recall that early nervous feeling about the Young and Old Bears that was there before we escaped. But I do not give up trying.

A year will roll around before Carl's *Abraham Lincoln: The Prairie Years and The War Years* one-volume edition is out. It will contain a Preface written in 1926 and never printed. The words are ones he often uses nowadays, "In the time of the April lilacs in the year 1865, a man in the City of Washington, D.C., trusted a guard to watch at a door, and the guard was careless, left the door, and the man was shot, lingered a night, passed away, was laid in a box, and carried north and west a thousand miles; bells sobbed; cities wore crepe; people stood with hats off as the railroad burial car came past at midnight, dawn or noon. . . ."

The piece ends, "The facts and myths of his life are to be an American possession, shared widely over the world, for thousands of years, as the tradition of Knute or Alfred, Laotse or Diogenes, Pericles or Caesar, are kept. This because he was not only a genius in the science of neighborly human relationships and an artist in the personal handling of life from day to day, but a strange friend and a friendly stranger to all forms of life that he met.

"He lived fifty-six years of which fifty-two were lived in the West—the prairie years."

My father had been forty-six when he wrote that. Now he is nearing seventy-six. When the birthday comes, newspapers front-page-headline the Preface along with suitable cartoons and editorials. He reads the whole thing in a half-hour television broadcast. It is reviewed, "Sitting quietly in his living room chair, with gaunt face, straggling white forelocks and deep-set eyes, with loose shirtcollar and old-fashioned bow tie, the aged Sandburg looked almost a part of history himself. . . . To at least one viewer, the half hour turned prose into poetry, a TV show into an occasion and a simple scribe into a saint." And the *Saturday Review* people ask him to read it as the first of a series of records they are putting out.

It is October when the book is released at last. Helga is mentioned in the "Acknowledgments" as one of four "faithful toilers on an incessantly changing manuscript." The other three are my mother and then two of my father's "women." One is something like a daughter, a friend of us all, Marjorie Arnette Braye. The other, a dancer as well as "toiler" has sent Carl her photograph which he has put away. Between her made-up eyebrows is the Indian red Brahma spot. The hair is black and glossy, the lips red. My father admires her.

Paula does not ever use makeup (barring a bit of powder for a formal occasion, a suggestion of lipstick) and does not share Carl's feeling for this person. When he invites her to Connemara, my mother strides about like one on a warpath. In Janet's autograph book is, "Dearest Janet, If anyone wants a guided tour of the Country-side or the Mountain-side, or the Animal-side—with a charming companion to conduct it—then Janet, a sweet young lady, is the person to call on. Many thanks for your Sweetness." And so on. Before long, the visitor is frozen out.

Uncle Ed does the endpapers for the book, using graphic photos of a hand of Lincoln and a life mask. On the "Dedication" list, "To Edward Steichen, whose projected photographic exhibition 'The Family of Man' will register his faith joined to Lincoln's in the unity of mankind and the hope of 'freedom for all men everywhere.' "

Helga has been around during Carl's long years on Lincoln. I was five when the Preface was written by the little barn in the weed-high lot behind our house, where he sat in the burning sun. And now thirty-five as the last of the typing is finished. The final line of Carl's book goes, ". . . the prairie years, the war years, were over."

"There is a pair of shoes love wears and the coming is a mystery." These are lines in a poem in *Good Morning, America* called "Explanations of Love." Are there women now (and have there been) in Carl's life whom he enjoys besides Paula in a loving way? Who knows? Some say so. Letters came to him (and will come until his last) during his life from women and he saves them along with the rest. Are there fragments that are implicative? Leafing through them, I look for answers.

"To have you here was like the bracing whiff of salt air and pound of surf when one has been too long away from the sea. . . . It was raining—we were on Wabash Avenue—and you gave me some advice or other about something. . . . Lord, it will be good to see you! Already I look forward to it. Don't fail to come, please. . . . Hoping you will be out this way and that we can arrange an engagement—and perhaps take another tramp in the rain. . . . You talked to me about Katherine Mansfield once while we walked along the shores of Lake Michigan. . . . Do you remember a rainy walk to Goose Island when we both cut assignments and I sang you the Adam and Eve Song. . . ."

And, "There are so many ways in which I might write to you, Carl. So many things that I might say to you. But they are not necessary. This is enough—no? You have never been a dream in my life but a strong and vivid reality. If I should happen never to see you again, nor ever to read another word of yours, that presence would not fail me. Muna." The last is a poet and writer I know later in life—Muna Lee, his friend since early Chicago poetry days. I never asked Muna why my father meant so much to her. It is not my way.

In reading old letters, there is one from another poet, dated 1920, "Dear Carl Sandburg: Your fine letter came to me a day or two ago, and I have been living largely on the joy of it ever since. I am sending you below an as yet unpublished poem which will tell you perhaps how the myth of you turned into reality for me.—

'Goodbye,' you said, and your voice was
an echo, a promise.
You turned to go, a grey iron ghost.
The night took you.
Insubstantial as air, stronger than iron,
You were here and had gone.
Your voice was an omen, an echo.

With every good wish for a New Year of splendid 'breakfasts-to-come' for you and those you love, Faithfully, Babette Deutsch."

Both these women, whose works I admire, speak of reality. Casual? Passionate? Fleeting? Enduring? Helga, leafing through the old papers, bless her, reflects. She writes to an author out west, a "woman" from the old days, Evelyn Wells, long ago a reporter on the San Francisco *Call,* one of a few remarkable American females then whose sole income was from her writing. She replies, "Maybe you want to know of our prowls in the second hand shops on Third Avenue, hunting Lincoln pictures and materials. In New York he saw a publishing friend who was divorcing his wife and your father was morally outraged. His indignation went deep. . . . He was as great a friend with women as with men and wherever he went there were many and he was taken around. . . . At the end of that wonderful New York month, he became weary, unhappy, unlike himself. Finally he told me that he was sick for home, and he went back to Michigan and I never saw him again. I feel I know you, because you, young and unknowing, did not realize you were part of a strong and affectionate chain made up of many, crossing the continent. . . . He once said, 'I could have made an awful fool of myself over women if it hadn't been for my work.' . . ."

Late in Carl's life, in the New York apartment of aficionados (followers of Sandburg), pictures will be taken of my father and Marilyn Monroe dancing and drinking champagne and doing his exercises—bending the knees, holding a book high. Lovely Marilyn, thirty-eight, leans close to then eighty-four-year-old Carl, a cigar stub between his fingers. She gives him her phone number and autograph, "Just for Carl." They are two legends, aware of cameras and their image. If it leads to a bed, don't I bless it?

Other stories are bruited about when my father reaches those twilight years. There he is being led (like a dancing bear) by "hostesses" who clean and brush his suits, send out his shirts, perhaps rent a tuxedo for an appearance at their favorite "supper club" where he stops the show. Other friends whisper to me in those years of a movie star or two aside from Monroe. And why not?

Carl has written hundreds of poem about love.

Sweet lips, there are songs about kisses now.
Looking backward are kisses of remembrance.
Looking ahead are kisses to be wished-for.
So time is counted, so far back, so far ahead, in
measurements of sweet kisses.

I could love you
as dry roots love rain.
I could hold you

as branches in the wind
brandish petals.
Forgive me for speaking
so soon.

Perhaps his love life away from home will forever elude. Perhaps answers will come. All I know for sure is that my father liked leaving home and he liked coming back and whenever he returned, he spent hours over the days with Mother in talk. He held her hand when she was near him. She stood in his arm. He came down from his bed in the top floor in the nights to hers below. In his early *Chicago Poems,* the middle of one goes:

But leave me a little love,
A voice to speak to me in the day end,
A hand to touch me in the dark room
Breaking the long loneliness.

And looking through the glass backward in time, there I am in 1954, living with the Young Bear in my (our) house, unable to let go of the Old Bear in my other (their) house. It is an ancient pattern harking back to pre-Bible days, a problem for many women caught between two loves.

Birthdays.

For Kenneth Dodson's book, *Away All Boats.* It has been published and not by Harcourts, where Carl pushed it and where it was turned down, but by Little, Brown. And now it is bought up by Universal–International studios. Lo, it will be made into a film, while *Remembrance Rock* sits on the shelf. Well.

For Uncle Ed. On the twenty-fifth of March he will be seventy-five and "The Family of Man" is about to be born. Over the years, my uncle tells me sometimes how envious he is of women who experience the bearing of a child. No man, he says, can imagine it. Now it is a different kind, but pain it is in the laboring for this show. The trustees of the Museum of Modern Art are giving their hero a party. He has been director of their Department of Photography for seven years, since 1947. Instead of a medal, the trustees are establishing "the Edward Steichen Photography Fund for the purchase of photographs for the Museum Collection as a way of perpetuating his and our faith and belief in photography as a creative art." The announcement is made at the birthday party to 1,250 prestigious guests at glittering tables set about in a Museum Hall. Paula is there at her brother's side. And Carl.

A third birthday. For Paula, who is seventy-one on May Day. Her brother surprises her. She writes, "Dearest Helga and all—Maybe we are not a proper family, letting the days slip by without communications. Anyway when you write, Helga, it's like a bushel of letters and I see you all—the house, the brave young trees, Paula on her bicycle. . . . I can read between the lines that John has two new customers on his paper route and his business is flourishing! May 15 was our Goat Show and we took Toggenburg Champion, Best of Breed, Best Toggenburg Udder & Best Udder in Show with Jahala. . . . In Nubians we took First Junior Kid, First Dry Yearling, First and Second in 3-to-4-Year Class, First in 5-Years-and-Over, and First in 2-Year Milkers. Bebe also took Best Nubian Udder. . . .

"Did Janet tell you that Uncle Ed conspired with the maid to get a Birthday Cake for me May 1st, decorated with Dogwood blossoms and candles galore . . . ! He kept the cake in his room! . . . He arrived looking tired and left rejuvenated. . . . Janet is busy with the kids and Margaret with the flower garden. . . . Love to you all always. . . ."

How serene my mother is off at the Goat Show, honored

as her little animals win their laurels. How blessed that in that day, nearly twenty years past, we brought home the Tom Thumb Dairy group! What would Paula's letter to Helga, telling of her brother's "Dogwood blossoms" cake have contained if our life had gone another way, away from the land and the beasts? Do goats ever stand still, as cows will, waiting for a hand upon them, a feed pail? No. Their nature is to approach Paula in greeting at once, mingling their fragrant breath with hers, nibbling at her hair wisps, leaning against her side.

Over the years, since the first ones were born, there has been a procession of silken-coated Nubian babies and soft and fluffy Toggenburg and Saanen ones to be received wet from the mothers, to be hurried through blizzard, rain or sun to the kidding boxes in the Big House. There the first feedings take place and the baby animals lie upon laps or spring about on the rug in the dining room to the pleasure of the family. How they satisfy my mother! Perhaps their being there is another birthday gift that surpasses all, even the surprise "Dogwood blossoms" cake.

July 1954. "Dear Buppong: It was nice to get your 'love and business' call. Of course we want John to go, since he is needed. He is lucky. I hope he spends plenty of time with you on the work. . . . Now about payment for working with you, . . . we will leave that to you! . . ." Art and I and the dog, Leif, are going to the beach for a week and John argues about missing that. My father's money is an outright bribe and is not for my son but for me (my car has broken down and our finances are limping). And so my child is put on the train for Connemara. Paula and I will join them for my second week of vacation later in the summer while Art is off in New York.

Something else is in the wind and I like it. Carl wants to give me his manuscript collection. Mother writes, ". . . When you come, Helga, we can pack up the manuscripts for shipping to you. This was a wonderful idea of Dad's to give them to you who were at his side preparing the Mss. in the first place. I'll try to stock up with boxes, etc. The men fixed up & painted the old flat-bottom rowboat for one lake—the canoe for the other. John will enjoy the boating. . . ."

And then my mechanically oriented son, from the farm as time goes on, "Buppong and I have recorded on 9,600 feet of tape and recorded for 5:80. We plan to record on 72,000 feet of tape. This tape will be sent to Columbia Records who will make an album on Carl Sandburg. Mr. Murrow is going to come the last week in August. . . . In the chicken yard there are nine roosters and 27 chickens. One chicken laid a three yoked egg." And so on.

And later, "Last Sunday Mr. Middleton invited me over to his house to swim and to have lunch and supper. His cousin, Tito, came over. He lives in Panama and is up here in a summer camp. We had great fun swimming. Mr. Middleton would throw in money and we would dive in after it. I got about 45¢. Buppong gave me a knife that his father (August Sandburg) made." And so on.

And, after Paula and I arrive a month later, to his stepfather, ". . . I can now dive head first in the water and I go swimming every day. I wish we could go to the beach, but Buppong says we have to stay to be on TV . . ." While the children spend time on the boats in the lakes (John now wears an ancient hat of Carl's, a gift, sporting a rooster tail feather securely driven through the felt), I am going through Carl's papers.

My father likes the idea and comes downstairs to join me. We are surrounded by dusty stacks of shelves that fill the cement-floored room. They contain quantities of different-sized labeled cartons of clippings from magazines and newspapers and boxes of letters (answered or not) and lines of volumes (fiction, children's stories, old tomes, whatnot) eliminated from the upstairs library and extra copies of his books, first and later editions. A fireproof safe is there (its combination never used) for manuscripts that will go into the bank vault or are being worked on.

Carl wants his papers off his hands but cared for. Due to dampness, there are rustings from paper clips and staples. Silverfish have made lacy patterns. The papers need arranging, assessing, sorting, protecting. And I am to find a final resting place for them somewhere. He composes a document for me to type for his signature (with Paula as witness) that he has given to his daughter, ". . . the manuscripts and related material of my published books including *Abraham Lincoln, The Prairie Years and the War Years, The American Songbag, Lincoln Collector, Remembrance Rock, Always the Young Strangers, Early Moon, The People, Yes* and other books of poetry. . . ."

He drags an ancient chair over and sits near. The air is cooled by the dehumidifier. For this moment in time, I am in all ways content. My father is talking to me. There is no need for answers, except in appreciation. This is the scene back there in the past. Her hair is graying. Blue eyes intent. An appreciated Working Woman, not just an amanuensis (Milton's three). And he? Deepset hazel eyes. An old blue shirt, collar open, sleeves rolled. His pants are baggy, shoes aged and comfortable. Loving. Liking the familiar father-daughter pattern, close. His voice, remember? The timbre. He speaks of how sometimes when he is on a stage with the guitar and singing, it suddenly comes to him that he does not know which song it is or how many verses he's gone through or where he is and has to collect himself.

He tells how when he first began talking on a platform,

he was unsure of himself and when he stood up to speak the word would not come and he would draw out that word that he was on until it did! He is glad that when he comes to Washington he can stay at my house and not at the Cosmopolitan Club where once he had been put, ". . . that mausoleum of respectability!"

He gets up to stand and watch over my shoulder. He pulls a piece of paper and then another out of its place and begins to read from them. His words beautiful and apt. He settles back in his chair. Helga watches carefully, so that she may replace the papers where they belong. I am possessive about my new treasure and can't wait to unpack the whole lot in my study.

And then the boxes are delivered to the freight office and I am on the train heading for home and husband and job. Little Paula stays with John Carl for the coming of the New York television crew. That is what their grandfather desires. My mother sends the check for the summertime children's visit and, "We are really busy with Murrow and his party of six—wonderful hard workers all! 14 hour shifts for the engineers! John is alert to everything—and Paula likes Mr. Murrow! So it's something they'll remember. . . ."

During that filming, which lasts five or six days, Edward R. Murrow and Fred Friendly stay at the farm, the rest in nearby Woodfield's Inn. On the pillared front porch, Carl is asked, "What do you think is the worst word in the English language?" "The one word more detestable than any other in the English language is the word *exclusive. . . .* when you're exclusive, you shut out a more or less large range of humanity from your mind and heart. . . ." "Carl, would you rather be known as a poet, a biographer, a historian—or what?" "I'd rather be known as a man who says, 'What I need mainly is three things in life, possibly four: To be out of jail, to eat regular, to get what I write printed, and then a little love at home and a little outside. . . .' " "Now, Carl, you have got all four of those things, right?" "In a way of speaking. . . ."

The show is aired on October 5, my mother advising, "Particularly listen whether you hear the bird calls as they put a CBS microphone on the Bird Feeding Station. Also listen for the Rooster as the sound man took special pains to do justice to our Rooster Choir! . . ." Two days later on the seventh, the one-volume Lincoln is published. As the reviews come in, they vary from objecting that the condensing has been done at all, to praising all out that it has. And so once more that is that. What next?

Another visit from Carl. He comes to Washington to open the Library of Congress "Poetry Series" on the twenty-fifth, "The poet, dressed in evening clothes but wearing brown shoes, . . . spoke in a deep melodious voice, etc." And then he is in our living room a few days later, the twenty-eighth. We are listening to the evening news, "Ernest Hemingway today won the 1954 Nobel Prize for literature. The fifty-six-year-old novelist will receive a gold medal and a check for 181,646 Swedish crowns—about 35,000 dollars. . . . Hemingway said he was proud and happy . . . but he thought Carl Sandburg should have won it. . . ."

We turn off the radio and Carl asks Helga to ring up Herblock at the Washington *Post,* busy on the next day's cartoon. He asks Herb to meet us all later at Harvey's in downtown Washington for dinner (Helga will pay the bill and let Mother know the total, as is the custom!). And, "Herb, you go on hitting the ball, catching flies with one hand high in the air. I rate you above Willie Mays." He tells him what Hemingway had said and mentions the story about the old Roman who was asked why there wasn't a statue of him and the old Roman, "I'd rather have that question asked than have a statue!" Carl, "I'd rather have the question asked, Herb!"

He turns the phone over to me to get in touch with a secretary to hunt up Hemingway's address at his *finca* in Cuba. I am to phone in a cablegram: "YOUR UNPRECEDENTED COMMENT ON THE AWARD DEEPLY APPRECIATED AND UNDERSTOOD IF ONLY AS FELLOWSHIP BETWEEN TWO ILLINOIS BOYS STOP. . . . WITH EVER LOVE AND BLESSINGS FOR YOU AND THE UNFORGETTABLE LOVABLE MARY WELSH OF BEMIDJI STOP LUCK STARS BE OVER YOU STOP MAY THE ROAD TO HELL GROW GREEN WAITING FOR YOU CARL SANDBURG."

A nice stroke for my father, who will eight years later be handed the same prize in the same second-hand fashion by John Steinbeck, the next American receiving it for Literature. "I'm glad to get it but oh, how I wish it could have gone to Carl Sandburg. Damn it. He is America."

Hemingway's wife, Mary, has been a friend of Carl's from their days far back on the Chicago *Daily News.* She writes him now and then. Once, "You remember how young reporters hero-worship sometimes? I guess you knew I was hero-worshiping you on those afternoons, still as bright as fire in my mind, when you used to amble into the society department and talk to us. Though it was an unconscious good on your part, that was a lovely thing you did for a girl who seemed to feel machines and organization eating into the very core of her. And it was long before that that I felt I really knew some part of you—long before when I first read your Chicago, with nothing but pines listening in Minnesota. . . ." When he sent her *The People, Yes* twenty years ago, she called him "Dear Great American" and, ". . . you are the one American poet who has grown these last dreary years. And how you stand out with new stature among all those who have shrunken." And that "Ernest knew and said you are the master—'maitre—maestro'—of us all, the big ones like him and the tiny ones like me."

The odd little news item—the fifty-six-year-old Teller of Tales giving his prize second-hand to the seventy-six-year-old Veteran—travels around the country in the press. Hemingway responds to the cable, along with Mary, and Carl says, ". . . One result of your warm-hearted and record-breaking comment is that you have sent Hemingway readers to Sandburg and Sandburg readers to Hemingway."

Mary has already given my father her award. She has written him that she keeps *Complete Poems* beside her bed "in the same company I've kept beside my bed for years, in Cuba or travelling—the Shakespeare Sonnets, Cecil Day Lewis' translation of The Georgics, M.B.'s Les Fleurs de Mal, and Paul Scott Mowrer—with some transients, of course, but these are the original company and I hope you approve of them."

And Mary again, "No one vested me with the authority to create a barony for you, but nothing I know of in our Constitution . . . denies me the right. And in these days of status-seekers and status-symbols, it seems both useful and appropriate, also inexpensive. This way, we're not going the whole hog, for Baron is the lowest rank of the British nobility, just two cuts above a knight (I made Ernest a knight years ago, but we kept it secret) and one cut above a baronet—modest enough. In the old days, if I read correctly, they made men barons for bravery, prowess in war and ingenuity in politics. I dub you Baron for having fought the brave, brilliant, honorable, uncompromising but ingenious road in the battles of our time. With affections and respect from your commoner."

So there.

"Dear Helga, Mother and I talked today about the way you saw a target in stenography and toiled your way into it and made your Mt. Everest. We give three cheers for your birthday and for all of you and yours. Buppong." And Paula, "Your new job sounds exciting! and important! We are proud of you!"

The cheers are for getting through a night school stenographic course in shorthand. I have begun to dream in squiggly lines and dots and dashes. However I am now a GS–5, my salary increased to a gallant $3,410, and cleared by the FBI to handle security files in the Office of the Keeper of the Collections at the Library.

My life is going beautifully. Not Art's. He quits his high school teaching job, fed up. He applies for a job in the Manuscripts Division. This I do not mention in lengthy correspondence with the farm, describing the happy processing of Carl's papers and the weekends in the Shenandoah in an old cabin lent us by Eric and Lois Sevareid. (Since his television show, Eric has been too busy to go.)

When the word is out, Carl and Paula do not admire the Young Bear's move. Hasn't he left a perfectly good position that supported his family without another in sight? Isn't their daughter employed and supporting him? Is he intending to live off the sale of the manuscripts? Why are the grandchildren not here for the Christmas holidays? (They had other plans.) None of these questions is broached.

A rift is beginning between my father and myself. I am glad of my new life and its freedoms. I like the conventional family scene: Father, mother, son, daughter, dog, cats. I wish for the addition of visiting parents and sisters. It doesn't work. How can it? It is an age-old scene for women, caught between the Young and the Old Bears. The Unfamiliar with whom we journey away from the Familiar. Ruth. I proclaim my loyalty. I intend to make my climb up the Mountain work.

Take the Old Bear. He is an item in Walter Winchell's column (regarding his uncombed hair). He appears on comedian Steve Allen's show (and is a hit, exchanging ad-lib cracks which, in Allen's words "had the control room in a panic."). He has been voted an outstanding artist by the National Arts Foundation (along with Pablo Casals and Sir Jacob Epstein). He accepts a scroll from the Civil War Round Table in New York (as "the Lincoln of our literature"). The John Henry Faulk Program features "A Salute to Carl Sandburg On His Seventy-Seventh Birthday" (which includes a long-distance interview from Connemara). Ed Sullivan puts him in his column ("He has lighted enough flames in his lifetime to get along without the dim flicker of candles on a cake"). *Newsweek*'s "Newsmaker's" page, ". . . Pointing out to the Overseas Press Club that he himself was seventy-seven, Sandburg said, 'That is a crapshooter's number. You're sure to live through that year.' "

Take the Young One. He makes a decision to try his hand as a television actor. He knows the stage profession and has friends in New York in the field. He goes there, staying with his parents. Sends postcards home, "I'm a man who gets murdered. Tune in early to catch it. It's a living. . . ." He works "Studio One," "Omnibus," "Danger," others. If anything takes off and a livelihood seems possible, we'll move to the big city. He has a casting agent, is busy with rehearsals, shops, visits and occasionally comes home for a weekend. He is giving himself a few months to see whether it will work. He wants Helga to quit her Library job and make her income on typing theses at home. He urges and she is willing. Helga is jumpy. We have loud and lordly fights. No winners or losers.

Uncle Ed. His child, "The Family of Man," is born in New York on the twenty-fourth of January. Carl does the Prologue as well as the captions. The poem about "There is only one man in the world" and the rest of that, is there. No problem between those "blood brothers" ever! The exhibition will tour the states while crowds line up. Nine million people of thirty-seven nations will see the sixty-nine overseas exhibits sponsored by the U.S. Information Agency. Paula goes to New York for the opening. She and Carl stay in a suite at the Gotham Hotel. Uncle Ed and Dana are in the adjoining suite. The four have breakfast together. Is their pleasure marred a little when, after Helga and her "angels" are mentioned, the failings of the Young Bear and the new development in that area are gone into?

You see, the day before the opening and before Paula arrives, my father is at his usual New York hotel—the Royalton and not yet over at the Gotham suite. Art phones him there. His friends have urged him to see whether his father-in-law can't open a few doors for him. Art feels the same. Why not? He puts in the call. The seventy-seven-year-old Grizzly is busy and has no intention of getting involved with an unemployed son-in-law. He says so shortly and that he "ain't got no time for visiting" and hangs up.

The approximately thirty-two-year-old Young Bear is enraged and insulted and puts the incident in writing on a postcard for the attention of wife and children. Helga is not in the least surprised. She would not have minded the click of the phone. But she is not a Young Bear. She is a daughter.

The holding pattern begins. Paula writes, "Dearest Helga. . . . I finally decided that I could make a quick 3-day trip of it—never left the Gotham Hotel except to go to the Museum—so I saw the Show and had a visit with my Big Brudder. . . . Margaret was just over an attack of flu and was rather weak. . . . I thought of trying for a short visit with you, but I decided against risking another day as Margaret's vitality was low and I feared she might neglect taking her medicine regularly which could lead to real trouble. Margaret has not had a seizure for over a year. . . . Deep love from all here always. . . ."

Their restless son-in-law is writing to Helga that she is to stop communications with the farm. He damns the Big Bear for all of his ways. By the end of March, Art is home. He has had a nibble on a writing job in Washington he wants to look into. I "tender my resignation from the employ of the Library." My husband has another idea. He will begin a book. *The Red Pencil.* Concerned with the travail of a high school boy, Jesse Wall, who is continually "red-pencilled" by the teachers and administrators of his school.

April. I hear from a Lincoln dealer and collector and family friend, Ralph Newman, interested in the assemblage of papers my father has given me. He writes, "I will check in at LC around 10 Thursday morning. . . ." I am no longer there, since the first of the month. Carl, at the same time, hears from Prof. Bruce Weirick at the University of Illinois in Urbana, "Dear Carl: . . . . This week I got a letter from President Morey asking me to find out if you still think cordially of letting us have your library, manuscripts, and the Steichen photographs. . . . so that we may get about the too long neglected business of setting up a center of Sandburgiana here in central Illinois. . . . Are you interested? . . . Call your shots! Love and best wishes. . . ."

Carl is having thoughts of his own. He composes a letter to his daughter. It goes into detail about what he has on hand. Letters. Tapes of lectures and broadcasts. Notebooks. His library. Photographs. Notes. Memoranda. Unpublished manuscripts. Items such as a slave auctioneer's cane and blacksnake whip. First editions of his books going back to the first ones. Foreign translations, ". . . including

Always The Young Strangers in Swedish, Portuguese and Chinese."

He continues, "I have, of course, told the prospective buyers of the manuscript collection in your possession. What is proposed is that if we make a package deal and the price to be paid you is somewhere between $10,000 and possibly $15,000, I am to pay you $5,000 this coming autumn or winter and $1,000 each year thereafter. . . . Sincerely and faithfully. . . ." He does not send it.

Carl plans to deliver the message in person. He comes through Washington in late June when Uncle Ed is here, setting up a "Family of Man" exhibit in the Corcoran Gallery of Art. My uncle is on radio and television and is making personal appearances. Our papers are full of it, "CAPT. STEICHEN AT 76 JUST HITTING HIS STRIDE," and so on. Uncle Ed is on the cover of the *Saturday Review* and was featured in the May issue of *Life,* along with old studies of Rodin. The February *Life* had put a "Family of Man" photo on the cover and a twelve-page spread inside!

And so Carl appears at the Office of the Keeper of the Collections. His daughter is elsewhere, not here. The staff is requested to put in a call to her home. I am asked to dinner and accept. Just me. Come into town and we'll meet.

That evening Carl rattles a paper or two beside my glass of wine and proposes to give me $10,000 for my Treasure. Will I budge? The collection is mine! A tie to my past. I refuse. Never. Carl states that he has a secret buyer for all of the papers and wants the manuscripts included. And he judges that it is best for all of his papers to be in one place. Is there really a buyer, the daughter considers, or is he regretting the gift, due to the shortcomings of the son-in-law? No. The manuscripts were given to me. I have labored on them. Bought new files for them. A dehumidifier for their comfort. They are mine!

The dinner is ending. Will he come to my house? He is "on the outs" with the Young Bear who has left his profession and is idling. He has plans for the night. He will stay with Marjorie and Bill Braye in Baltimore. I dial the number there so that he can talk with them. He returns to the table. "Life," he says musically, "is a series of relinquishments." Helga feels the truth of it as the air that she'd hoped to clear, is foggier yet. I drive him to the train station. There I get Connemara on the phone for him. Mother. We talk back and forth of this and that. I see him safely, sturdily, onto the Baltimore car.

After the report is received in my home, Art, whose rage has not abated, composes a furious letter. He explains his Young Bear position. He also points out the Old Bear's specific problems with relationships and life and how he might solve and mend them. Helga sees the frenzied letter before it is mailed and feels that the catharsis, the purification, for her husband, may give him relief (The Last Word!) and our life will be simplified. I feel the pain and in my fashion, no inclination to stop the tide (King Canute!). My husband returns to his desk and his wrestling with his new manuscript, cleansed of his ire.

THE RIFT

THE SUMMER moves into July. Helga receives a brief communication (typed by him and signed CS) from the Old Grizzly that he has just recently come upon the misplaced "printer's copy" of the Lincoln manuscripts that should have been in my collection. He does not suggest that it belongs to me. I at once put his missive into the file and refuse to answer or think about it.

August. From the Shenandoah Sevareid cabin, by candlelight, Helga writes to "Dear All" (true to the holding pattern she is establishing with Paula). About how Eric and Lois are "somewhere on the continent. . . . it is isolated—lonely—crickets, mayflies, various night-insects, tree-frogs—and 2 exuberant whippoorwills breaking the dark." Reports on the children fishing, Leif hunting frogs, the cats enjoying grasshoppers, the "privy, swimming in the nude, spiders in the bed, no rugs, worm-spotted apples, wild blue & blackberries, rinsing out the clothes & drying them on the ramshackle board fence . . ." And then sending photos of "apples, girls, tomatoes, trees, gourds, boys—and even gardenias and roses. Love . . ."

Mother, bless her, by return mail, "All happy to see the pictures of John and Paula. . . . Paula seems to have made an extra big spurt in growth the past year, but she'll never be as tall as her giant brother. . . . These photos are almost as good as seeing the children. Of course you know that we would love to have them for a visit anytime. . . . Dad is writing steadily as ever, only fewer hours at a stretch. Margaret takes daily walks with Dad—otherwise she explores the whole world of books—and politics too. Janet manages the kids on her own. . . . We can see that John takes special pride in the tomato vines . . . It's nice that Paula can have a good horse to ride. . . . Love from us all . . . ."

What I do not say in my letter is that we have our two typewriters with us at the sunny cabin and while the children and the dog and cats roam, I am on a well-paying thesis job and Art is finishing his novel. Unlike my father, I will pull a string or two for his son-in-law if I can. I write an editor I have met and vastly admire in New York, Pat Covici. He is Steinbeck's editor and when in New York eight years ago, he gave me an autographed copy of *The Wayward Bus* just out. Would the editors at Viking Press take a look at *The Red Pencil*? And I add that Harcourts does not know of this work. By return mail, Pat writes to send it on "at your earliest convenience."

Helga is regretting her refusal to return Carl's gift of the manuscripts in her study. They are necessary to complete the collection. His papers should be together in one place. She wants to be rid of them and their memories and will put the money he wants to pay for them into the market or bonds for the children. I talk with Mother on the phone. She will discuss this with Dad. We speak of the "angels."

Carl dictates to his secretary a rather formal letter regarding the payments. $3,000 down and the rest in yearly installments at 6 percent interest. He states that "Your collection was a gift from me, and when you return that gift, I give you an equivalent gift in money." And, "If you wish to accept this offer on the terms stated above, sign below and keep one copy of the agreement, and return one copy to me together with the paper that I signed on the original gift of my manuscripts."

"Dear Dad, I am enclosing herewith the paper that gave me title to the mss, as well as the agreement and carbon that you sent for signing. I don't think you and I need signed agreements. . . . I am on a rush job (typing a thesis in Italian for the Universite di Milano regarde le biografie a le storie di Washington Irving!) but will be finished soon. . . . I can't believe this is the end of September. . . . John is very serious about his first year in high school. . . . love. . . ."

He does not reply. But his daughter knows where he is always. There it is in the press, how he "will be seen on two nation-wide television programs in October"—a reading from *The People, Yes* for some NBC spectacular and then on Murrow's "See It Now" discussing Andrew Johnson, who succeeded Lincoln as president. "Recently Mr. Sandburg went with a CBS camera crew to Greenville, Tennessee, where his part of the program was filmed in the little tailor shop that Johnson owned early in his career."

Then something wonderful happens to Helga. She begins a journal on the fourth of December of that 1955, in which her heart is written out for the next eight years. In the first pages are comments on a program of reading she's launched on of the books of writers she admires that can stand at her shoulder and silently help as she puzzles out their philosophies and techniques.

And in the pages too are lists of the ways and forms of the characters that are beginning to live in my mind and on paper as I begin my first sustained writing of fiction. My tale will be of farms and the ways of country people and animals. There will be goats and a strong-willed daughter and a powerful father.

By the first of the year, my husband is off in New York again for television acting work. He visits Pat, who has turned down *The Red Pencil*. Art mentions that I have begun a novel. It is true that Helga watched, helpless, as his book grew and took form and she had no control.

There is the vivid scene in her mind. Hadn't she been instructed by Carl in those lost days of locks that turn and lighted lamps and cigar smoke, back in the lovely Connemara room, with the comfortable chairs and an occasional "loving cup" of wine? His voice in cadence, "Swipes, writing is just putting down one word after another."

And so the letters go back and forth between Paula and

Helga. Wistful on my mother's part. Mine still doing my best to coax at least some of my family (count Carl out) into my territory. Each of us, mother and daughter, with a Bear whom we cannot turn from the direction he has taken. Paula (Helga has observed this since a small child) has always let Carl go his way. In this affair he stands firm in his rage and no persuasion by a woman could move him. Helga? How could she turn her husband (in his rage)? Although she mourns the rift, there is peace too. No more nervous moments. Within her family, there is stability, contentment. She has chosen.

And the letters. Paula's to Helga tell of the doings on the farm and missing the two "angels" and can they come to visit? (The Young Bear has put his foot down in that arena. No visits. Like hostages being held!) Helga's about this and that, no reference to the crux of the matter (everyone is quite aware of that), but about doing "supper over the fine fireplace coals, and the cats and dog toasting themselves. . . . We have all become serious checker players. . . ." And so on.

Christmas comes and goes. "Let the children know what gifts you selected for Buppong's and Gramma's presents to Paula and John—Bushels love. . . ." "Dear Mother, Your X-mas boxes were lavish. . . . But Paula, nearly 13 now, wears a 14 Pre-teen and wouldn't fit into the beautiful outfits you sent. . . . As to John, the 15½ shirt was perfect but the sweater too small again! O dear! He is a hefty fellow, broad in the shoulders and I get large or x-large for him . . . We're having a very green Christmas. Love. . . ."

And Paula to her namesake granddaughter, "It's a year and a half since we saw you, so you've perhaps grown a lot! I hope with all my heart, that you and John will visit us next summer, like you used to, during school vacation. Yesterday Buppong and I were looking for your little moss garden on our way for a walk along the Memminger Path—and we couldn't locate it. Last summer we could always find it—but the heavy fall rains and then the freezing with fallen branches have hidden the little moss garden. . . . Gramma."

In his study Carl puts together a little poem that Helga doesn't come across for years.

My little exiles the banished ones
the heart keeps turning to them
memory will not be still
remembering how and what they were
the faces and words of them
hope works on how and where they are
how they laughed and ran and slept
their utterly somber faces thoughtful
their utterly reckless singing gayety
their perfections of grace and manner
their ease and quiet at going lonely
to each of you I say across empty miles
"whither goes thou little pilgrim?
do you sometimes remember Gwawmaw and Buppong?"

There is Helga in her study, immersed in the growing stack of manuscript. She sees the girl, Ellen, gathering apples in the orchard in the valley below the farmhouse, her dog close at hand, her doe about to bear her young. The countryside is clear in her mind—like a Breughel painting. I am tense and thrilled.

My mother writes me of the quiet Christmas, the walks with Carl. Love. And I return, ". . . Maybe in spring you can get on the train with the girls—and we can take a gander at the cherry blossoms and be critical about them & then come home and have wild ecstatic remarks to make about our own pink dogwood and young bearing apple. . . ." and so on. And always saying "love," both of us.

Carl? His likeness is in my morning paper, observing his seventy-eighth birthday and saying that he will "sit and look out at the Great Smokies and work once in a while . . ." And that he sometimes feels he has "lived past my years." On Lincoln's Birthday, there he is on television, controlled, assured, white-haired, like a patriarch in his black bow tie and suit, with André Kostelanetz and doing that "Lincoln Portrait" again, this time for "The Ed Sullivan Show." Our local critic the next morning, "There's a lot of ham in poet-historian Sandburg. . . . who has the face of a Biblical prophet, speaks hesitantly, sometimes slurringly. But he can communicate every measure of emotion contained in a pure line of writing. . . ."

There is more about my father in the press. *Time* reports how the University of Illinois got a "good bargain for $30,000." And lists with a careless wealth of inaccuracy the various items included in the "private library, now housed at Sandburg's North Carolina goat farm."

Do I care? The first part of my novel is with Pat Covici, ". . . . I hope for your personal opinion on this secret venture. . . . And since it's typed on old stationery that I'm using up, with an old address, for god's sake don't return it any place but here . . ." And Pat, "We like much of your projected novel . . . ." and how it is having other readings. ". . . I like your dialogue and I like your character of Ellen. . . . Do let me hear from you. . . ."

It is an odd time in Helga's life, feeling her writing power (along with innocence and ignorance) and uneasy that her secret will out. The letters go back and forth. Lengthy criticisms from the Viking editors arrive. And, "Dear Pat, I am surely beholden. . . . When I am prepared to send you another draft and further material, I will send it on to you without hesitation. . . ."

April. The scene shifts from the piled study desk to Carl's room in New York's Waldorf-Astoria, where he is giving an interview over scrambled eggs and coffee for New York reporters. That night he is to receive the Albert Einstein Commemorative Award of $1,000 and a medal. Carl tells them that while he never met Einstein, back eleven years ago, in August of 1945, in the time of the atom bomb dropping on Hiroshima, he wrote "Mr. Attila." The press prints it, pleased.

They made a myth of you, professor,
you of the gentle voice,
the books, the specs,
the furtive rabbit manners
in the mortar-board cap
and the medieval gown.

They didn't think it, eh professor?
On account of you're so absent-minded,
you bumping into a tree and saying,
"Excuse me, I thought you were a tree,"
passing on again blank and absent-minded.

Now it's "Mr. Attila, how *do you do?"*
Do you pack wallops of wholesale death?
Are you the practical dynamic son-of-a-gun?
Have you come through with a few abstractions?
Is it you Mr. Attila we hear saying,
"I beg your pardon but we believe we have made some degree of progress on the residual qualities of the atom"?

June. No letters have gone to or from Connemara after January, as the camps settle, the seige holds and the Rift takes a wide swing apart. Paula sends a last-ditch handwritten letter as to whether the children are coming for the summer.

"It is Buppong's dearest wish, and mine, to have our grandchildren here for a visit with us. I'd think, Helga, that you could spare them for two weeks out of fifty-two! . . ." and more of the same.

Helga would be happy to oblige. However, at the head of her household is the strong-willed blond-headed Bear, who will not. He is at his desk. He wants to write out his rage. A number of drafts are gone through and the result is a single-spaced typewritten red-hot message, containing a history of grievances, and a list of the injustices done to their son-in-law, who has "given us only the rarest kind of devotion and for this we three bless him." And on and on.

It is at this time that Helga is "written out of the will" by her father, an action for which she thirsts! The message is an angry one, and protests her people not responding to invitations to come visit and, ". . . I believe that the children are not bean bags to be tossed back and forth between a disunited family. John's memory of our visit two summers ago is that when we wanted to leave we could not. Paula's memory is of Dad's saying that if she didn't stay, he was going to find another granddaughter. And I was bought off, against my judgment, tongue-tied, bullied by Dad's saying he'd get another daughter. . . . I wonder if you or Dad have any suggestions. Deepest love. . . ." And it is given into the hand of my postman with righteous fervor. So there.

A week later, on the twenty-seventh of June, I follow it, as Janet's birthday comes up, with a gift for her. She thanks me and, ". . . . I think of you quite often. Tell John Carl and Paula that I think of them too quite often. Write soon. Loads of love . . . ."

It is during this June that Carl composes one of his mystic poems and gives it a mystic name. It goes partly,

Consolation Sonata

These poplars dream,
still or shaken they dream:
they never come out of it:
to this dreaminess they are born.

Consecration is a flower,
also it is many vegetables
or again it is neither,
not a flame of rose seen
nor a new potato eaten:
it is one tumbling moment
flowing over from a bowl
of many earlier moments. . . .

Kiss the faint bronze
of this garment of the sun.
Kiss the hem of this spun fire
brought from a smoldering,
leafed out in handspreads,
two four five handspreads.

The sun burns its gold
and this to you
is home and mother.

The night frames its stars
and this to you
is a book and prayers.

And while Helga does not see the poem (it is by his typewriter and not for printing yet), in the current *Look* is a spread of photos of my parents and there are my sisters, unfamiliar in clothes I do not know. The guitar is about. It is a serene scene. "Sometimes I play for Janet and Margaret and Paula, but often I play at night, in the dark, alone. . . ."

And, "I went to the feet of Jesus and quit smoking." There are the goats and the barnyard and the dining room table. Nostalgia. A look at them. Far away. ". . . . You know, when you're over seventy, a day is an awful lot of time. . . ."

As the summer lingers, I go with Art to New York and while he is busy, have a talk with Covici. Pat is intrigued with the Rift and feels I should think of a book on Carl. I am disinterested, enthralled with my new field. Feel the safety of fiction and intend to make my statements there.

The country? The polio vaccine is developed and the four of us have shots regularly as advised. The flame of freedom burns in Poland and Hungary, while the Russians continue their efforts to put it out. Here "We Shall Overcome" is heard in a louder and yet louder chorus. In September, the presidential campaign is under way and our hero, Adlai, is persuaded to throw his hat into the ring again (Carl's voice is in on the persuasion, and he will help when called upon). Again, however, as destiny rules, in November Stevenson is defeated while Eisenhower takes a landslide and "Tricky Dicky" is along for the ride.

My sole correspondent from the farm is heard from, ". . . How do you like the way the election turned out? I hope Eisenhower lives his full term of 4 years and doesn't die. I hate to see Nixon as president. . . . What grades are John Carl and Paula in? Write soon. Loads of love, Janet. P.S. I think of you quite often."

I now have a New York agent. A friend of Art's—Richard Gilston of the Literary Department of MCA Management, Ltd. They handle playwrights and Art knows him through his stage contacts. He writes me: "First off, I think your novel is tremendous—moving, compelling, exciting, warm. . . . Suffice to say that I was deeply moved and completely engrossed and do not doubt that Pat Covici will react the same way."

Heaven. Manna. While I respond to Dick's letter, I also enclose a short story called "Witch Chicken." And, "I have an idea for another one, but hate to waste the time if there is no outlet. I am collecting material for another novel now. . . ." Mid-December and the news. Viking does not want the book. Four editors read the manuscript. They liked it but it needs work and "a vast amount of cutting" and so on.

Helga's elation in her work is untouched. And she sends a holding letter to the farm, "Dear Mother—We are going to New York for five days or so after Xmas. Would you like to come and stay with the children then? Or better yet, you and dad both? love. . . ." Carl will not set foot on his son-in-law's territory. Women are not the same. Paula's letter later, "Thank you for the happy three-day visit with the children. They have 'grown up' since their last visit here—so mature—so well-balanced—so sweet-natured as ever! they always were 'mature' for their ages—and it was fine to see them as sweet as ever—now that they are 5′5″ and 5′7″. . . ." She adds a "P.S. Dad will be on radio January 6—4:05 P.M., 'American Minstrel.' "

She sends her granddaughter the photos the three took of each other, ". . . . Buppong says it's almost like a visit. . . . and you were the gracious hostess—delicious food etc. etc.! . . . You and John made me very happy and proud!"

The tall territorial Grizzly's birthday again—the seventy-ninth. It is a Sunday afternoon. A fire burns in our living room, Leif and the cats sprawled before, the children alert, the insecure Blond Bear in his easy chair. We are following up on Mother's "P.S." The show has been recorded by Joe Wershba, our family's friend and one of Murrow's "second generation" boys.

The guitar and the song I sing:

I've been wandering, early and late,
New York City to the Golden Gate,
And it looks like I'm never gonna cease
My wandering . . .

The familiar lost voice on and on. Most of the talk, the opinions, the humor, I've heard before. The tender sweet guitar.

But it's a long long while from May to December
And the days grow short when you reach September
And I have lost one tooth and I walk a little lame
And I haven't got time for the waiting game. . . .

Helga hones after the Old Bear, denied in her life. This I do not say as the household takes up its ways again and the voice comes up and fades off as the show ends:

Love, oh love, oh careless love,
Love, oh love, oh careless love,
Love, oh love, oh careless love.
You see what love has done to me! . . .

The Young Bear has a good job now in a Washington university. He walked into the office of the president and offered himself as Director of English Composition and has been put on the staff as an assistant professor. He's given up, for the moment, being an actor or writer. He keeps a close eye on my productions and their hoped-for sale which I do not relish. My typewriter is busy. I have a dissertation to finish and a 400-page thesis waiting in line. Besides the second novel.

What of Helga's literary efforts? Random House turns it

down. Easter and waiting for further word. My son spends his life in his room, now a licensed ham operator. My daughter rides Ginger, a neighbor's horse, in a local show, wearing old jodhpurs of mine and a visor cap. Helga stays in her study steadily.

The eighth of May. It is sold! A leaping heart! To a new firm, McDowell Obolensky. And that feeling is "that this will be either the biggest thing since the Bible, or that it will die with a Jurassic thud. He inclines toward the former opinion himself. . . . They will have an option on your next novel. God, isn't this exciting! See you soon. Dick."

David McDowell is my editor. I like him and he becomes my friend. I am heady and hurl myself into the revisions he wants. Summer and the cabin in the Shenandoah again where the hot dry grass beside it is sweet-smelling. The hay has just been cut and the overpowering nostalgic scent sweeps up the hill. The fish are plentiful. The dark woods call for young exploring feet. The lake is icy cold.

Do you see the scenes? The daughter with her loved family and her new happiness. Paula at Connemara with the girls. Her restless husband? Where but high over Chicago in his first helicopter flight. Carl has been invited by the Chicago Dynamic Committee to visit all over the place (including the high ride) and then write a new poem about Chicago. It is forty-three years since *Poetry: A Magazine of Verse* came out with that first "Chicago."

Henry Luce is Carl's fan and has *Life* do a big spread. He writes from his *Time* office that "Your message to America and the Americans is the finest thing LIFE has ever had the honor and good luck to publish."

We live in the time of the colossal upright oblong.
We are meeting in the city where the skyscraper was born. . . .

Millions of horses vanished into horizons of thin air
to be replaced by millions of steel tractors,
skyways and airport timetables . . .

Take a look at the nation again. "We are not afraid," sing the people. In September the Little Rock showdown. There goes Governor Faubus leading his jeering crowd and the National Guard to stop the nine black children from entering his Central High School. Ike stalls. The federal court orders the guardsmen removed. Federal troops are sent. The students walk through the doors. The first civil rights law since Civil War reconstruction days is passed by Congress.

October. *Sputnik I* ("Fellow Traveler") takes off, the size of a beach ball, man's first earth satellite (going to pieces four months later). November. *Sputnik II* is launched, a thousand pounds and carrying Laika (the dog dies after a week and so does the satellite before long). Molotov is exiled to Siberia. Khrushchev replaces Bulganian as Chairman of the Soviet Council of Ministers. He goes to Peking where China's Great Leap Forward is happening, led by Mao Tse-tung. More than half a billion peasants are put into twenty-four people's communes and promised food, shelter, clothing and child care in exchange for owning no private property.

There is Carl on "Meet the Press" explaining how Lincoln would have handled the Little Rock situation, "He would be holding daily conferences with the NAACP. . . ." Regarding *Sputnik*, it "is a testimony that man, whether he is Russian or American, wants to know about the spaces beyond the earth . . ." and so on and on.

The scene shifts from Carl enjoying himself on Lawrence Spivak's show to his daughter, where delicious excitements fill her heart, unknown to him. The title of her book has been decided. *The Wheel of Earth*. From Gilston at MCA, "It's always nice to send checks—here's one for you today. $450 advance due on delivery of THE WHEEL OF EARTH." She is thirty-nine. When his first recognized book, *Chicago Poems* was published, Carl was thirty-nine.

The climb up the Mountain of marriage so far survives. There are battles. Weeping. Despair. Loud shouting and stamping. Wrath trembling in the very pit of the bowels. See how she is stirred! (Love also in that part of her life. The bed. Desire.) Her second novel has for its lead characters a strong-willed girl (another one), the *deus ex* her *machina* a weak-willed husband. Helga's writing has become the center of her life.

Now sometimes she does a radio interview. Or a pre-publication party is thrown for *The Wheel of Earth*. She is writing more short stories and Dick Gilston sends them on the rounds. She takes a temporary job at the Library of Congress for John Wells Davidson on the Woodrow Wilson papers. David Mearns comes out of his office, "What is going on between you and Carl? Has he read your book?" She is polite, evasive, gentle, noncommittal. And, "No."

And then in the household, there is a new situation. As my son matures in body as well as mind, his stubborn and unique nature becomes more evident daily. He is sixteen. A Little Bear. His stepfather, the Big Older Bear, has what Helga considers an overzealous disciplinary attitude towards John's progress in his conversion to Art's own ideas about culture and etiquette.

On being instructed to "make conversation" at the supper table, the Little Bear balks. Thereafter comes a directive. He will have his tray in his own room, deprived of his family's company. So the boy, in heaven, retires to Merlin's Cave. A natural scientist since the age of three and a half when he ordered everyone away from his electric train ("I can wun it myhelf!"), John stays an enigma to my "logical" literary professor husband, barely eighteen years older. (In time John will get his Ph.D. in scientific fields.)

The Table Conversation Battle takes up a lot of noise and time. There are others. The War of the Bears is on. My feeling for my son is and will remain such that it hurts my heart in love. This feeling, which is not concealed, does not help the step relationship. Paula, female and wily and pretty, survives.

John's job, where he makes his living after school hours at a nearby golf driving range, is one where his talents at running the pick-up jeep and his other duties are respected. One evening he receives a directive from our professor that if he is not home from the range by ten, he will stay out until two. Sure enough he does, in the doorway, in the rain. Stubborn. Silent. A little pale. His dark red curls matted. Asking no quarter, on his way in life. My hero—my Little Bear.

Time wheels in its pattern. The moon waxes and wanes. In the web of the stars is the new unstable one that is clear and brilliant, sparkling and tumbling through Orion and out of sight—*Sputnik II*. 1958. Carl turns eighty. In March, Uncle Ed is seventy-nine, Paula seventy-five on May Day.

Her Christmas letters, like ones coming by ship from another land, had reached us. "Dear John Carl—How's this air-plane view of your old home? . . . You can even see the little round pool in front of the house! We hope school is fine this year and your short wave set doing all you want it to do! Love from us all, always. We are all lonesome for you! Gramma."

"Dearest Paula. . . . We had a very happy Christmas here too. And I thought of you all and knew in my heart what a happy Christmas you were having too—as I saw last Christmas how wisely you live finding happiness in worth-while things—so mature you & John, for your years. Love to you all, Gramma."

"Dearest Helga. . . . You and the children were especially in our thoughts during this holiday season, with remembrance of my happy visit last year with Paula and John. Many things we do not understand—but we love you now and always the same as ever. Your loving Mother."

And my reply, as from a distant island, with never a whisper of the lovely novel-child on the way, "My dear Mother" and about the going of one of our cats at eleven years of age. "It was strange at first, for the children were three and five when we got her—somehow she was a part of our daily living. . . ." About working for John Wells Davidson. And "Love to you all. . . ."

Helga's book is not yet even in galley proof. But she has seen the jacket. And it is splendid—white on red and a pastoral farmland scene! Her heart is hot. David writes that the galleys will be arriving in pieces and she is to "work around the clock" on them so the book meets the publication date of 18 April. The head salesman, Henry Staden, is in Chicago getting in touch with the people at Marshall Field's, where there will be a special book display and they will push this one. Pat Covici sends a letter, "I am very anxious to see the publication of your first novel. . . ."

Meanwhile the short story "Witch Chicken" is moving around. Dick writes, listing the various places and that "I got a notification the other day from the Virginia Quarterly Review about the Balch prize contest and have entered it. It is not at any rate, moldering. . . . Love to the young equestrienne and the engineer and the scholar and always, to you. . . ."

And then! "By the time you get this note, I will probably have spoken to you over the phone. . . . You are now the first prize winner of the 1958 Emily Clark Balch contest for your story WITCH CHICKEN. Along with this comes a check for $675—your $750 less our pound of flesh. I couldn't be more delighted. . . ."

Helga sends a hasty reply that she'd "had a sudden thought. . . . Surely you entered the story under my literary name, Helga Sandburg? Will you set me at rest on this? . . . ." And, "Dear Helga: Set your mind at ease. Sandburg you are."

William Carlos Williams, the poet-critic-doctor, likes Helga's book. Flossie, his wife, reads it aloud to him. He tells David, ". . . crazy about it—love and congratulations to Helga—would like to meet her." Williams is reviewing it. (He slammed my father's *Complete Poems*, ". . . Carl Sandburg petered out as a poet ten years ago. . . . His poems themselves said what they had to say, piling up, then just went out like a light . . . 'Chicago,' his first brilliantly successful poem should have been his last. . . ." And more of that.)

Henry Staden, the sales manager, is setting up guest speaker arrangements. Booksellers and book-and-author dates. He phones the news. There will be a "Monster Rally" in Marshall Field's where they are fans of my father. One reviewer says the book "has the courage to have innocence." The sales staff will use that for a catch phrase. William Carlos Williams will be on the flyleaf of the finished jacket, "Never since Emma Bovary sickened and died has such a female spirit as that of this farm girl from Kentucky been presented to us. In Ellen Gaddy, Helga Sandburg has created a memorable character."

And then a story for me. Henry is with the Field's buyer, Olive Peterson. She tells him how she was in her office at the *Tribune* with Fred Babcock, Fanny Butcher and Polly Goodwin. Carl is there. Polly mentions Helga's novel. Carl,

"Helga is back in the old pattern of her days. The camaraderie, the gaiety, the ease, the understanding, the acceptance."

"The three-year-old in sailor suit and round cap stands on the steps beside the sixty-six-year-old in full dress uniform with Commander stripes."

“Paula signs over the goat herd to Helga and gives her a paper, ‘I have also leased the pastures and the barns . . .’” (Jackson, Helga, Brenda)

“My sister is in her mid-thirties. Her hair is dark. Her laugh is sweet. There she is on Blueberry . . . John Carl is on Patches at her side.”

“My parents like Art . . . He gives me snapshots of himself taken there beside a great silver bomber.”

"'Dearest Swipes, Tell Snick on even days I love her the same as on odd numbers. Dad.'" (Photograph credit: Dana Steichen)

"'Dear John, You are my grandson but I can tell by your letter you are my dear old friend . . .'" (Photograph credit: Dana Steichen)

"Their nature is to approach Paula in greeting at once, mingling their fragrant breath with hers, nibbling at her hair wisps, leaning against her side." (Photograph credit: June Glenn, Jr.)

". . . we have our two typewriters with us at the sunny cabin and while the children and the dog and cats roam, I am on a well-paying thesis job and Art is finishing his novel."

"The scene shifts from Carl . . . to his daughter, where delicious excitements fill her heart, unknown to him."

"The visiting pair are recognized and Russian photographers want to have their pictures taken with Steichen."

"When he develops the photo back home, Uncle Ed writes 'King Carl & Fool Carl' on it. That is the beginning of the nine-day look at Sweden!"

"Helga's third novel is going well and will be ready in October . . . I am on a Georgetown University Writers Conference panel with Katherine Anne Porter, in heaven." (Photograph credit: Detroit Free Press)

"Mother photographs Carl at the table with Snick's arms about him. Their relationship remains a rock of love."

"Harry keeps in touch with me, seeing to plane and train reservations and a hotel when I go to New York . . ." (Photo presented to and inscribed for Helga) (Photograph credit: Don Hunter)

"Carl is tremendously happy. He carries the post card I mailed from Florence, . . . It is sepia-toned and does not illuminate the new auburn hair color I'd adopted . . ."

"'Dearest Carl—how we all wished that you could have been here . . .'" (Uncle Ed and Mother on Connemara's front porch)

"'. . . Ed, Joanna, John, Helga and Little Paula were all here. I missed you more than ever . . .'" (Uncle Ed and Joanna on Connemara's front porch)

"When in Washington, he visits the White House. Helga is along. Stewart Udall, our Secretary of the Interior arranges it all." (Photograph credit: The White House)

"In the Oval Office, Stewart and Helga sit on one of two sofas, Kennedy is in his cushioned rocker and on the other sofa is Carl, a bit of the smoldering cigar still between his left thumb and forefinger." (Photograph credit: The White House)

Dairy Goat Journal

February 1962

Volume 40, Number 2

*Mrs. Carl Sandburg, Flat Rock, North Carolina, was presented a handsome, framed photograph of her record-breaking doe, Puritan Jon's Jennifer II 9*M T121022, at the convention banquet at last fall's American Milk Goat Record Association meeting. In making the presentation, R. W. Soens (right), secretary of AMGRA, pointed out that the award was made for "years of service and devotion to the dairy goat industry . . . with emphasis on your program of carefully planned breeding over the years." A metal plaque on the frame is inscribed "Puritan Jon's Jennifer II 9*M T121022, 4-0 305 5750 191.0, Production Champion—All Breeds." Frederic Knoop, Cincinnati, Ohio, prepared the photo and frame.*

"How easy it is with my mother. Here she comes with a picture of herself and Jennifer . . . on the cover of *The Dairy Goat Journal*."

“A few days later, I arrive. John is here, ‘Hi, mommy cool. I get up at 5:30 and quit at 5:30. I’m a farm boy on a twelve hour day!’”

“Out on the porch, he, ‘She is a great daughter we have.’ She, patting his cheek, ‘Ah, indeed, Buddy.’”

“Barney. Stunningly handsome, graying hair and wild blue eyes, aggressive determination in all ways. A surgeon! An Author. A four-star Lochinvar . . .”

“. . . our new President Johnson . . . invites Carl to come with Paula to the White House in April. He has asked Uncle Ed and Joanna too. And then here they are. Mother, just eighty-one and not giving a fig for fashion . . .” (Photograph credit: Robert Knudsen, The White House)

"The New York *Times* headlines, 'JOHNSON STAGES A BALCONY SCENE.' And 'Hey down there!' called the President . . . 'Hey! Here's Carl Sandburg. Don't you want to ask some questions?' "

"Helga goes to find the guitar and gives it to Carl. He fumbles a while, hunts chords, returns it to me."

"In the long evenings, there is talk. And music . . . I am happy with the sweet-toned instrument . . . And Barney says in the night, 'I've never before been to a house with an undivided feeling of peace!' "

"'Two children turning pages in a big book under a high tree. May all the gods of luck watch & speak wisely with them. Love and love . . .'" (Carl and Paula on the porch on Connemara)

"Helga's tale is done. The moonlight of the present meets the sunlight of the past. The window, the glass of memory we have been looking through, shatters and is no more." (Photograph credit: Josef Krames.)

"What name is she using?" Polly, "Helga Sandburg." Carl, "Oh, capitalizing on the family name!" Polly, "Well, you gave it to her, Carl, didn't you?"

Helga is beginning to have strange bright dreams. She puts them down in the journal, "Dad had a book published in collaboration with my name. Produced it triumphantly with Harcourts editor, Kitty McCarthy. It was a dreadful thing with old type and photos. And I tried to be polite about it, knowing I'd been taken, wanting to discern if he believed he was helping me (he thought once of collaborating in a book on Taliesin) or thought he was putting one over, making out on my publicity! These dreams as a rule are astonishingly vivid. I hope one day to put them to rest."

And then the strange bright dream becoming a reality. Another call from Henry. The publicity manager at Field's has dreamed up a project to take a television crew from Chicago—Fanny Butcher, Babcock, Bradley, Harris, and more—coming along to Flat Rock. There Carl will introduce his daughter. $500,000 worth of publicity! Helga is appalled. "No, Henry. Never." Why haven't I told him that I haven't seen Carl for three years.

I will not be bought. Emotionally I know I am right. The fiasco would be intolerable. Critically, intellectually, I feel secure in my decision. Professionals must separate. Carl is at the end of the road. I am at the beginning. I will not lean.

The home scene. The household professor agrees with my decision. However, he is firmly critical of the speech I have prepared. Much too literary to be read to a crowd. Changes. Is my husband beginning to fancy himself as Pygmalion and me the ductile Aphrodite? This I do not mention.

Another call from Chicago. The big rally for Helga's book at Marshall Field's is all off unless their plan is followed. Reconsider. Fanny Butcher, friend of the family since "Chicago" was published in March of 1914, will review *The*

Wheel of Earth and has offered to talk with Carl. His editor, Kitty McCarthy, at Harcourts is going to speak with him too. She will get him alone and see what happens. She knows of the Rift and suggests there might be "a new relationship" resulting from a "get-together."

Helga makes terms. If he will introduce me in a Chicago *Tribune* office or on Field's stage or in a Lake Michigan outdoor setting in some way that suits him, all right. But I will not have my arm twisted by Field's. I will not go into his arena in Flat Rock. The sales people are looking at tomorrow's dollars. Helga is taking the long view of a literary future. She is frustrated but clearheaded. Feels that his ghost will forever bedevil her! Henry again, "Carl is willing, provided he gets the two grandchildren." "No."

Helga's household. Silent banging mornings. Gestures abrupt and things thrown rather than set down. The air is quite alive with electric charges. A little like Connemara at the last back there. And the War of the Bears proceeds. The lamp crashes. Glass splinters. Low voice of command. The Little Bear will not retract whatever began the Battle. And the War with the Wife too (remember he is five years younger than she and also his book was turned down). Furious. Picking up everything in the study that night that is breakable (and some not) including the Venetian glass birthday bowl. Smashing that. Berserk, hurling this and the other upon the walls. Her desk a disaster. In the next evening, on return from the Wilson papers in Washington, all is clean and a bouquet of roses on her desk. Well.

My peripatetic wrath for my husband and his uncertain temper continues as the days march on. (And it doubles my fury for my father, the Grizzly.) Why not some sympathy, understanding for the household Bear? There is the unbudgeability of the Young One (he swept up the glass). The fact of Helga's coming fame (notoriety?). And she is entirely too blithe. In heaven. Confident. Glory. Hauteur. Assurance. Joy. All calculated to drive a man crazy.

Is there love at night? Not touching, the bodies. Helga puzzles on it. How wise Paula seems—tending, fostering, pacifying genius. I have witnessed Carl in towering rages (not quite equal to the Venetian glass one), but I was never somehow touched. As a child, I saw Paula retreat to the shelter of a closet while the storm raged. That household is directed easily to the pacifying of its hero, the Big Grizzly. Not this one! And sometimes at night I weep in the bushes by our little house's side, thwarted in the image I want of the husband going his way, me mine, and happiness therefore.

It doesn't work. "Leave him," say the children. "No. I will do this my way. You'll have your own households some day. It's my life." I have taken the first step down the Mountain.

Through a glass darkly I see her there. The triumph! Plastered in the Washington *Star* (Sunday, 6 April 1958 edition), as well as various papers around the country. My friends keep mailing clips to me as the days pass. "SANDBURG'S DAUGHTER WINS $750 STORY PRIZE" and the picture (holding a copy of *The Wheel of Earth*) and caption, ". . . all kinds of love." Look at her. Never a day like this one. All mine! Not father. Not husband. Not boss. Mine! My story. My book. Through the glass, see her face glow, the secret delight!

My close Washington friends put a red rose by my plate when I go to one of the luncheons where we meet in the city. They are Lois (Mrs. Eric) Sevareid, Helen (Mrs. William) Costello, Lillian (Mrs. David) Cohn, Sally (Mrs. Scotty) Reston, Benny (Mrs. Howard K.) Smith. They all have famous husbands and they all are like my mother—tending, fostering, pacifying, (fighting?) genius in their ways. I love them and cherish my secret—the hard new work, writing.

There are calls for radio and television and newspaper interviews and appearances and for speaking engagements. *Time* is on the phone. Dudley Doust of the local office. He wants Helga to say that the New York rumor is true—the loving uncle and powerful father in the novel are *her* uncle and father. They discuss this around the mulberry bush for an hour. He hangs up, unsatisfied. When Henry hears of it, he sighs. "Sales lost in that, you know!"

Luncheons as a celebrity! At Eugene and Agnes Meyer's (Close to Uncle Ed. We speak of him. And Agnes and I become friends. She wants me to give her "editorial help"!). Sydney Hyman (his book is just out). Carleton Smith and his French wife, Anne. They want to help. Max Freedman at the *Manchester Guardian*. He calls with tickets to a show and dinner in mind. Helga wants to go. Art calls Max a sneak. Max says, "Your husband is civilized surely." "No. Primitive." Well.

Then the "literary" speech. The first presentation is at the Washington Booksellers (critics, publishers, book people, no public) on April 16. My husband is there on the podium. And my children. I do not freeze. Henry is happy, "Be yourself always. Marvelous!" Not the professor, who hands me a note as Henry and I board the sleeper train for Cleveland and the next event and he returns home with John and Paula, "Terrible. Jaw frozen. Louder. Slower." "Svengali incarnate," she sighs and goes to the parlor car with her sales manager for a special liqueur that he (a gourmand) knows of.

The same speech in Cleveland at a Book and Author luncheon. A wonderful time. Then Helga's first experience in an airplane. To New York and talks with David McDowell and Ivan Obolensky. Interviews, appearances, and the rest. Among them Helga misses the Dave Garroway "Today Show." Why? Well, the producers tell Henry that they featured Carl a week or so ago and don't want two Sandburgs so close together. That blessed name!

The American Booksellers Convention in Atlantic City (Eleanor Roosevelt was asked and turned it down). "Use that same speech," says Henry. The audience is enormous. I have never seen or been one of a congregation like this one. I am lined up with the others who will sit at the head table and we march in. During the talk, there is a certain "twenty-twenty" joke of my father's. I am speaking of my childhood and various areas I did not then understand. This crowd on hearing the punch line, stamps their feet and roars. This has not happened before.

Norman Cousins is there at the head table. Long ago we met at a World Federation crowd in Asheville when I lived at Connemara. Now he asks for the speech to put in the *Saturday Review.* Carl's joke? A man is at a racetrack. He never bets until he receives a sign. He notes his parking ticket is number twenty. So is his seat number. He has twenty cents change in his pocket. Overhead a plane flies by with twenty on the wing. A horse comes up called "Twenty Grand." He bets on him. And when Twenty Grand comes in twenty leagues behind the rest, the man gets up, stamps on his hat, yells, "God damn that son-of-a-bitch Roosevelt!" A debt to Carl, that joke.

The reviews of *The Wheel of Earth* come in from McDowell Obolensky. They are pleased. Breathlessly, each week Helga leafs through magazines in the drug stores. In May, *The New Yorker* reviews the book and to a wild heart beat, she reads to the last line, "This first novel is a triumph of storytelling." And then the genius on whose poems and stories she has been weaned in her adolescent years, is there in *Esquire.* "DOROTHY PARKER ON BOOKS: Miss

Sandburg is Carl Sandburg's daughter, but with this, her first novel, she stands well on her own." Helga leaves the drug store with ten *Esquires* under her arm.

It is time and I mail three autographed copies of my novel to Connemara. The first response, "Dear Helga, Thank you for the book that you wrote, that you sent me. I like the title of your novel. The daffodills, forsythea, star magonia are blooming. I had a nice Easter. Did you. . . . I think of you, John Carl and Paula quite often. Loads of love, Janet."

And then another, its tone not unexpected, "Dear Helga, Thank you for the book, although I can't take what is written on the fly-leaf too seriously. There are some beautiful spots in it; I think you are at your best in writing about nature and the animals. It is a little extreme for my taste, though, which is not surprising considering that we differed about Jean Stafford and a few other authors. I hope it makes the best seller list. Congratulations on the prize-winning short story. The title is intriguing. Love, Margaret."

Along with my mother's copy, the usual hope is there, "I'm wondering if you'd want to come for a visit in late May or early June, maybe bringing Margaret. . . . I'd like you to meet some of my friends—and of course want to see you again and visit. If Dad came too, that would be swell. Love as always. . . ."

"Dearest Helga. . . . We all thought your novel very fine—and the short story *a really great story, an enduring work of art. . . .* What could be better than the prospect unfolding for you of a life-work of creative writing! Nothing could please me more than a visit with you and the children. Margaret is not well enough. . . . Salutations to you for the hard long labors—and the beautiful work you've done and will do. Love as always and ever, Mother."

On the same day that I write confirming her train arrival time, Carl sends her a little note.

Dearest —
Here's first time
you done seen
yr daughter in
a best seller list.

Carl

Helga sees an Associated Press piece on Carl in which he "slapped the arm of his chair. 'Why don't you ask me how I feel about my daughter having a novel out? I believe it is a great novel—extraordinary for a first novel. She's going to write novels as long as she lives.' The blue eyes glinted. . . ." How like my father! Afraid of my book when first he hears of it. Of course. Then listening to what others say, looks into it himself. And there you are. Helga sees him clearly, speaking to the press—old and tall and lean, brown age spots on his huge hands. His eyes shrewd, merry, eying the reporter under the green eyeshade.

I know where my father is at all times. Someone sends me the New York *Post*'s Leonard Lyons' column, "The Lyons

Den: THE VISITING POET: Sardi's was studded with stars of Broadway, but all eyes were on the tall, gray-headed man sitting at the round table—Carl Sandburg, who now raises goats in Flat Rock, N.C. He's in New York to record his poems on nine L.P.'s for Caedmon."

There my father sits among the gathered crowded tables. The dark walls are papered with photographs, sketches that change (with fame) continually. Glasses clink. Silver. A cigarette. Linen. Whispers, laughter, murmurs. How perfectly he fits in. The waiters know him. He hungers, back at Connemara where Paula is, for the excitement of adulation. He has something to say! And Lyons and others come, pencils in pocket, to listen and record. Helga has been to Sardi's and knows. Not Mother.

There she is at seven in the morning, on the train up from the south. Helga meets her. (The last of the Woodrow Wilson boxes are catalogued and that work is finished.) I am free of schedules and have been making lists of questions and want her to tell the grandchildren of her early days and about Oma and Opa. There is a sack of dahlia bulbs among her parcels, that she's dug from the front garden. I am hungry to see her and she is beautiful. White wisping hair back in a knot. The grace of her face more accented with time, the elegant nose, cheekbones, a Steichen classic mouth. She looks up at me as we walk to the car, pleased. Her child.

Paula has questions for Helga as they go over the bridge into Virginia. "Isn't it embarrassing to be asked if you ever see Dad? Won't this worry the children when they are in school?" I shrug, "They say our grandfather lives in North Carolina and we haven't seen him in three years. Our father teaches at the university. He is a professor with strong notions on education. Our mother is probably writing another book. As for me, I'm interested in so and so." Mother doesn't buy this but lets it go. Peace is her nature.

The visit becomes a wonderful one with only a single terrifying story, as from a far country. She shows us photographs she has brought along of Joe and Adaline's children. A pretty daughter of seven with red curly hair. And a sandy-headed little boy, four. They visit the farm sometimes and Adaline still calls her "Mom." Our household leader does not want any contact with that part of Helga's life, but she'd like to get the stepbrother and sister into the picture!

The "terrifying story"? "Dana died last June." It is like news brought by slow ship to Helga! When Dana arrived with Uncle Ed at the farm, Mother noted that she seemed tired. Didn't walk with the others. Leukemia and fatal. My uncle is devastated. Mother is amazed that his grief is so intense. He took leave from the Museum to stay with Dana at Umpawaug. They phoned Connemara no oftener than usual. It was her wish.

"When she died, my brother simply went to pieces. All of his will left him and he became so lethargic that he could not lift a hand. I was surprised!" He can't stand Umpawaug just now and has gone out to stay with one of his protégés in California. He walks among the ancient redwoods. He begins to paint again. He had a stroke at the end of 1957. Agnes Meyer had told Helga at her party, but not of Dana. I'd thought little of it, my uncle seventy-eight.

There was the strange stubbly beard and mustache and sideburns, matching the bushy brows, in the December *Saturday Review* article awhile back. The grim look in the cap and gown in June, his hands at an awkward angle, the gold ring for Dana on the finger and no sign of the frizzled later beard. She'd been dying then. Mother hopes that by now her brother has shaved. "He is a handsome man and I do not like the beard at all!"

Dana kept writing on a book she called *Beethoven's Beloved*. Mother says, "E.J. wants to finish it. She worked hard on it, would go until noon, then tear herself away, go to the icebox, walk around the house once and back to work. She was obsessed with getting it done."

The stunning auburn-haired wife, an actress at sixteen, later George M. Cohan's leading lady. Fifteen years younger than Steichen, always wildly in love with him. And now betraying him. My uncle had planned that Dana would outlive and care always for him. A strange man with hungers, speaking always with passion of his mother, Oma, who brought him across the ocean at eighteen months. Fabulous and famous Edward Steichen photographs in galleries about the world of those two women!

Paula brings out her camera. The three are photographed before the poplar trees she once planted ("You can't have a yard without a tree!") on her first visit here. Her arms linked with granddaughter Paula, a head taller, and with John Carl, a head and a half. She tells them stories, detailing the history of Oma and Opa's lives. When she and Uncle Ed were small, Oma made "Mr. and Mrs. George Washington" costumes for them with velvet britches and lots of lace and afterwards the two played out in the barn, wearing them!

Margaret? "She is more alive mentally than ever." She's written stacks of papers on different subjects, got printed in the *Capital Times* of Madison, Wisconsin: "MARGARET SANDBURG SAYS." And she is painting in oils. Janet? "Busy as ever." So. Daughter number three?

Mother tells that when she heard I was writing a book, there were grave doubts. She has the two-page single-spaced many-drafted "chronology letter," as she calls it, and thought it showed no understanding of human relations. "I read the book and was amazed." She has an item Carl gave her to bring along. The novel is on a best seller list—fifth of seven, just above *Of Love Possessed*.

"It is a great book. Not the greatest, but great." And she adds firmly, quietly, "Dad thinks this too."

Dreams. Assailing Helga secretly in the dark nights so she wakes worrying in the stillness. Wanting them laid to rest. Done with. They are written out in her journal, looking for exorcism. "A dream last night. Dad and Mother standing there with me and declaring my independence (again!). I will make my own way, husband or no. And their indulgent smiling faces (frustrating!) and my husband (Joe-Art) laughing. Later saying goodbye politely to them and kissing Dad's smooth cheek and him being busy and hurrying past me. Dreams. I am aware of the implications. I suppose I will always fight the uphill battle (Sisyphus?)."

"Constantly, the dreams. Dad, Mother, Uncle Ed, sometimes my sisters in strange angry alien roles, pitted against me. Unfamiliar. Humiliating me in public as well as private groups. Dreamed last night of being seated in a large audience where I am to speak. Suddenly Dad appears in the doorway, a sweater (to disguise himself?) over his head. Mother is with him. With glad hands, he is drawn in by the public, who remove the sweater. He is given a good seat and when Mother looks over at me, I smile in greeting. She turns away. Then he gets up to examine some paintings on the wall and to comment on them in his engaging rambling way. He is taking over my ground. I say, even though mortified, 'Hush! Shhh!' And he sits down."

Two bones Helga worries at in her new feelings of freedom: her family (written out of the will and wanting that) and her husband (handsome, tall, engaging, with his pipe and his droll ways, insisting on the role of mentor, guide). She is on the Descent from the Mountain. It is a dark time in her life. Lots of yelling. Big blowups. Guff about divorces back and forth. "Well, go then!" "You'll see. One day!" And so on.

The darkness is lighted by Helga's work and her pleasure in the beauty of the growing daughter and son. She is driven intensely by the fact that she labors in her father's vineyard. She wants to sacrifice herself on the altar of rigorous lonely long hours of work. Why doesn't the Bear of the place, who wants to be a part of it all and is firmly and steadily rejected, ever understand me? Dissatisfied with Helga's friend, Dick Gilston, at MCA (responsible for the Balch prize), he is negotiating for a new agent. And that's that.

More work comes along from the Library of Congress. John Wells Davidson wants me on the Wilson project again—as secretary for the editing and publication of the president's papers. Now she rises at five, the old farm milking hour (the second novel, *Measure My Love,* is with McDowell Obolensky and she is starting a third, in between the short stories), writes till eight, off to work at nine and home before six.

A little brightness. Davidson honors my lecture commitments and I am to give a talk to a National Council of Jewish Women chapter. Take the train to New York. On my own, in heaven, leaving a Growling Bear. On the way is a handsome mustached Lochinvar, who asks me to the bar car for a drink. While there, the train halts briefly at Newark. For a moment Helga's mind goes to the little red plaid bag (dear possessions—new glasses, silk robe, earrings, gloves, my speech) and on return to her seat near New York it is gone!

My speech! Her Lochinvar goes with her to the chief of police's office, while another passenger (gray and tall), stands back there calling, "Are you the lady who lost the bag? Can I help? Do you need *money?*" The police take David's phone number. I wave goodbye to the nice Lochinvar and call John Davidson who is coming into New York for a conference on the papers. He will bring the carbon and meet me under the Grand Central Station clock at an allotted time. A secret adventure. No one to shout, "What the hell were you doing in the bar car!"

My stage appearance is well received. So is the one the Grand Old Bear is making in the Hollywood Bowl. Bing Crosby is chairman. Norman Corwin has scripted the "two-hour show, featuring luminaries of stage, screen, and television, the Roger Wagner chorale and a symphony orchestra. . . ." Carl's audience is vast, the ovation sweeping. His next occasion will be on the Milton Berle show. As for Helga, when she gave her last speech, the introduction went, "And now I give you the famous daughter of the famous —oh dear, I have forgot his name. Carl—who is it?" And the question at another, "Tell me, how long as it been since your father passed on?"

March 1959. An invitation comes in the mail and Helga hastily declines it. "THE LIBRARY OF CONGRESS AND THE LINCOLN SESQUICENTENNIAL COMMISSION REQUEST THE HONOR OF YOUR PRESENCE AT A PREVIEW OF THE LINCOLN SESQUICENTENNIAL EXHIBITION TO BE OPENED BY THE HONORABLE RICHARD M. NIXON AND THE HONORABLE SAM RAYBURN ON THURSDAY AFTERNOON, FEBRUARY THE TWELFTH, AT TWELVE-FIFTEEN O'CLOCK IN THE GREAT HALL OF THE LIBRARY OF CONGRESS, WASHINGTON, D.C. THIS CEREMONY WILL FOLLOW THE JOINT SESSION OF CONGRESS. PLEASE PRESENT THIS INVITATION AT THE DOOR."

Helga is in the kitchen of her house, just home. The phone rings. Art answers, "Hello." And draws a blank. Again it sounds. He picks it up. Carl's voice, "May I speak to Miss Helga?" He definitely does not like the article Norman Cousins printed in the *Saturday Review*. (My speech at the American Booksellers Convention in Atlantic City with the "twenty-twenty" joke and a few candid remarks about my childhood!) "That was not the girl I knew." "But I'm not your little girl. I'm grown." "Where do you come off with that stuff!"

And the daughter goes into explanations. Reasonable. She was after interpretation. It was a speech, not an article. And so on. He states that he told Patterson, the associate publisher and his personal contact there, what he thought of it. And then, "Uncle Ed will be in town. Have you seen the beard?" "When would I have seen it! We're the oddest family." "As odd families go," he replies. "No," I counter helplessly, "we are the oddest of odd families."

He would like to talk to the "little ones." Each of them reacts in the same fashion, "Oh, no! What'll I say!" John Carl is witty, "You can add another 'uh' to make it a twenty-minute speech!" (The papers have reported Carl saying, "I tried to make my address nineteen minutes and fifty-nine seconds. I only had twenty minutes.") Paula struggles through, vivacious, bright.

Helga comes back to wish "Justice Orville Brand Windom" (the grandfather, "Bowbong," and also narrator of *Remembrance Rock*) the best of luck. And he ends the call in his noble way, "Not since that eminent historian George Bancroft addressed the Congress in 1874 has a civilian been asked!" So there.

In the morning, the secretary of the Manuscripts Division calls Helga. Carl is in David Mearns' office. They would like to see me, the two of them. "But I'm busy just now." "They leave for Congress at 10:30." It is after ten now. Helga hangs up. "The bastard!" she tells the room.

Carl calls again that evening, "Did you see me on the tube!" And, "Are you going tonight?" (A talk at the Library of Congress, the invitation to which was turned down summarily along with luncheons or whatever.) "We can't. Art has a thing at school. A literary club. John just got in from the library. Paula is away baby sitting. I am reading proofs on my new book." (Of course, we heard the tape address on the radio at 11:45 in the morning. Saw the television recast at 2:30. Would hear his Library live broadcast at 8:30.)

"Well, I'll be calling in mid-March to stop by. And say, you didn't send me a copy of your book. What the hell!" "I mailed one to the girls and to Mother. Shall I give you a copy of this one when it's out?" No reply. A grunt or two. (Because his answer would be a question. I am his daughter. I know his ways! He will never say he wants my book and I will not send it.)

It is four years and three months since we all sat here and the radio reported on Hemingway's personal award of the Nobel Prize to Carl. Helga is so bitter! She will not be wooed. She is so enraged! Even her husband is surprised at the breathless fury. She will not come at anyone's beck or call! She will never follow. Never. What will come of it all?

The morning Washington papers are splashed full with accounts. The New York *Times* does an editorial and gives him their front page spread along with a three-column photograph of Carl at the lectern backed by President Nixon and House Speaker Sam Rayburn in their high presiding chairs. They print the full text of the speech and "SANDBURG ON LINCOLN HUSHES CONGRESS. Poet Casts Spell on Joint Session With Moving Eulogy." Isn't my father a wonder!

> The poet moved to the rostrum where presidents and statesmen before him had looked down upon the assembled leaders of the Republic and began to speak in vibrant, whispered cadences, "Not often in the story of mankind," he began, "does a man arrive on earth who is both steel and velvet, who is as hard as rock and soft as drifting fog—" And down on the floor of the House the spell of poetry legend began to take hold. His voice was quiet, occasionally hoarse and quivering with feeling, often vanishing to a sibilant murmur. When he finished and stood looking out over the House, the emotion he had aroused broke in a thunder of applause. Moving with great dignity, he stepped down from the dais and moved across the well of the House to leave.

Does Helga like the talk? There before her television? Carl in his black suit and black bow tie. Standing magically among the war- and-peace makers, a battery of microphones before him, television cameras grinding, photographers snapping. The diplomatic corps, the Cabinet, the small-portfolio functionaries, the Congress assembled.

She is standing and doing something. Dusting. Peeling apples for the kitchen. Anything. Not sitting in a chair and watching. She is restless. It is all familiar material she has heard forever.

The dog, Leif, is gone. Five weeks ago. I miss his daily presence, sympathy when there were tears, undemanding companionship. He was ancient for a Doberman, eleven. The vet said it was like an old car, lots of things to go wrong. Leading him to the bare clean cage, past crowded ones of all sizes and full of all sorts of creatures, yowling, meowing, shrieking, barking. Sitting by him and staying until the breath quieted, ceased.

A small tragedy. A little sorrow. The old fellow liked to take walks and rummage about. Only one cat is left of the happy crew of three. She is aging. Tsum-Tsai in her basket. I lean to scratch her ears. The old dear dog is so stunningly absent.

Helga's stories and poems are selling. I am speaking continually at campuses, Fine Arts Festivals, clubs. I relish the travel, seeing my country. Journeying past the sprawling midwest black-earth farmlands and into Willa Cather's country. I meet poets, professors, writers. At a Pennsylvania Contemporary Writers Conference Malcolm Cowley likes my talk, ". . . straight from the shoulder to a target somewhere below the belt." And at a party one evening struts with body rolling, right arm extended, hand on hip, cake-walking and renders "The Bastard King of England." Helga has not heard it. Carl taught his daughters no such songs, though he knows them as well as Cowley, ". . . For in the ride the French King's pride had stretched a yard or more! . . ." And so on.

The new novel, *Measure My Love,* is out in April and the Washington *Post* invites Helga to their book-and-author luncheon. The critics are nice. The *Saturday Review* puts it among the ten novels in their "*SR* Suggests 41 Ways to Spend 3 Months" list and Walter Winchell in his "New Yorkers Are Talking About," mentions "Helga Sandburg's beautifully written novel. . . . She is poet Carl Sandburg's heiress. . . ." Well.

Summer begins. John will be going to college in the fall and during the summer sells encyclopedias as well as holding onto his job at the golf driving range on weekends. Paula is working at some five-and-dime and taking night classes. The last little sorrow. Tsum-Tsai's basket is stored away. She has joined Sa-Wang and Leif. (A small Blue Persian kitten is here, Mr. Shams, helping the healing.)

The shouting matches do not diminish. Declarations are made as to philosophy, silence, deaf ears. Helga walks away, weeps no more. An idea has been yeasting. Eve's. A plan. There is a way. Clearly, she is trapped out in suburbia with her sweet house, her gallant trees, her tomatoes. A new way of life.

She calls forth all the deadly female wiles, honey-tongued. The Bear is beguiled. Remarks are slipped in now and then on the pleasures and delights of a Washington apartment. Surely the marriage will benefit! John will be off to Virginia Polytechnic Institute in the fall. It works. By August a picture of our home and piece of land and Mother's trees will be in the Better Homes Realty prospectus. Like a dream, the gate is opening a little, the slow sure way out of The Garden and down The Mountain.

The third novel is begun, set in the sand dunes of Michigan. I am looking back into roots. I need to examine grains of sand, tracks of sandpipers, gulls, beetles, crabs. And to be sure of the color of the lake when the wind is still and when it blows and how the sun feels and slipping into the water in the dark nights. I am going home. It is mid-July and we are taking a Greyhound. Helga will write a short story on the way. Paula is along and we stay with old neighbors (The Holdens. Helga and Carl would stop there on their oldtime walks.) I am filled with longings for my beginnings.

Carl is about to look into roots too. With Uncle Ed. It is mid-July. Back at the time of the speech before Congress, there had been a notice in the morning paper, "Sandburg and Steichen are going to Russia. . . . 'We'll be Fuller Brush men,' said Steichen. 'Together, side by side we'll go,' said Sandburg. . . ." and so on. Now there is my father again in my *Post,* smiling, fedora in hand, with my bearded uncle (His arm in a sling. Bursitis. Also, says the press, "The arm was injured in a fall while ice-skating recently."). Uncle Ed firmly holds the arm of a beautiful lady, Carl on the other side. They are descending the steps of our Russian Embassy.

Helga has been wondering about Uncle Ed's love life, with Dana gone so long now. The beard here is trimmed neatly as well as the gray sideburns, his hair is carefully combed. Perhaps there is a special lady somewhere. In the past March, Steichen had been on the cover of the *Saturday Review* and was speaking of new disciplines, of photographing a little shadblow tree endlessly, of experimenting "in new directions as a painter." He is just eighty, a year younger than Carl.

My uncle holds the beautiful lady's arm and there is a decided twinkle in his eyes. The *Post* says, "She is Tamara Y. Mamedov, second secretary and cultural affairs attaché at the Soviet Embassy." And, " 'Our Russian trip begins here,' said Steichen, taking his hostess's arm, as they walked down the three steps of the Embassy. 'Remember what you told me,' Sandburg's voice boomed mellifluously to Mrs. Mamedov as he took her other arm, 'You said you would have lunch with "Da Lawd" of photography and "Da Lawd" of writing.' "

Can you see why the press enjoys Carl? "Snow-topped, cherry-cheeked Sandburg as usual wears a loose bow tie." And how he has "threatened to get himself a balalaika in Moscow." And then quoting Uncle Ed, "A friend told me, 'When you two fellows walk arm in arm down Red Square, then that's the end of the Iron Curtain.' " He is to open "The Family of Man" in Moscow on 25 July and Carl is along for the ride. They will go first to Paris and there board a Russian jet for the Soviet capital. Russia will be the thirty-second country the exhibit has visited.

Helga wants no reflections of glory. Bent her own way now, she wants nothing to do with either of them. The overtures to the family to lure them onto her territory got nowhere, except for Paula's flying visits. She is wary of gestures from the Great Bear at this time. It is also in her nature to be thrown off by unexpected phone calls. Warn me by letter or slow boat!

Here is the picture. It is six in the evening of the day before the pair will leave for New York. Helga is mixing bird feed, her arms deep in the supply bucket. Cracked corn, bread crumbs, raisins, currants. The phone and his voice. "Snick?" (Could it be "Swipes?")

"Hello, hello. I'm in the grain and all dusted up." "Going to Moscow." "Have a fine trip." (Cold as ice. As if speaking to a planet, wishing he would go away. Leave me alone.) "Well, well. So it's you." And something about hearing that John Carl was on a trip in Alaska on a motorcycle. Disclaiming knowledge of the report, "John is working as usual. Paula has a job." And on being probed, "In the local five-and-ten." Then soon, "I'll be ringing you again at the end of August." "Fine, fine. Goodbye." Art comes in from showering and raises his brows at the brief and cold tenor of his wife's words. Fiddlesticks!

And there they are at Idlewild, the reporters hovering and snapping and grinding away. Carl waves the fedora. Uncle Ed's arm remains in its sling. They board the Pan Am jet and in Paris are whisked past customs by the State Department people. A day later there is my father, bless him, making headlines again, "SANDBURG LOSES PASSPORT ON TRIP. . . . REDS OBLIGING TO SANDBURG." How do you lose a passport? Leave it in the Paris hotel drawer or basket? Did some cleaning lady toss it out? "Soviet officials smiled and disregarded the lack of travel papers which the white-haired octogenarian said he must have mislaid en route to Russia."

And there you are. The world takes care of Carl.

What will the visit to Russia do to these two old men in my life? No women are about and Carl wears the same baggy pants and soft blue short-sleeved shirt throughout the trip. My uncle has his 35-mm. Nikon by its strap about his neck. The Moscow Friendship House people have them to a party on the first day and poets and artists and writers are there. Carl gives a talk. He jokes about the newspaper *Pravda* (Russian word for "truth"). "If the two of us were witnesses under oath, would we be asked, 'Do you solemnly swear you will tell the *Pravda,* the whole *Pravda,* and nothing but the *Pravda*?' "

The next day "The Family of Man" opens at the American National Exhibition in Sokolniki Park. Crowds of Muscovites troop through. Premier Nikita Khrushchev comes to look. The visiting pair are recognized and Russian photographers want to have their pictures taken with Steichen. The Soviet press says little about the show, but the radio reports that it has the largest attendance of any of the other features of the American exhibition. Uncle Ed stands back and watches and says he is reminded of the Japanese poem: "When you look into a mirror you do not see your reflection, your reflection sees you." He thinks that's what happens here. The people participate. He photographs them doing it.

Carl goes to a reception at the Writer's Union and takes over. A group of famous Russian singers are about to perform. Carl stops the show. He has found an English-speaking young writer who has translated some of *The People, Yes*! He calls him up to the platform to read. Everyone loves it. Then a guitarist begins to perform and stops and turns the instrument over to Carl. He sings for an hour. Unabashed. The audience is charmed.

The next day the two go to the spare dark office room of the editorial staff of the monthly *Foreign Litre* and Carl reads them the talk he will give on Lincoln later. On the small crowded table are a bowl of grapes, a package of Russian cigarettes, a bottle of red wine and many glasses, most nearly empty except for the two in front of the visitors from America who want to keep their heads.

The Russian stint of the trip lasts a full two weeks. Carl writes a few letters to America. Some to Paula. And one that involves a new character in this story—Joanna Taub, twenty-five, slim, black-haired, lovely, long-limbed. In the past January, she had handled the American Airlines account when Carl took the pioneer flight of a Boeing 707 jet from New York to California. His "Reflections" were recorded and played on the airlines' coast-to-coast radio "Music 'Til Dawn" program. Carl loved the assignment and Joanna had caught his eye. He gave her the one-volume *Lincoln* and *Home Front Memo* and introduced her to Uncle Ed at a party in New York.

Joanna and Carl get on. She has told him that he is "as warm, strong, merry, human, deep and wise as his writing." Now her letter informs him that she has just been handed a copy of the New York *Herald Tribune* "with a wonderful picture of two singularly *un*-weary looking travelers and a report of 'thunderous applause' for a performance by a certain American poet who is 'loved and admired', it says here, by the American people! After such spectacular first and second acts to this traveling show, what will the Paris Finale be like? . . ." The twinkle is there in my uncle's eyes when he peruses Carl's letter. He glows.

Stockholm. The sixth of August. Carl waving his felt fedora, Uncle Ed natty. From the dark feeling of Russia to sunny free Sweden in one small flight! Cousins, diplomats, photographers, little children, flowers and kisses meet the two. Hans Hammarskiöld is there (a friend, one of his photographs is in "The Family of Man"). His camera is at the ready. His two small daughters. His wife, Caroline, who is at once on Uncle Ed's arm. He stayed with them in Stockholm when scouting for foreign photographs. When Susanne, the older, was born, Uncle Ed became the lucky godfather.

On their first night in Stockholm, they are guests of the *Hotell Reisen.* And what happens? Why, a guitar is brought over in the evening. Carl sings and plays and is still there after my uncle is asleep. The next morning the pair sally forth in the company of the press, Uncle Ed elegant in a light-colored summer suit, Carl still in the same blue shirt under his suit coat. His bow tie is a polka dot. His pants are comfortable.

There is a statue the two are visiting near the Royal Palace. Carl has seen it before. In his one excursion out of America to Scandinavia as a reporter in 1918 (when Helga was about to be born). It was winter and the sun rose at 8:30 in the morning, set at 3:30 in the afternoon. Now it is summer and the days are long. Then he was forty and wrote Paula that "there was a thrill about seeing the soil of Sweden, setting foot on it and hearing the speech of one's forefathers spoken by everybody and on all the street signs."

He wrote a poem back then. It is the reason they are visiting the statue. It is in *Smoke and Steel*, the book dedicated to Uncle Ed, "Savior Faire."

Cast a bronze of my head and legs and put them on the king's street.
Set the cast of me here alongside Carl XII, making two Carls for the

Swedish people and the utlanders to look at between the palace and the Grand Hotel. . . .

If the young men will read five lines of one of my poems I will let the kings have all the bronze—I ask only that one page of my writings be a knapsack keepsake of the young men who are the bloodkin of those who laughed nine hundred years ago: We are afraid of nothing—only—the sky may fall on us.

The towering bronze figure before my father and uncle is set on massive blocks of stone and surrounded by a heavy linked chain. This is a charismatic handsome bold young king. His left hand is outstretched and the right holds an unsheathed long sword. Always Carl (he is Charles XII's namesake) has had a fancy for this countryman and once thought as a young student of doing his biography. In 1904, when he was twenty-six he published a small book, *In Reckless Ecstasy*, and in it was "Charles XII, of Sweden."

Though I have ranged the annals of the past
And cast my eyes on many sovereigns of yore,
Ne'er have I seen a royal one like thee,—. . . .

Immortal Swede! Across the years
There comes to us a glint
Of how a man should laugh at luck;
And whether it was sleet that beat athwart thy brow,
Or sunshine bathing thy proud locks,
Steady and straightforward, smiling,
Did you face the shifting stars of Destiny.

And so the two arrive at the statue. Steichen directs Carl to stand before it and stretch out his right hand (the king points with his left) and hold the faithful soft cap in his left hand (the king his shining sword in his right). Carl has a quizzical happy look. The Nikon clicks. When he develops the photo back home, Uncle Ed writes "King Carl & Fool Carl" on it. That is the beginning of the nine-day look at Sweden!

Hammarskiöld spends time with my uncle, visiting museums and galleries and meeting Swedish photographers and looking at their work. Carl is whisked about to homeland ancestral places. A hundred miles out of Stockholm is Appuna, birthplace of his mother, Grandma Sandburg. He visits the grave of his grandfather Anders Persson and the farmstead where his mother was born, the church where she was baptized and confirmed in the Lutheran faith. Cousins, relatives, reporters observe and aid his progress. Translations abound. An emotional time for my father.

He is continually on the move. On the thirteenth, leaving Uncle Ed in Stockholm, he is again on the train, along with reporters, Hans Hammarskiöld, cousins, relatives, heading back to Appuna and also to Åsbo, Grandfather Sandburg's birthplace. At the station, as he gets off the car, a group of waiting serenaders in old-time costume, burst into the "Song of Östergötland." Carl stands with the white golfing cap (the fedora is for formal exits and entrances) over his heart, at attention. Flowers, embraces, curtsies.

There are seven cousins and thirty relatives among his following. Gifts are given. Letters and photographs and Bibles are shown. Carl walks out into a field and picks blades of grain. The paths have been raked. The present owner of the farmstead weeps from emotion and delight. A long table is spread with white linen and set out on the grass under the trees. Coffee and sweets and flowers and more memorabilia to look over. A cream cake is brought out, *"Valkommen till Åsbo"* among its decorations.

Their time in Sweden is almost over. Their traveling bags are stashed with mementos to go on top of those from Moscow. The pair visit the prime minister. And then a train trip to the University of Uppsala where Carl gets an honorary degree and a cannon salute. Finally a visit to King Gustav VI Adolf, climbing the palace steps and to the king's study to have a chair by the desk and talk. And to be pinned with a gold medal hanging from a blue ribbon, inscribed *Litteris et Artibus*.

Paris. The Hotel Continental. In the mail is another from Joanna, "Dear Mr. Sandburg, Having captured Moscow and conquered Stockholm, what are you doing to Paris? . . ." And he sends a note to Connemara, "Dearest. . . . We went to Rodin's tomb and museum Sunday & Ed was marvelous in commentary & illumination. Soon now to London & New York & talks with you. Your Carlo."

Continuing the theme and setting of homelands, Helga too has been to hers. Carl visits his maternal grandfather's grave, and I mine. Opa's at the little Riverdale Cemetery on the road to the Three Oaks High School. Oma's ashes were laid to rest with his body. The arborvitae Mother planted on either side of their stone is now taller than Helga and Paula. "STEICHEN. Mary 1854–1933. JOHN PETER 1854–1944." We visit all the sites of memory. The Elmhurst childhood house. The railway station where Carl had taken the "Owl Train" back and forth to his Chicago *Daily News* desk. Helga photographing all, noting colors, scents, sounds. Dwelling on beginnings, Paula feeling it along with Helga.

And then back to the Holdens' to stay out our week by Lake Michigan. A letter comes that our home is sold to an army major and I am to wire at once that I approve the deal. We will move out in mid-October to a Washington flat. Heaven waits.

While "Aunt Ruth" Holden and Paula discuss life, Kenn and Helga talk. He is an old friend besides neighbor of

Carl's. We speak of the Rift. He saw Carl recently at Purdue where Carl was giving a talk. "What's wrong in hell between you two, Carl?" And the reply, "We don't see eye to eye." "Don't worry, Kenn. That's a pretty good answer." And Kenn telling of old days when we'd stop in and he would ask me, "Why do you keep nodding at everything he says? Why are you always agreeing!" And Helga then, "Because it's the truth."

November. We are in the Washington apartment at last. Tall-ceilinged, high-windowed, many-closeted, old-fashioned. John Carl, a cadet, his curly dark red hair ruthlessly crew-cut, is having a wonderful time at Virginia Tech, his own turf. He couldn't wait to go.

The old plague of my father in the night, "November 21. Had an odd dream. Caught sight of Dad in the other room, very clear, after sitting down amid audience at the Library of Congress, looking forward to hearing a performance of something. John, as a little boy, was with me. Dad made some kind of dramatic statement, about how he'd heard there was a daughter in the audience. He went about looking in people's faces, finally arrived at us. Said, 'How do you do?' to me and all the while John kept watching my face, not looking at him. Then he left. It was all fairly peaceful, except I had the old anger, that he subjected me to his performance!" Well.

Where is the man of the dream now? Out in Hollywood, writing Paula, ". . . Am recording 3 platters of songs here. . . . Love, blessings & kisses. . . ." And then Norman Corwin's dream coming true! *The World of Carl Sandburg*. Bette Davis and Gary Merrill in Washington at Constitution Hall. The Washington *Post* calls the event "glittering."

It is Davis' first national tour along with her husband, Gary Merrill. He looks a lot like a young Sandburg, black hair falling forward over his strong face. The show was awhile taking off, the company traveling by road to cities in New Hampshire, Massachusetts, Connecticut. Then it received unanimous enthusiastic press praise in Philadelphia at Symphony Hall, where two performances took place.

Inside the *Playbill* sold in the lobby, is the pretty picture taken at Connemara when Ed Murrow's crew came—Buppong singing, playing the guitar, Paula laughing, twelve-year-old John, Karlen Paula with her little white Saanen kid. Beneath the caption, "The World of Carl Sandburg." On the biography page is the photo ("Carl Sandburg and grandson") taken that Christmas back in 1942, when the child was a year old and reached for Buppong's nose.

Carl is in town for the Thursday night Washington performance. We do not go. We read of it in the papers, ". . . He'll be in the box to see and listen. . . . Will he speak? 'If there is a loud outcry for "Author," ' he grinned. . . ."

And what of Uncle Ed? Something wonderful happened on his return from Paris. Twenty-five-year-old engaging Joanna. Carl calls his "black-haired correspondent," who comes along out to Umpawaug. There formal salutations are dropped and between them they now are Carl, Joanna and the Captain.

Carl tells her, "I told you you would be good for him." And her response, "Why, it was you brought me to him!" (Carl keeps this exchange in the little notebook he carries.) Joanna has a singing voice. To go along with it, on Carl's advice, she buys and learns to play a guitar. He is so pleased with her accomplishments, that he gives her one of his traveling lute-shaped ones. So she now has two and the guitar and song have become a part of Joanna's way of life.

By mid-November for them *terror!* My uncle is alone in his New York flat. A stroke. Commanding his body, he finally reaches a phone. Is able to dial Joanna. He speaks, "Come." She does, sees him to the hospital. By December, he is healing and when she visits his room, she brings a guitar. And then when he is home at Umpawaug, she spends the weekends there, leaving the lute-shaped one with him.

Paula is elated. She names Joanna "the angel" and those two become close. The bright spirit saved her brother's life! Joanna and Uncle Ed will marry before long, the one twenty-six, the other eighty-one.

Christmas. Helga announces her new address to the family at Connemara and that now there is "quick and easy access to Union Station" whenever anyone plans a stop with us. And too, she mails "To Mother with love," the latest magazines where her short stories are printed. Back on that lecture trip west, she wrote a poem about deer that appeared in the mountains. When it is published, she sends it to Connemara also and Paula responds, "Dearest Helga, Dad will be much pleased that you inscribed your poem 'On the Sixth Day of April' personally to him, and I'm sure he'll enjoy reading this poem, so deeply perceptive of Nature's moods, and with your rare gift of words making all come alive. . . ."

And more from her, ". . . I wish that you and John and Paula could see Connemara in this heavy blanket of snow—18 inches in the front pasture with drifts over two feet. Hundreds of birds come to our feeding stations. During this heavy snow, Margaret scatters sunflower seed, hemp seed and cracked corn on the snow banks under the pole-feeders for all the new arrivals from mountain & meadow. It was thoughtful of you to send me the Opa poem and the short story about the Daeman Bird. You have a born poet's gift with words—and we are proud of you and proud that you work and work—writing. For this is hard work—not soft—creating POEMS! . . ."

How wondrous she is. And she mourns and it hurts me,

". . . We had a lovely letter from Paula and from John too. These letters deeply moved us all. Connemara carries so many memories of the children—John's favorite retreats on the sheer declivities of Big Glassy—Paula's little gardens & miniature waterfalls. When a new bird visitor arrives or the young Mimosa blesses the flower border or the perfect rainbow arches over the pond, we think that Paula & John should be here to share these precious moments. We have their letters to bless all our days—with bright hopes for Paula and John in all their years to come. I know they are both very proud of you—and you—Helga proud of them! Always love from all here. . . ."

Spring break for John. And then summer. Paula is off to Camp Dunnabeck in the Adirondacks, a counselor and heading the riding program. David McDowell writes that his publishing firm is breaking up. The copper-eyed, long-blue-coated Persian cat, Mr. Shams, watches until I have a tray, then puts a paw up and dips into soup or whatever dish and settles back to lick his pretty toes. John has landed a summer job (after walking the streets for three days!) in an office position for Americana Corporation.

And so there I am in the Washington flat, after seven years, restless, of roaming the Mountain. I am reaching the long winding way down. Worrying over leaving "the loving arms," over the unconventional aspect of a couple splitting. Convinced that my nature is not good for the Bear. That loneliness with integrity is what I want (in trade for marital affection). If he is rid of me and his borrowed "notoriety," he can save himself. He is thirty-six.

Helga feels she is old, set, resigned. A heavy veil lies between her way of thinking and her husband's. She subverts her better judgment continually in the name of peace. She wishes to be pure and uncorrupted! She has grown sly and hides her stories when they are returned and the correspondence on them. The last he saw from the *Saturday Evening Post* editor, brought a raging tirade. Helga likes the editor, her mentor! And the walls shake as the Bear looks for control. Helga is aware of the frustration she engenders.

And so I give out the news, say my piece. I'm not a good wife. I don't give a good goddamn about your work. Here I go, the millstone removing itself. An ashtray flies. Threats of strangulation. Loud sounds. And a compromise is suggested. Time to consider. There is a beach cottage of a friend of his. Go there and think things over.

Helga is not averse to time alone. Getting used to loneliness. The Snake and the Apple in the Garden gone from her life now!

Part Seven

THE TRAVELERS RETURN

BUT FIRST I find a lawyer and have the initial separation paper drawn up (and presented although not accepted). In the District there needs to be a legal separation for five years before divorce is possible. The stocks, bonds and bank accounts are laid on the kitchen table and split down the middle. The apartment house owner has a flat that suits Helga in size and price. She carries in boxes, begins to divide the library in half. *Cry the Beloved Country* here, *Too Late the Phalarope* there. Commotion. Violence. Trembling. Then quiet and discussion and the beach-house proposal.

The cottage is cool and still, bare floors, a canary in a cage, a refrigerator that runs softly. She brings typewriter, journals, books, scrap paper, materials for a new speech. Her life is spread about the room. She is absurdly content. She writes the farm, without a whisper, "Dear Mother. . . . Enclosed are shots of the two inordinate young people—John in his 'whites' and the child in one of her personal creations. . . . I do hope you can plan a visit to Washington this fall. . . . But I'll write you later. . . . and try to nail down your bringing one of my sisters. I am here alone at the empty cottage of a friend, luxuriating in utter silence, sun and the rest of those things. . . ."

Done with love. The stifling feelings. The stammering unhappiness. The thing that's like moonlight flooding and birds calling in hot nights. Now only herself alone in the moonlight. (A little pain of unhappiness for him.) The debt to Joe and to Art. To the first for taking me from my family into the golden life of the farm and its reality. To the second so that I was stirred into writing (and also for removing me from the family scene!).

Now I will write Joe and send the photos of Paula and John in uniform. Now I will insist on my family coming to my new Washington place! I'll invite Carl to take my children out when he is in Washington. The children will make an excursion to the farm.

The utterly still house. The little Volks, strange and lonely out there, waiting (bought with the first $1,500 on *The Wheel of Earth*). The white road like snow. One's soul is chilled. It is like a quiet empty death. Yet there is the one warmth: oneself. Saying Corinthians 1:13 aloud every night just as I go in, "Though I speak with the tongues of men and angels and have not charity. . . ."

Flowers arrive. A dozen glads, stark and funereal, and signed with my husband's name. (I am crazy about carnations, roses.) The hot sand beach nearby. Lying half asleep, replete with the heady feeling of brilliant sunlight and washing waves. The clear masculine voice, "Don't I know you?" "I'm from Washington." "Of course you are. Me too. State Department." A Young Lochinvar, browned, tall and a shattering sweet laugh.

Now that Helga has descended the Mountain and is striding straight away from it, to her surprise, wonderful years in the Garden (vowing never to be there legally again, though!) begin. A cocktail beach party tomorrow night and will see the Lochinvar on the beach in the afternoon.

And then the week is up and back in Washington, as inexorably committed as ever. Mother's response to my letter comes, ". . . Yes, time goes by—and life. Both your sisters would love to see you and I can't help wishing that you and John and Paula could come here for a visit with us all. You know that this has always been our dearest wish. . . . Your ever-loving. . . ."

Helga has strange dreams of violations while the packing goes on, the painting of her flat before she can move in. She tells Sally Reston of it and she and Scotty offer their house (they are off to Los Angeles for a month) as a haven. Lois

Sevareid calls to say that "Alabama is a one-day divorce affair and reasonable." Helen Costello sympathizes (her marriage is like a rock and romantic!). Helga does not mention her State Department Lochinvar, who keeps in touch, takes her to a little French bistro and about.

In the morning Helen phones again. There is a letter from Sally for me, sent from the Biltmore Hotel in Los Angeles in care of the Costellos and dated July 6. "Dear Helga, I've been worrying all the way across the country about you! In the last rush to get away, an old friend of ours, Professor Bruce Weirick (English—University of Illinois) called. He is a great admirer of your father's, was responsible for the purchase of his manuscripts by the library there. Telling him about our summer plans, I mentioned that you might be staying in our home while we were gone and why. It was an inadvertent remark I immediately regretted.

"To my astonishment, he suggested calling your father to tell him about your decision. I told him, of course, I thought this improper interference by an outsider in your affairs & asked him not to do so. Shortly afterward, he called to say that he'd talked to your father's secretary in New York, and that she had called your mother & given her the news! I was appalled, told him your situation was difficult & I thought this kind of meddling might do no one any good. He promised to call the secretary back, repeating what I had said. Dear Helga, I hope no irrevocable damage has been done here & that this will not add unnecessarily to your anxieties just now. . . ."

Helga does not mind in the least and sends Sally a card saying so.

Of course, by now I have written, "Dear Mother, Here I sit in Scotty Reston's study. Sally, who is my dear friend, offered me this place. . . . I had told her as I am now telling my other friends, and of course you and my sire—Art and I are separating. This is a long tale and this decision of mine isn't sudden. My art has come in the way. I think it robbed my husband of that ego he stood sorely in need of having assuaged. I don't know. Anyway, what I do know is that he was unable to cope with my new master. It is destroying him, I am sure. . . .

"At any rate, that is enough on that. I have leased an apartment for the children and myself. On Wednesday the moving is done. I spent a profitable morning with the painters ('Just a bit more of that green in the gray! No, too much. Now a little more gray—now a little green. There—hold it! It's perfect.'). I've come forth in the battle of the household goods, a bit bloody perhaps, but yet unbowed. My main need was my library and in its name have given up such useless utensils as Mixmasters, vacuums, tea tables. . . .

"I have this tendency to say take it, take it, take everything. Leave me my soul. It is all very grand and dramatic and probably worth it. The Costellos—Helen and Bill—are on their way over. I've left the door unlocked and they're to come up here. Helen is absolutely appalled by my attitude in this. She's Scotch. . . ."

And that I want to go to Connemara. And the children. "Perhaps for a few days in early September? . . ." Honing for the time.

At the same time that Helga is engaged in all this fine drama and is dashing up and down the dusty floors of Indiana Avenue's second- and third-hand furniture warehouses for bookcases and old chairs, a dining table (she intends to entertain!), and the rest for her flat, where is Carl? Why, into another venture. He is seated in his great cedar chair on

Connemara's white-pillared front porch (bow tie, old vest), deciding on a deal he cannot resist. Doesn't try to. Lucy Kroll set it up. Paula doesn't think it will work but time will tell. Lucy has put in a clause that he can quit at any time.

Carl will sign a contract shortly with the Greatest Story Company (Twentieth Century–Fox combined with George Stevens Productions), providing for his employment for six months during the pre-production period of the film, *The Greatest Story Ever Told*! He gets $125,000 plus expenses which includes a paid room at the Bel Air in Beverly Hills. He is having a wonderful time. Let the past go. What does it matter that his book to follow *Always the Young Strangers* (and titled *Ever the Winds of Chance*) languishes in the ground-floor safe or in Paula's safety deposit box at the bank or in a few carbon chapters on a shelf at Harcourts?

And this is hardly his first Hollywood experience, says Carl. In his days as movie critic back in Chicago, he's gone to see films with Groucho Marx, who was supposed to wake him a little before the show was over but by then they both were asleep. Groucho came out to his home in Elmhurst. And he'd done interviews with all the stars of the silents. Once D.W. Griffith wanted him to do a movie about Lincoln and Carl said he'd cancel his lectures and bring along his Lincoln collection and he wanted $30,000. Griffith offered ten. So, "We got Stevie [Stephen Vincent] Benet for the job. Stevie was good. I forget the name of the picture."

Remembrance Rock is mentioned. Sitting on a shelf. Too much for any of the directors to handle. Carl also reveals that he has been transferred from his expensive hotel suite to a smaller one, despite the fact that he is not paying the rent. It was too far to walk from one end of the place to the other and it was too gaudy for his taste. "They had silks on the beds that would be all right for Marilyn Monroe, but not for me."

And lastly, "No. I will not give up my home in Flat Rock and move to Hollywood." So. What next?

August 1960. The wide canyon of the Rift, in an instant, slams together and it is as if it had not been. Phones and letters are employed. Helga's third novel is going well and will be ready in October (Dial Press wants it). The separation papers are signed. I am on a Georgetown University Writers Conference panel with Katherine Anne Porter, in heaven.

Mother reports that her brother married the "angel" on the nineteenth of March and that it is "confidential" although she surely doesn't see why. Uncle Ed's stroke affected his speech and he had to learn to talk again and now speaks perfectly. He still has a slight limp and can't write legibly or work at the Museum. He'll be eighty-two next year and the Museum of Modern Art is going to put on a big birthday bash which will include an exhibition "Steichen the Photographer" featuring sixty-five years of his work. Joanna has thrown herself into the project and they have 30,000 prints to choose from.

Right now the "big brudder" is in a slump and everyone is worried. Some kind of virus, they think. Mother is going to visit him along with Margaret and will Helga come along? And she adds that back there when Uncle Ed had been told of everyone's dislike for the son-in-law, he had said, "Don't blame Helga. She has to sleep with him!"

More news. Aunt Mary, three years older than my father, died two years ago in July of 1958 at eighty-three. My favorite aunt! All this unknown to Helga! Like learning of Dana's going long after it happened. By slow boat or horseback relays, a message delivered by a passing traveler.

"Dear Mama, It would be very nice if you came here

overnight before going to New York." There! I'll have them on my territory. Of course they will come. Will Janet accept Mr. Shams, our copper-eyed beauty (rock-sterling disposition, affectionate without being subservient, ping-pong-ball mad) as a gift? She will. (One of the clauses in the separation agreement stipulates, "The husband shall have the right to visit the Persian cat known as Mr. Mohammed Khalid Shams at all reasonable times.").

As for Hollywood, Mother writes, "Dearest, Here is Helga's address and phone number. Paula arrives tomorrow or Sunday and will stay till September 3. All busy here with preparations! I have my reservations arriving Washington by train Sunday morning September 11 when John & Paula will be home all day. Monday Helga and I leave for New York to see the big Opening September 15, and we plan to go to Umpawaug for a day before. What hotel do you suggest as most convenient for you as of course we both want *to see you* before we visit Uncle Ed & Joanna.

"Helga says that she and the children will come here for a visit for the Thanksgiving Day school holidays. So Margaret has much to look forward to. Perhaps you could fly here at that time and make it a real Family Reunion! Love always to you and Bless you for the phone talks! P.S. Helga sent Janet a very lovely Persian cat 'Mr. Shams'—deepest blue with copper eyes. Ling-Po doesn't mind!"

The end of August. The Georgetown Conference. One of the nuns, "I didn't know your father was married." She dwells on it and then, "Do you know if Frost is married?" And again, "What's it like to be Steinbeck's daughter?" Their faces enthusiastic, shining. And Helga has been asked by the Unitarian Center of Bethesda to speak one Sunday. They have put in a call for a minister, who will not come until January. I plan to use Revelations, "And God shall wipe away all tears from their eyes and there shall be no more death, neither sorrow, nor crying, neither shall there be any more pain: for the former things are passed away." Mother likes that. It is also in Helga's present novel.

She is on a schedule to get the book written and typed. And it is time to look for an agent for her work. And to find a lecture bureau. Would Colston Leigh (they handle Carl) take her on? She writes Pat Covici, who may recommend her to an agent or two, that "I have no idea where Mr. Steinbeck lives or if he's in the country, but I thought he might enjoy this from the Georgetown nuns. I'm coming up to New York in October and if you'll be there, would very much like to say hello to you. By the way, you may be interested to know that my husband and I are separated. It seems a wise and not unhappy thing. I hope you are having a good summer. I am busy, poor, and working hard. . . ."

Pat replies that "John Steinbeck will be pleasantly surprised that all of a sudden you are his daughter. Since he has two sons, you would be, I am sure, most welcome. I wasn't in the least put out when I learned that you and your husband are separated. I would love to talk with you. . . ." My life is coming together and I am heady with ambition.

September 11 and Margaret and Mother are at the door to our flat. Helga has a sister and a family again! Paula puts on the pot for coffee. John takes the coats and settles the bags. Margaret tries on all the dresses she brought along to decide what to wear when. The energy of my mother and sister astound me. I feel frail, exhausted, young. In the evening we click on the television to catch Buppong on John Daley's "What's My Line?" My father too, astonishes with his energy. A Hollywood celebrity now. And Norman Corwin's show, *The World of Carl Sandburg* (Bette Davis now with another leading man), is about to premiere on Broadway. Carl's name in lights!

In the night, still talking, Mother urges me again to accept money. (My pride is cracking. She is beautiful.) "My brother wrote home once that he was broke in Paris. He was very young, just twenty. Oma emptied the cash register drawer and sent it all to him. She didn't know where the next month's rent was coming from but then there were orders for lots of hats in her millinery shop and there you are!" As for the former spouse (about whom Helga will hear no ill spoken) Mother quotes easily in her literary fashion, *"Der Mohr hat seine schuldigkeit getan. Der Mohn kann gehen."* ("The Moor has served his purpose. Let the Moor go.") I like that!

Morning. We three are off to catch the train for New York. John is at his office, Paula in school again, as we take the elevator down to the street. The wind is high. The taxis are filled as they whiz by. My hat blows off and I run and a cab stops. We get in. "Helga is the Angel Gabriel," declares Mother. Over and over. She is happy. At last!

The October issue of *Playboy* is on the newsstands of Grand Central Station as we three get off the train in New York. Inside is "A Portfolio of Carl Sandburg". Illustrated. We buy copies. We have an hour to wait before the train leaves for Ridgefield station up in Connecticut. Helga phones David McDowell. She has the manuscript of her new novel (*The Owl's Roost*) in her bag and he wants to go over it before my return to Washington. David is a little of a Lochinvar now, newly divorced. He'll be right over. Helga settles in the seat by Margaret to read Carl's poems. One touches me.

LOVE IS A DEEP AND A DARK AND A LONELY

love is a deep and a dark and a lonely
and you take it deep take it dark
and take it with a lonely winding

and when the winding gets too lonely
then may come the windflowers
and the breath of wind over many flowers
winding its way out of many lonely flowers . . .
so you can take love as it comes keening
as it comes with a voice and a face . . .
and you put it away for a keen keeping
and you find it to be a hoarding
and you give it away and yet it stays hoarded . . .

like leaves of windflowers bending low
and bending to be never broken

Mother gets up to call Carl at the Royalton. He will not come out to Uncle Ed's, she reports. Too busy. *The World* will be at the Henry Miller Theatre on Wednesday, the fourteenth. Two days off. And they've got him on a heavy schedule. The "Today Show." The "Tonight Show" (he's getting Joey Bishop, not Carson). And ten, more or less, radio and television appearances. Then later today he goes to the theatre to meet the press and accept a scroll (for the fourteenth time) proclaiming "Carl Sandburg Day" in New York. He'll see us on our return.

David arrives and helps us on the train, carrying the three suitcases and stashing them in the overhead rack. He is handsome and able and in my handy journal is the note, "I saw David's eyes when we said goodbye. The rest of the time it wasn't he. I closed myself in his eyes when we said goodbye."

And then, "There's Steichen," says a passenger behind me as we reach Ridgefield. I have not seen my uncle (except in magazines and newspapers) in a long while. He looks like a man out of a Sergei Eisenstein movie or an Ingmar Bergman! High boots (there has been a hurricane). Sharp coat. Small dark blue beret. And the beard. How different he is from

Carl, who never knows what he is wearing. My romantic uncle was always a poseur. (John Carl has a little of it in him. He wants a cape. Who wears a cape?) Mother says that when Uncle Ed came back from Europe as a young man, he wore a flowing black cape! And now the beard and the young wife. The costume. The flair.

As we get down from the train steps, he goes straight to Paula. Margaret and Helga just stand there with the bags. Uncle Ed clasps her. His adored "Little Sister"! Protracted, he kisses her before all the curious people and passengers. And his hurt dazed eyes. Mother, female, is strong. He is not. They both feel it. We ride to Umpawaug with my uncle at the wheel of his open-topped Lark through the back roads of the Connecticut countryside. Blue sky. Cumulus clouds. The sun nearly ready to set.

That night he opens two tiny chilled splits of champagne, having "just a taste" himself. He seems truly ill, shaky and pale and with those ravaged eyes. Helga tries getting used to the change. You see, my mother is *unchanged*. Just as she was in the days of the Tom Thumb Dairy in Michigan.

The doctor has ordered that he is not to drink. A silver tray of bottles and ice and glasses has been set out earlier. No one has come near except Helga, pouring seventeen-year-old smooth scotch with soda and having a cigarette Joanna found for me. My uncle arrives at my side to put a smidgeon and no more of the amber liquor in a glass. The "angel" comes and takes it from his hand and adds it to mine (with an angelic smile). He accepts the act, rueful. Joanna does not drink, she says, except for wine. My mother and sister drink nothing. They do not do that at Connemara. They have no need!

The twenty-six-year-old angel seems younger than I had thought she would. A child, who tends him a little commandingly. Like a daughter. She has fine full breasts and a talllimbed handsome body. Her face is slim, a wistful mouth with a scar to its right. (She had her own airplane. It crashed and Joanna walked away.) There are a few gray hairs in the glossy long black locks. She has a horse and is jumping hurdles and all.

My uncle admires that. He holds her elbow tightly and Helga thinks, "Oh, be gallant. Make her content!" Wondering if she wants a child. Is she pregnant? Would she dare? Her dress is a little tight. She is wise and bright and very beautiful and good, thinks Helga, scotch and soda in hand.

At the supper table my uncle says (fiercely) over and over, unendingly, unwearying, as if through him he also lives—my father's name and deeds. And then Joanna must have her pilot's license transferred to her new name and address. She should have her sanity questioned too for marriage to him! They seem good for each other. He spoils her, wanting to know her each wish and repeating her beauty to her continually. Joanna's mother is not yet used to the situation, "Help me to get back my little girl."

I have no idea how my uncle feels about me and my return to my family. When I go off to bed down in the lower level, he kisses my hand. The room is tiny. My bed narrow and soft. A delicate Matisse on the whitewashed wall.

In the dawn, the lake outside is spread with waterlilies. All of us assemble early at the breakfast table in the big windowed room to catch Carl on "Today." Joanna brings a tiny dish to her Captain with seven different rainbowed pills. Mother speaks of the Hollywood contract and how it took twelve sheets of paper to accompany the first payment check. "I buy my own stocks and bonds," she states, "and plan it all myself."

Then there is Carl, telling of George Stevens' pictures. How he sent Stevens a copy of *Remembrance Rock* after seeing *Giant*. They became friends after that. Carl feels that there is poetry along with the American dream in Stevens' productions. And *Giant* is more important, as far as the youth of the nation go, than any of Shakespeare's plays.

Carl also makes a few electric remarks about the condition of the motion picture industry in many areas. "*Ben Hur* was a monument of tripe! And DeMille's *The Ten Commandments* as well."

Uncle Ed is glued to his face and words. They all are. Helga is the only fringer, watching them, not Carl, whose face she is familiar with on the tube. I am eager to meet my father.

Everyone troops out on the sun-filled lawn where a hammock has been stretched between trees. Uncle Ed goes to lie in it. Joanna gives him a shade for his eyes. On one side stands Mother, her head into the sunlight, leading with her chin, waving her hands and nodding for emphasis. On his other is Joanna, her hands on him, smiling as she crosses one shin backwards on her calf in a half-dance.

How they dote on him! Joanna, "Is that pillow in the right place?" Mother, whispering, "Perhaps at the shoulder?"

The brother and sister talk at length of Oma's death there in the sunlight, and of Opa's too. They detail the deaths until finally, having followed each to its conclusion, he rises and stands, almost fainting because of the change of position, holding onto the hammock with both hands behind. "Now it is time I go in and call my doctor." Mother says fimly, following him, "Well, for the kid we had with pink-eye, we changed vets." A joke is made of this. But she repeats it, meaning it, "Try another doctor!" How strong the women seem. And he feels it, sighs, "I've always thought myself indestructible and now I'm not sure."

They verge on politics during the visit. Paula is an out-and-out supporter of Jack Kennedy, ". . . our best chance for improving the status of America among the nations of the world," and so on. Her brother sees it differently. She waves her hands (still in sunlight) and says (to clobber him), "You don't like Kennedy's teeth!" And she goes into the time of Kennedy's PT–109 boat disaster, "He towed the boy for five miles and made that Boston fellow swim who wouldn't swim!" Nevertheless, my uncle does not like Kennedy's face. He shakes his head, "Huh, that fellow! Hummm."

I leave them, put on a bikini and go to the lake. The water is stinging cold and lovely. Drying, Helga lies on the pier planks in the pale sun and the wind blows up and she feels her luck.

That evening, when I have my scotch and soda (still solitary), Joanna finds more cigarettes (Benson & Hedges) and Margaret takes one too, bold. Joanna says she smokes sometimes. I know she does not now because her husband cannot (doctor's orders). And she plays a folk tune on her little recorder and her Captain conducts, elegantly, pleased, tired. And the lute-shaped guitar.

As I went out one fair May morn
Down by the flowing river,
The birds they sang, the lambs they played,
And pleasant was the weather.

It was hand in hand we trudged along,
Pleasant was the weather,
And many flattering tales we told,
As we trudged along together. . . .

When I look at my uncle, holding to his eyes, he responds, nodding, "Yes, um, ummmm." I seem separate and foreign and an entity around these people, who are of course, obsessed by the illness of Uncle Ed.

And then morning and our bags are packed and we will leave in a party for New York after lunch. Today Uncle Ed seems more cheerful. Although still withdrawn and afraid of me, he finds more things in common with his niece. He is no longer the stranger. At the lunch table, he heaps his portion of salad onto my plate and more of the hot mushrooms with sour cream and tarragon. He says that at the age of seven, Oma sent him to Pio Nono College to be educated by the priests and taken off the rowdy streets of their mining town in Hancock, Michigan. Then when he made his navy application and they asked his college, he wrote in "Pio Nono"! And when he left Hancock at seven he remembered a forest and a large pond he loved. Returning, a child of nine, he found a mud puddle and three trees.

We are all in the Lark, heading for the city. Open top. Blue sky. Cumulus clouds. Uncle Ed wears a pre-First-World-War wide-brimmed black hat. And I feel pleasure in our lovely angel too, a vision.

At the Royalton, Uncle Ed leaves Joanna at the wheel and sees us into the lobby and that we have rooms. (They will go to their apartment off in the city and meet us at the theatre.) Mother and Margaret have Room 1007. I have 1001. And my father has been in his 1010 a few days. As I leave my uncle to take the elevator up, he kisses me warmly and like his old self. "God bless you," he says clearly and there is no hesitation of his words.

We are due at the theatre at 7:30. Our tickets are waiting there. My family assembles for a light supper in Mother and Margaret's room. My father is casual. We are cool. He has a list of arithmetic problems for my children and reads them off while Mother arranges a plate for him.

1. There was a zebra with 5 stripes on one side and 6 stripes on the other. He got sick and lost one stripe. How many had he left?

2. There are 10 apples in a blue wheelbarrow.
   12 apples in a white "
   4 apples in a red "
   2 apples in a pink "
   How many apples are there in the blue wheelbarrow?
3. There were two one-legged men in a room, one with cropped ears. How many men were in the room?

Carl is pleased that we have seen the *Playboy* issue. Ben Hibbs rejected the poem Helga likes, says Carl with venom. And, "It is better than Shakespeare's sonnets and Elizabeth Barrett Browning, too." So there.

And as we eat a little, Mother, "Now, if you're not too busy, you sign here and there and there, Carl." "Up here?" "No, down here." "You just tell me where." A little business, she calls it.

Nobody asks Helga how her work is going. Carl does not ask. He says his work in California makes him think of Michelangelo planning the Sistine Chapel. And, "I sent you postcard pictures of the Bel Air, Buddy. Ain't it the nuts!"

Then, "Are you going to change clothes?" she asks. "I'll change to a black tie." "It's time now," she says.

He stands. Takes a hard roll from the plate. Prepares to return to his room (Mother and I will see him to his door). "That'll make my breakfast." He puts it in a paper napkin and sets it on a paperback book. To Mother, "That looks like another book, eh?" And, as we leave together, to Mother, "You carry the roll." Helga has forgotten his ways!

As we part at his room door (he doesn't need us), he turns to me, "And did you bring a manuscript up with you?" They go and Helga shuts her door and rushes to the journal, "He asked me! HE ASKED ME! I THROW MY CAP IN THE AIR! HURRAY HURRAY! He cares!"

Will Helga ever understand Carl? Complex. Unfathomable. Coming from old-country roots. Here he is in this lonely time, away from Paula and home and celebrated wherever he goes. He is sought out by (and seeks out) women. Mother gives them no competition. Her hold on Carl is an anchor of mighty love. There are plenty of ladies to draw upon, to become caretakers. To keep him clean. And then to lead him to late-night festive gatherings, to exclusive restaurants, to supper clubs, to cafes, to their apartments. He is a star sensation among celebrities. A performing lion or bear, led on a string, who often roars or growls and shows his claws, but not to them!

Carl, enchanted (as with our Joanna), gives one and another a guitar to hang on her wall, so she can report on how she practices and keeps her nails trimmed. And then the instrument is there (even if dusty) when he comes to visit. Wanting comfort, solace, companionship. I know him well. My father needs a continual small captive audience to listen to him read his new (and to re-read his old) poems and pieces, chunks from the books that he looks at with the kind of awe creative people (he is not unique!) have for their works. He rewards his aficionados with copies of his present and past performances, with letters, sometimes a wire from the solitary Bel Air suite.

Carl is a natural "night owl" seeking company. Are there beddings? How can I know (or care)? Once I asked a Hollywood actress, whose name I'd heard mentioned, and she laughed, "Oh, those stories. I only remember meeting him once." And Paula keeps her cool. No leashes.

This evening, at our little supper, Carl's suit had been clean and fresh. That would have been due to the concern of one of his ladies, his hostesses. That morning he gave an interview for the New York *Mirror* and without putting on his clothes. (The suit was at the cleaners.) The report goes, "Carl Sandburg lay in bed in silk corn yellow pajamas, a bandana around his neck. The shades in his hotel room were drawn, the tables and chairs loaded with books and papers, the guitar that always goes with him was in its case on the floor.

" 'I had a long, mean night last night,' he said in the semi-darkness. 'Stayed up with a couple of beer drinking friends to watch the Jack Paar show I had taped. Didn't make the sack until after two a.m.' Weary or not, the eyes flashed, the voice rolled out like soft thunder, 'My wife and daughters are moving in today. I'll behave. Oh, they're fine, fine.' Proudly he added that one daughter, Helga, had published two novels and was working on a third. . . ."

In the evening, Helga is to pick up the tickets. She is in heaven, showering, dressing (sunburned from Uncle Ed's pier), "chief cook and bottle-washer" again, back with the family! There are only four tickets, says the agent. Mr. and Mrs. Steichen and Mr. and Mrs. Sandburg. "Your father slipped me a curve!" cries the manager. I assure him that Margaret and I will sit in the aisle. Before long, two more are found.

Out on the bright-lit sidewalk is Joe Wershba (He writes a column for the New York *Post* three times a week now. Also visits the farm and makes recordings of Carl for CBS radio and television.) and what is the red-jacketed book he carries? Waving it grandly to Helga's delight? Why, *The Wheel of Earth*. He thinks it is a "country Dreiser" and bought a dozen copies and had them shipped to Connemara to give away.

Helga is out there looking for Carl and the rest. It is nearly curtain time! And then Uncle Ed and Joanna arrive in a flurry. My uncle wobbly, the angel stunning, the press cameras grinding and clicking. Helga gets them in while Joe holds the tickets for the others. And there they come spinning up! They had a cab driver who had never heard of Henry Miller's Theatre and had been going about. The ladies' stoles are flying. Very elegant. Mother looking Spanish! They are whisked to their seats. Margaret and Helga dash for theirs.

Walter Kerr will report later in the *Herald Tribune* that it must have pleased Bette Davis to walk onto the stage that night "and find herself nearly blown through the back wall by the size of the ovation. . . ."

Of course, Gary Merrill is absent. *Time* (not sparing its natural ferocity) reported in the spring how that "Terrible-tempered Bette Davis, 52, charged her fourth husband, dour Actor Gary Merrill, 44, with extreme cruelty, asked for alimony, will have a new co-star, etc." Leif Erickson does not light the same spark as Gary, but it is a fine show. Norman has interpreted Sandburg and the audience is happy.

Even "Fog" is there, in the first half of the show. Bette leans across her lectern into a neo-blue light. Whispering about the little cat feet, the audience on her side. Gary had done the "Monkey of Stars" poem when he was with the show and now Bette.

There was a tree of stars sprang up on a vertical panel of
the south.
And a monkey of stars climbed up and down in this tree of
stars.
And a monkey picked stars and put them in his mouth,
tall up in a tree of stars shining in a south sky panel. . . .

It was only a dream, oh hoh, yah yah, loo loo, only a dream, five, six, seven, five, six, seven.

At the end of it all, the stage goes black. Curtain. Bursting applause. Margaret and I stand to clap with the rest when the author is led onto the stage to be seated by the performers on a "throne" chair where his books are stacked about.

Afterwards we go, by taxi, to Upstairs at the Downtairs, all of us transported. Helga loves the quintet show. If only my father did not absolutely require the limelight! He does not view the cafe group silently. When a cigarette is mentioned in the review, he calls out from his table, "Plug, plug, PAYOLA!" He is drinking. Unruly. Ours.

Finally he decides to leave. He is bored, tired. Gets up from the table, says something about late nights, staggers a little. Mother goes to take his arm. Margaret and I follow. Can you see them, the daughters back there, delighted to be together again? Close. In the familiar scene. Loving the man, with eyebrows raised at his ways. Helga is back into the swing of it all without the smallest effort.

At the Royalton, Carl comes with us into the lobby. There he hesitates. "You go on to bed," he tells us, gentle, mild. (Are we in his way?) "You need the sleep. I'm gonna take a walk." Paula pats his cheek. The daughters stand back.

And he goes down the street alone. A frail man. Paula looks after him, "Really I don't see how he stands it!"

But I do. The "night owl" is restless, not ready for sleep yet. He needs to play a guitar or read to someone or talk. He is going out to find an audience.

In the morning, again through the glass (in the dimness) looking back through the years at a bright scene. Sunshine.

Helga in her Royalton room 1001, propped up in bed. Pillows. A towel about her hair just washed. Breakfast at her side and two morning newspapers brought with the tray. In both, photos of Bette embracing Carl after the show, rolling her lovely eyes at him, still with the long white gloves on. And in one, "Make no mistake about it, Sandburg has become a cult. He has a large following. So, for that matter, has Miss Davis. But we couldn't help thinking that 'The World of Carl Sandburg' would have been more at home in a hep espresso cafe. . . ." Perhaps.

Helga, in heaven now, is busy at her own affairs. Calls. David about the manuscript. Lucy Kroll, to ask about what we spoke of in the lobby, that I need an agent now, someone dynamic and not connected with my father, not knowing his name! And calling John at home to read off any letters of interest. The American-Scandinavia Foundation has a grant to send me partway to Finland! The State Department will take care of the rest. Paula is coming to see the show. Complimentary tickets from the manager. John will not make it.

Harry Golden phones me. I met him last night for the first time. So begins a devoted and humorous and delightful and lasting and valued relationship. Love at once. Harry says, "I hope when I am eighty-two I can dance with Bette Davis and write poetry for *Playboy.*" His best-seller *Only In America* (Carl did the Foreword) came out three months after *The Wheel of Earth*.

Harry's picture is on the jacket of *Only In America* along with Carl. The one is rotund, wears glasses, carries his fedora. My father wears thick wool vest, bandanna, work gloves in hand and his axe. Then the New York *Times* reported that "The next Golden work—aside from The Carolina Israelite—will be a book about Carl Sandburg."

I had seen the notice and at the same time heard from a

Chicago friend and bookman, Ralph Newman, who liked *Wheel* and was selling it in his Abraham Lincoln Book Shop and wondered whether I was about to write something on Carl. Ralph said, "It will be much needed. . . . Too many of the persons who have written about him (or will write about him) don't know very much about him. . . . I have been in this business for almost twenty-seven years and have met some rather exciting personalities, many of whom qualify under even a strict definition as among the world's great, but Carl is by far the most complex and fascinating and yet unfathomable personality I have encountered. Only those who have known him briefly set down confidently to write about him. . . ."

And then walking about New York with Margaret. Carl has two collections of poems (some new ones) out, *Harvest Poems 1910–1960* and *Wind Song* (the latter dedicated to the little exiles). Paula goes with him to Harcourts where he will autograph copies. And they want to see the show again and Bette. Not the sisters. We go to Le Valois for trout. And to *Hiroshima Mon Amour*. All the while, striding down the streets, ordering our food, studying the shop windows, Margaret talks. On and on. Politics. Harry and the new idea of a book on our father. Her voice never ceases, like dove-cooing. A wonderful time. We like the idea of Ma and Pa not having the daughters tagging along.

The next day, we do a bit of shopping and they are gone (not Carl). Mother back to Connemara, in heaven and with the American Milk Goat Record Association meeting coming up shortly. (Janet will go with her.) Margaret stopping off in Washington where she will stay with Marge and Bill Braye and come to me when I am back on Sunday. By then Carl is in Beverly Hills.

He writes Mother about his life. In bed at his Bel Air suite at midnight (he does not say he has been out with George

Stevens and dancing at a Hollywood party too!). Doing his exercises and reading. The studio car arrives just after noon. The actresses are lovely and just right for the parts. He gets goat milk three times a week. His two-room office is elegant, his name in brass letters on the door. His secretary (sent over by Norman Corwin) answers the phone, "Carl Sandburg's office." "It's worth a nickel to hear," he reports. And, "I love you a million bushels. Carl."

Helga, back there in the Royalton Hotel room, the sunlight pouring through the windows, had been starting a letter to Carl. Then in Washington, after my sister's visit, I put my feelings into words. Not stammered out loud and seeking an answer. But a silent message he could go back to and review (instead of stomping roaring out of my sight) and perhaps understand his daughter's ways. At any rate, the letter is composed, typed and sent.

It begins, "Dear Dad—I've been meaning to write you. . . ." And goes into details about the children and their lives and, "I'm sorry the years have gone as they have, without you knowing each other, but that is the way of it." And, "I hear all sorts of splendid reports about you from the four corners of the world. I am to be sent by the Finnish–American Society to visit Finland for ten days next spring. I hope to make the trip a Scandinavian one and include Sweden." His old homeland would be part of the trip in the spring and the State Department would get involved also and book Helga for lectures in England and on the Continent.

The letter goes on that "This week I'm typing up my book which will run near 450 pages, and then will spend two weeks in New York. I need an agent. . . ." It ends, "Will you please take good care of yourself? I mean things like the right vitamins regularly, and doing Captain Rice's Daily Dozen twice a day, and not letting anybody push you around, and getting all the sleep you can sleep, and being furious when you want to be, and happy when you want to be. . . . This is a Delayed Love Letter. . . ."

Carl does not send a reply nor does Helga wait around for one.

Helga returns to New York. Gets a new and tough agent (who did not know until he'd taken me on and was leafing through my two books that I am Sandburg's daughter!). Also Colston Leigh wants me for a month a year of speaking on the platform. Then there is the sermon to be "preached" at the Unitarian church. And Helga is ready. A driver will come to pick us up tomorrow. Then on Monday Paula and Helga will head for Connemara and a week there including Thanksgiving. Mother says Carl can't make it. He is due in Hollywood.

A Writers Conference is in town, including some Russians who want to meet Helga. There is a grand Saturday night party. Lots of poets. I get in at three and head for the kitchen to make toast and tea and settle down to get things together for the "sermon" in the morning. There is a note on the table from Paula that an important call has come in.

Early in the morning, Helga draws a bath, planning to prepare slowly for the day, a bit shaky from lack of sleep. Puts her head into the kitchen where Paula is, "What's the VIP call?" Buppong! And he's at Connemara for the day only. He wants us to fly down at once. Paula jumps to the helm, calls the airlines. Helga dashes through a bath, packs bags, wakes John and we are gone.

The driver assures us that she will speed to the airport from the church. Don't worry. The talk goes well (Paula thinks it a "bit over their heads"). We are exactly on time for the flight and half-sleep through to Asheville. Mother is there, shining.

Helga's "letter" reaps its reward. My father is not like the Carl of New York. Is it because we are at Connemara in the old scene? Is he more at ease with only his family around? Whatever, he looks healthy and grand. His nice little soft beard! And so tender with Helga. Perhaps he has forgotten that I write.

I drive him into Hendersonville in the afternoon. Paula is at the barn with Mother. Carl has little errands. His Marsh Wheeling stogies at a certain drug store. Chewing gum at another small place. And a haircut at the Crystal Barber Shop near the railroad tracks. The barber pole is of iron, an overturned boiler tank set up long years past. The metal is eaten through at the bottom and the red-white-and-blue is mottled with rust. The barber welcomes him and I wander across to the old feed store for a while.

The Golden Place again! In the late afternoon, all come together on the front porch. We are setting out on a walk. The high whine of the warm autumn wind is in the ancient pines overhead, as if someone is coming on wings and with the wind, passing on. The bushes of laurel overhang the Memminger Path. The sunlight reflects and glints off the evergreens, their leaves and needles like stars on a green sky. Walking through the drying pasture, the falling sun is golden and blinding, lying low on the hill crest ahead.

At the barnyard, the milking is over and the goats come out for companionship. They nuzzle my mother. They chew on Buppong's sweater sleeve. Paula points out Jennifer, Mother's pride and world champion and her creation. She is soft brown coated, with tiny ears, a Toggenburg, amber-eyed and gentle.

Leaving the animals calling after us, we head for the Great Rock. My father bends and picks up various stones. Some are set with lichen or a kind of soft green moss. He inspects them and puts certain ones in his pocket. Then he stands tall and makes a speech, addressing one and then another of us, "We don't ask. We don't put it to you, comrades! We DEMAND!" And Mother softly, "You have nothing to lose but your chains." He turns to Helga, triumphant, "I got four letters last month. Carl Sandburg, Hollywood, California!"

At the supper table (catching up), "Swipes? Snick? Did you hear the Mamie Riley song I gave on the Dave Garroway show? Ain't that an oddity? Out of the time when the Irish predominated in songwriters."

And, "Sophocles Papas is going to arrange a song for me to the guitar. You know Sophocles Papas? In Washington?" (Still catching up. How could we know, in another land?) "What the hell. Segovia sleeps there when he comes to town!"

Later, in the living room, the dishes put away, the night upon us, the family comes one by one to assemble in the lamp-lit place, taking various chairs. Carl begins reading aloud most of the long preface to *Complete Poems,* enjoying Helga, taking the bull by the horns, ". . . when you write in prose you say what you mean. That's Justice Holmes. When you write in verse you say what you must. Rhymes are iron fetters. It is dragging a chain and ball!"

He turns on me, "Ain't you glad you didn't have a book out last year! Don't be in a hurry to get published." And in a while, softly, "If you play it right, you may be moving into your greatest creative period."

I look at him carefully. He is mine. And unfathomable. His beard bristles. He doesn't bother to cut the cigar with his pocket knife. He tears the half into quarters. He lights the dangling end of tobacco shreds and smokes the piece down to a tiny bit. He is like an old Tolstoy!

To Paula, "Snick! Come February I'll be on 'Lincoln In Illinois.' Of course, you know Lincoln is dead. But I'll be resurrecting him all over Illinois!"

There are silences and bursts of speech. Snick goes to bring in a bowl of apples. Mother says that Harriet Monroe once lent her a long evening gown of yellow silk for some occasion. "Was it Miss Monroe's?" I ask. "Oh, mercy no. It was a sister's or cousin's. Beautiful. Of course, I had no clothes then. It was nineteen fifteen."

And Carl on his fable pieces, "I've got the darndest set—Hongdorshes, Hoomadooms, Onkadonks. Three, four, five stories for each. But I have only one ZWICK story. Z-W-I-C-K! 'A fat waddling zwick often asked, "Do I look as silly to a penguin as a penguin looks to me?" ' " And so on.

Then all at once (Giving the news. We've been separate. Off on an island.), "We have a contract where George Stevens gets twenty-five percent of the gross product from the picture. And I get two percent of his twenty-five percent. Lucy says her feeling is that this is all right."

A moment of quiet and then abruptly, "Now I can hate Art like I hate Nixon!"

Mother rises and leaves the room, "I'll just call my brother." After a time, she returns to report on her talk with Joanna. Uncle Ed is fine. There had been some kind of infection. A proper antibiotic was found and he is working eight-hour days now. The angel says he has regained more energy than she'd ever had in the first place. And there are great gray panels of composition board now stacked all about the place in the process of arriving at a selection of photographs for the birthday exhibition next March.

Strangely, it is as if Carl and Helga never experienced the Rift. I have not changed much over the years. But here is

Paula, seventeen, tender, womanly, grown. He brings out a scrap of paper from his pocket to read. "Just for the record," he says.

Sweet Anecdotes of Snick

Buppong: "Do you love me a million bushels?"
Snick, 6 years old: "I love a million bushels anybody don't hit me."
Buppong: "John, I think I'll cut your ears off."
Snick whispers in Buppong's left ear, "Don't do that, then when he is scolded real hard he can't hear it."

Late in the night the group separates (Janet long since gone). Carl has an idea and Snick follows him up the stairs to his room. He hunts in a closet and comes out with a lute-shaped guitar. "That is for you and John. One of you might want to fool around with some chords sometime. And there's Sophocles Papas, Segovia's friend and a guitar teacher, who'd give you lessons!"

With Janet too, it is as if time has not gone by. She is casual with conversation and embraces, sisterly, a little shy, as always. Mr. Shams is there, stalking a purple finch under the feeder with elephantine tread. (The bird is safe.)

And the camera. Mother photographs Carl at the table with Snick's arms about him. Their relationship remains a rock of love. The trio, Mother and Carl and Snick, stays close knit. With Helga and Carl there is the taint of the rebellious (but loving the while) and erring and stubborn and firm daughter.

The leavetaking. Buppong is to be driven to the airport off in Greenville, South Carolina, where he will take the plane back to Hollywood. We are all going (not Janet). His ticket is lost. That is, it cannot be found. Everyone dashes about. Searching. Like the eye of the hurricane, my father is calm. It is finally decided to go without it and buy a ticket on the plane. (Of course, on arrival at the airport, he takes a look into his little fat bag and there it safely is.) Well.

And photos at the airport, before the Prop-jet takes off. Carl with his daughter and granddaughter in his arms again. One on each side. And he beams! Then, fedora on head and valise in hand, my father waves from the door of the Golden Falcon Electra, off for star-studded Beverly Hills.

Mother writes him from her healed heart of the voyagers return from the distant land, ". . . now it seems like Christmas. If only you were here it would be complete. The New Order brings back the days at Chikaming and the first years at Connemara. . . ."

Remember the lute-shaped guitar that Buppong gave Paula? She set it in a corner of the apartment on our return to Washington and John eyes it with interest. The case is battered with travel and use, an adhesive-tape patch half-mended hangs on one side. The guitar itself shows signs of having been around, has elaborate scrolled giltwork set into the face. Sophocles Papas' studio is but four blocks from where John works.

How lucky that Carl was moved to present this particular instrument at this time! Before long classic guitar chords ring out in the evenings. A check and note have arrived from the grandfather.

Dear John Carl

This enclosure

for guitar lessons with

Pappas. It goes to you

near your birthday

& Xmas—even tho any

day in the year is one wherein

there is love of you from

Buppong

GEORGE STEVENS PRODUCTIONS

Sophocles is happy with his pupil and writes Carl that he is "looking forward to making him a fine guitarist. John told me that you sent him the money to pay for the lessons but I refused it. Your friendship pays for everything I may be able to do for the Sandburg clan. Affectionately, . . ."

Carl replies that Sophocles should have John sleep sometime, "or at least have a nap, in the bed where Segovia has slept. You can call that corner of your house Saints' Rest. Please know my heart is soft about what you see with such certainty in my grandson. . . ."

And now my father too is feeling the voyagers return. Was there anger in his heart? I am waiting to hear. At least the fire has died now and is ashes. John writes Carl words that enchant him, ". . . Using the guitar has greatly increased my knowledge of symphonies and the converse. . . . Mr. Papas' teaching is one of the most enlightening experiences I have had and I think he is one of the best and greatest men I know or can hope to meet. . . ."

Carl has his secretary copy the letters of the two guitarists. He mails them to Paula at the farm with his note.

Dearest -
a nice surprise
for both of us -
Carlo

And again to her, exulting, "What a grandson for us to have! What a sweet nephew for Margaret to have—hooray! Carl."

The boy gives him a further report that, ". . . I am finding that my ability to play the guitar attracts people. Tonight, on the way back from my lesson, the cab driver asked me to show him how to tune a guitar. In a short time I was showing him all I knew about the guitar and he was showing me what he knew about the harmonica. I must admit that the people in our apartment house must have strange thoughts when one of the tenants is playing the guitar for a cab driver on the sidewalk. Again, I would like to express my thanks for your giving Paula and myself the means for buying better guitars. Love . . ."

By now it is May and Helga has been in Scandinavia a month, lecturing for foundations and the State Department, a tour that leads me through Europe and Greece, the *Cote d'Azur* and Oxford, England, before boarding the RMS *Queen Mary* for home in August. When in Göteborg, I order a mandolin for John and a Goya classic guitar for Paula (now lured into beginning lessons with Sophocles).

In Milan, I send home an Antonio Monzino classic guitar for John. That one arrives by air in fine shape. As for the Goya, John's letter reaches me in Nice, ". . . Paula's guitar has arrived brutally mangled . . . the neck has been broken from its body. You have no idea what it is like to wait patiently for something and then receive it crushed, . . . etc." The Göteborg people replace it. Sophocles undertakes the repair of the mutilated treasure. And lo, an extra instrument! A proliferation of guitars. One for me!

Another happening that spring. The children's surname is legally changed. They pick their grandmother's maiden one and Uncle Ed's—Steichen. (Sandburg would never do! Only a daughter can handle living with that.) Mother, the Luxembourger, is happy, says that "Joe's people came from Bavaria and France and it seems suitable."

And Buppong tells her that their grandson ". . . is a love of a boy, and he's got some of the best of the Steichen and Sandburg breeds. I remember when you were in tears over that first marriage, and I said, 'I think it means we are going to have grandchildren, and it may be that they will be exactly what we want.' Now it has happened. You have done well all the way through, and I kiss you a salute to our progeny. Carl."

6 January 1961. Carl is eighty-three and away from home. A cake and a reception are provided by the Twentieth Century–Fox Studios. He tells the press that he "predicts he'll die when he is either 88 or 99 because two of his great-grandfathers died at double numerals." As for the state of poetry, it can be described "with the word you hear on airplanes. 'There's no turbulence.' " And as for President-elect John Fitzgerald Kennedy, "I feel good about him."

My family all voted for Kennedy. The inaugural is at hand. The coming president has invited 155 scientists, writers, artists, musicians, poets. All sorts of cultural affairs will take place. Classical music concerts. Shakespeare plays. He asks a noted poet to begin it all. Robert Frost, who did not vote in the election, busy out in California with poetry readings.

January twentieth. Our city is hit by an unexpected storm. Snow swirls. Temperatures plunge to twenty degrees. Our hatless eighty-seven-year-old poet's white hair blows about in the wind. He is swathed in overcoat and scarf. The January sunlight glares down. He squints at the paper (he worked till the last minute on it). Fumbles through six of the forty-two lines. Pauses. Mutters.

Vice-President Lyndon Baines Johnson leaps forward to shield the sun with his top hat. "Here, give me that!" cries the poet. It does not help. He thrusts it aside. The folks on the platform shift, a nervous laugh comes from the crowd. Frost gives up on his dedication poem and resorts to reciting one he and the nation know well, "The land was ours before we were the land's," and through to ". . . Such as she was, such as she would become!"

Ever since that day, new acquaintances and strangers have explained to Helga how sorry they are that the light bothered my father at Kennedy's inauguration. I write a poem about the event called "The Blinding Light." Our *Post* publishes it. Frost likes it and will be in Washington shortly and wants to see me. Carl likes it too and asks Helga if The *Post* paid her.

Our poet muffed it, muffed his chance.
Was it some mischief in the orb made her dance
Her rays on his words? Was it some voodoo
Made "this tribute verse" go all ascrew?
Nobody else cared; we hurled up our caps
When he began, "The land was ours—" Who minded the lapse,
Except he who'd praised the sun like a lover
And refused to believe that she'd thrown him over;
He stumbled through six lines until he realized the case,
I have wondered what he told her when he left that public place.
Was it, "Sun, I had a thing to speak there on art and glory,
And you made a fool of me. Now come on, let's hear your story!"

I am about to visit the farm. My father is home for a month, a special arrangement with George Stevens. Harry Golden is coming to talk about his book on Carl. And Mother wants me, ". . . the family together again—wonderful!" And sends pictures of Joe and Adaline's children, "their daughter of 10½ with a splendid Angus steer, her 4H project, and the boy with a pet kid. I thought you'd like to see it and maybe you'd like to show this to the children. Might fill in that background in the stream of life and experience. . . . Deep love always." Paula and John view their handsome half-siblings with interest. John, "Maybe I'll help the little shaver along some day—my half-brother. Ahem." (My son is nineteen.)

I look forward to seeing Harry, who visits the farm a lot and has become somewhat a member of the family. Harry keeps in touch with me, seeing to plane and train reservations and a hotel when I go to New York and introducing me to people when in my town ("Dear Carl: . . . I have to be in Washington on the 25th and am taking Helga to a reception along with Hubert Humphrey," etc.). When Harry gives me his books, he writes in *Only In America,* "Helga Sandburg:—Whom I found at Connemara—when I needed her most—to help with the next one. . . ."

And then the family. We are all characters in a Chekhov play, looking back into it. The lights are up. The Father, swathed in warm colored robes with strange foods on the table before him—tomato juice and harsh bread and yogurt. He changes directions frequently. "I wish goat milk. No, I wish yogurt. No, no more yogurt. I wish orange juice—fresh-squeezed!"

The Mother, huffy about a third long-distance call from some woman out in California (whom she disapproves of because she keeps bringing up *Remembrance Rock* as a possibility for the movies and Paula thinks it should be left alone), answering the phone and saying very distinctly, with irony, "No. This is NOT Mr. Sandburg. No, indeed, this is not MR. Sandburg." And then he is on the phone spilling his secrets, "This is a secret! Stevens just called. They are going to use the star of Ingmar Bergman's *Seventh Seal* and *The Virgin Spring*, Max von Sydow, for Jesus. No one is to know!"

The Returned Daughter, keeping the peace. Carl gives her his advice about lecturing, "Listen to the spots where you get a response, either by sudden quiet or loud cheers. Use these over. Delete the dull stuff." He rages about what

Colston Leigh pays her and is about to ask for a new contract for himself. She asks, "Sometime let me do my reading for you, with the songs! It is such fun." (Wanting to show off, eager.) He makes no response, goes on with his singing. (Malish. Bull elephantish.) But she is not offended. Peace.

The Middle Daughter. Bursting into loud sobs. Paula rushes in to see, "What is it?" A bit of wine has spilled on the white tablecloth in the dining room. Helga's doing. An unusual occurrence. Mother, "It is nothing. Just a cloth." All is well.

The Cherry Orchard. Hear the axes ringing!

And the walks. Gray and blue-white skies, woods of soft green, misted. One tree never falls. It is a leaning monstrous tree. "Other trees go," Paula says, "but that one has more strength than any of them."

"I am glad to celebrate the end of an era," says my father. And later, "A new era has begun!" And to Mother, "We have immortality after all. We are living in the children. Who would have believed it." He repeats it, "A new era has begun!"

Helga, "I'm happy. Deposed from the wifely throne."

Carl, "The poor king. Ointment of the anointed dripping in his eyes!" He is pleased with himself for saying that.

The two of them on the pillared white porch. Helga mentions a piece she is doing for *Holiday*. Carl says that he knows the chiefs there and when they last used a poem, he got $500. (Helga does not say that she is to get $750 if they like her work.) Carl does not want to hear of her. Not ever. It is only of he, he, he. Ah, Helga had forgot!

He wishes to guide me, sure that I am going to write about him, "Now, when you talk about that Lincoln job, remember I spent fifteen years total on it. And it nearly killed me. I turned down again and again Alfred's [Harcourt's] offer to lend me a couple of thousand. You mention that."

Again, I am working for him. It comes naturally, typing letters, cutting down old lecture brochures to get the picture off so he can autograph each for the hunters who aren't worth a better one. When I boast that my agent took me on, not knowing I was Carl Sandburg's daughter, he does not respond. He has let his whiskers grow long so he has a sort of shaggy gray wizzled look.

He comes upon a poem someone has sent him in praise. "Look at this." Helga, "I think it's nice, but it isn't literature." The rank anger, "You better look out with your stuff. You're wobbling!" (Carl cannot bear it that she has an audience. And I don't mind the sudden rage, although I weep a little, retreating to dash water on my face. But the blaze of anger I feel! It will pass.)

He goes back to the *Saturday Review* article, ". . . in which no story was told more incorrectly ever! Huh hah hah." Helga has her back to the wall. He is trying her, to see how far he may go. She could be touched off again!

Am I going too far? Trying to give a sense of how it was? The girl (woman) has been away in a far place, some island. The reconciliation is over. Now the skirmishes. Well, tomorrow Harry Golden comes and the tenor will change.

It does not change much. Harry is substituted for Helga. Carl rides him when they set to work on how his book is written. And when Harry says it will be done in a day or two, Carl tells him two or three at least. Golden is to do a telephone broadcast from Connemara that night at nine and the technicians are in the dining room. Carl, "I'll work on your manuscript right through your broadcast. Helga can read the poem 'Omaha' on it (making up). She's a fine lecture performer and you yourself said what you did about her voice being a 'Sandburg' voice!"

Harry is moved at the subject of his book going through it, "Did you ever try to write something about someone?

And then have him read it in front of you? It's tough. Don't you read it, Margaret, until it's between covers. Will you? It is a terrible thing to sit here and have him read it. The emotional impact is tremendous."

And so the evening goes. Carl correcting the book. He stops to insert a small knife blade into the bit of cigar he is smoking that has gone out. He lights it delicately. Golden is reading nearby. Mother amid the technicians, ignoring them completely as she corrects another section of the book. Margaret is in her room copying items wanted immediately.

The next morning. Carl asks Helga to stay over another day. She agrees at once. And he asks Harry to stay, too. He will improve the Golden style, he says. Midnight. A tussle begins about Frost and Sandburg and relationships. Carl says that Frost wasn't for the war and it was too bad. And, "Archie MacLeish had fellowship with me and we went over poems that could be made into war songs, set to music. There were none to be found in all of Frost." Then, "Archie states in an article in the *Atlantic Monthly*. 'Frost is our greatest living poet.' Archie is involved in literary politics!" He looks directly at Helga, eye to eye, "You don't understand literary politics!"

Harry, "How can we have a book about Carl Sandburg without mentioning Robert Frost exactly as I have written it?" Carl, "Robert Frost? You say there is a coolness between us? . . ." "But, Carl, it's all over the place that you and Frost are a little cool to each other." And so from midnight until three in the morning, we hear nothing else. "You think I'm cool to Robert Frost? You should reproduce the poem I wrote about him which you will find in *Complete Poems* in 1956 and to be reprinted now in 1961!" There!

Helga admires Frost, calls him the "good gray poet" and sees him at dinners at Secretary of the Interior Stewart

Udall's home. Lee seats Helga beside Frost. I like him telling the dictionary, "You are going to get an experience from me!" Helga does not say any of this to the present group.

Golden dislikes Frost, calls him "a nasty old man." When he was on a plane to Israel, along with Bob Considine and Art Buchwald, he discovered Robert Frost was there too. He says he tried to discuss Carl with him, "and all I could get from him was a grunt, and he tossed off, 'His daughter writes me.' " (That was the "Blinding Light" poem.) But Harry will not be turned.

Buchwald did a column on the trip. Frost saying of Carl, "He has a good heart. He says in his poetry that the people say yes. I say the people say yes and no. . . . But I have no quarrel with him. He's out there in Hollywood now with his name on the door writing that $5 million picture about Christ, and I suppose that's all right if you want to do that sort of thing. But I don't like people telling me we have the same kind of hair." And there you are!

One more day at Connemara. Setting to work in the afternoon and going through to a walk (Carl and Helga) at five-thirty. Golden scribbling in the chair, a glass of warm bourbon by his side. Margaret still copying (and making an extra carbon for my files!). Mother in the kitchen.

Janet comes in, loud. "This is important! Two does just had kids at the barn. There are five of them and we don't know which belong to which!" Later in the night, she comes to report to me, "Mother went to the barn and it was easy to tell. Two were already dry and the other three were just born." During the men's rumble of conversation, tiny wails like human baby cries filter up from the basement room.

Helga senses the barn on this visit through Janet, who goes by regularly, apron-clad, for the kid feedings which happen on schedule. She brings a different kid now and then for me to see. Tiny-bodied, long-legged, their hoofs soft and jellyish yet. Nubians. One red with a white star and foot. Another brindled. Another solid black except for a white spot. Mother says these are Brocade's finest yet. And how is it done? By breeding her to her son! (Oedipus.)

The shouting continues, "People will say this is one of the oddest biographies that ever came along. Jesus!" Harry is losing his color, "I wish the hell I'd written a biography of Napoleon." He buttonholes everybody to repeat this, even the cook. Four A.M. and Helga in the middle. "And you know in here you should put that speech I delivered about Albert Einstein. And while you're at it you should really include the one at the Albert Einstein School for Medicine." Golden sighs, "I want my words in this book and not yours, Carl. I want this book to sell well."

And then at last, back in Washington. Peace. My quiet flat. My Lochinvars. My work. My own.

And so it goes. Our lives separate and yet together. My Lochinvars come and go (never to be caught climbing a Mountain again). Carl comes to visit Helga's Washington flat. John puts on a recording tape that we let spin as the hours go by, to remember his ways. The faithful lute-shaped guitar is there for him to strum and sing to.

On a Monday morning it began to rain,
Around the bend come a passenger train,
On the bumpers was a hobo John,
He's a good old hobo but he's dead and gone.

Charley Snyder was a good engineer,
Told his fireman never to fear,
All he needed was water and coal,
Put your head out the window, see the drivers roll.

Jay Gould's daughter said before she died,
"Papa, fix the blinds so the bums can't ride,
And if ride they must, let them ride the rod,
Let them put their trust in the hands of God."

Carl is tremendously happy. He carries the postcard I mailed from Florence, off on that State Department excursion. He will pin it up on the bulletin board in Connemara's Farm Office! It is a photograph of Helga, well-burned from the Lido in Venice, wearing a gold medallion of the Madonna picked up in Rome, white gloves, little shoes, taken by the photographer-of-tourists who works the Piazza Santa Maria Novella. It is sepia-toned and does not illuminate the new auburn hair color I'd adopted (my father has forgotten and thinks it always was so).

He also carries my poem torn out of the June *McCalls*, writing Mother, ". . . I like it a little better than any poem she has had published. . . . ever yours." *The New Yorker* has bought one too ("Woman" wins the Borestone Mountain Poetry Award of $200 and also is published in *Best Poems of 1961*.). Meanwhile, my agent is peddling the short stories done in Europe.

My father, the eighty-three-year-old, still returns always to his desk out there in Hollywood ("wearing baggy grey trousers, a blue pullover shirt with prominent stains, and sandals . . ."). Mother, lonely at Connemara, writes him in her longing way as other visits take place, "Dearest Carl—How we all wished that you could have been here when Ed, Joanna, John, Helga and little Paula were all here. I missed you more than ever. . . . John was so happy to meet Uncle Ed, as he was only 10 the last time he saw him. . . . He had some good talks with Ed. . . ."

The nation, the world, stays in turmoil. Our young president has been tried. Russia holds the lead in space technology. Maj. Yuri Alekseyvich Gagarin circles the earth in *Vostok I* in 89.1 minutes. The United States sends two men on suborbital space flights. The border between East and West Berlin is closed and a wall speedily erected. Khrushchev plans to soon be busy exploding 25- and 50-megaton thermonuclear devices. The fires of war are flickering in Southeast Asia, Laos, Cambodia, Burma, Vietnam.

Carl continues to stand for young Kennedy and at Christmas Rose (Mrs. Joseph P. Kennedy) asks him to autograph seven sets of the six-volume *Lincoln* to put under the tree for her children. When in Washington, he visits the White House. Helga is along. Stewart Udall, our Secretary of the Interior, arranges it all. In the Oval Office, Stewart and Helga sit on one of two sofas, Kennedy is in his cushioned rocker and on the other sofa is Carl, a bit of his smoldering cigar still between his left thumb and forefinger. "You are one of the rare presidents who have style," he says.

JFK laughs, rocks, waves his hands, points his finger, listens. Carl praises, comments. The door is open to the wind and there are espaliered roses outside where the guard walks. Later there is a tour about the Kennedy private quarters. "And did Jacqueline put this in?" (pointing to kittens and bows) "And did Jacqueline select that?" (puppies and bows). All the while the photographers keep busy.

Out on the lawn, reporters. "Kennedy? He's a great relief from the press conferences of Dwight David Eisenhower. Ike. The most ungrammatical president we ever had. For insidious he says insiduous. . . . Ever since he left the creamery in Abilene, Kansas, he never bought a suit of clothes, never bought a meal, never out of work a single week or a day. All of the anxieties that go with a man in a free enterprise system. Oh, shucks!" The press has its story.

November. In the mail, "Dear Helga: Looking at your nicely embossed initials on your stationery I think for once

I should send you a letter. I stuck along with the ungodly late morning hours because there is only one of you, only one of Sophocles and one and only Herblock, besides other one and onlies. . . . John and Snick keep haunting me with their outer and inner lovelinessess. . . . Jesus! Swipes! Its good to know you under the NEW ORDER. Buppong."

And at my desk, "Dear Buppong—When your letter came to me I thought, now I am a woman truly blessed in love. It makes me very strong. . . . Do not forget that I have a large empty room for you if you are ever in this town and want it. Also other extry services supplied. I am at peace under THE NEW ORDER. Your child—Swipes."

So there!

And then a little longing letter to Paula to say that by February his stint will be over and that he will not make Connemara for Christmas. And that also he has come upon answers to some of his questions, ". . . In many ways all that I have found is merely a corroboration of what you and I already understood or suspected in our by-way cottage in Maywood. Well, it won't be so long before I'll be back. You three are the biggest thing for me anywhere, so much I have learned. Carl." How lovely for my mother! How brilliant he is, putting it into words. Her reward. Love!

She calls Helga to talk on the phone, asking, "How can people be lonely? The earth is the important thing, not people. All of you could die and I'd still not be lonely!" My mother!

Harry Golden's book is out, *Carl Sandburg*. It is wildly castigated or generously accepted, seldom anything in between. Those who rage forget that Harry has said clearly to all, "To begin with, anyone who wants to write the definitive biography will have to spend six years at the University of Illinois perusing and cataloging the Sandburg Papers. I am too old and too fat and perhaps too impatient to spend time with all those sources." The two, author and subject, charge about the country autographing the book together.

As for Helga, there in Washington, it is good for her to be in the company of Robert Frost now and then. Astonished at how warmly she feels about him. And for the first time, having an inkling of how people respond to my father. An aficionado. Frost queries me on my education and hearing that I have had little, says, "Me too." He speaks of the Greek he had for six years. And about Golden, "What does he do? Is it any good? He sat down in the seat across from me on the way to Israel. He got that seat so he could get something out of me!" I am dazzled and leave the party feeling the way people must when they meet Buppong!

Helga reports to Carl on the visit (along with a new gift), "Dear little Buppong, I saw Frost at a small gathering at Stewart and Lee Udall's. He spoke with affection of you. Your grandson is here for the holiday. . . . looking tall, winning, and with the stamp of his own life upon him. I've written a poem finally for John Carl and send it along. I love you."

At Twenty

The foreign soil is dusted on your shoes,
You, these many months gone, returned.
The arrogance of conquest is in your stance
As you hurl the door to and enter my domain.
Your fierce voice startles, used to a small son
Soberly erecting erector sets, not even swearing,
Conscientious, religious, within my hearing,
A gentle child! And I employing strong words at times
In a temper, being amazed and thinking you tender
And alien. You were a still boy, who now come
To my room with a loud sound like laughter. Why, I wonder,
Can I scarcely touch your fresh hard face? Stranger!

This evening I glance across to where in a chair
Your cradled guitar makes odd tunes from some land
Where women shield their faces and men go hand in hand,
And you tear open black figs large as oranges,
The pink flesh hot and sweet and sensuous.
You have lifted veils; you have with those men
Taken wine resinous, half-warm. There is brine
In your new beard, sinewy your different hand.
In the shadow your mouth glints telling of a dragon
And mermaids, of swine to men and men to swine.
Rocked on my knees in fever were you once mine?
With mouth then like a flower from which now I turn?

You do not know nor ever shall, tall one,
How frequently to my angel I mention
Your name in a bargaining fashion. Let, I pray, this rebel son
Outlive me! no longer any visible part to him.

And he? "Dear Swipes. . . . As a poet and a person you seem to me to be hitting a good stride and all the time growing. . . . We have plenty to gossip about when you may be getting down to Connemara. . . . I love you and I admire you and there ain't many papas can truly say so. You were born under luck stars and lets keep it that way. Sophocles *Papa*."

When I come to him at the farm in January, there is another little magazine under my arm to put into my father's waiting hand. *Seventeen* has just published "Mary Had a Redbird", a short story all about a bittersweet encounter of a teenage white boy and black girl on a Greyhound. He accepts it and says of the new novel, *The Owl's Roost*, "Have a copy of your book sent me with bill." "But of course, as soon as it comes!" "Well, then." Smoldering, appeased for the moment, "Write a love letter in it."

How much simpler, not to be a daughter of a writer! How

easy it is with Mother. Here she comes with a picture of herself and Jennifer the prize dairy goat on the cover of the *Dairy Goat Journal*. The women are so mild. We do not compete. We praise and endeavor to understand. An impossibility with this particular father and daughter.

Helga has new books in progress. A juvenile girl-and-horse story (Nancy, the old Golden Love!). A songbook of the music that has filled my life (*Did You Bring Your Guitar?*). And many Lochinvars in her days now. The Independent Working Girl. And all the while filling lecture bureau dates that fit neatly between quick farm visits. So I can keep track of sisters and mother and Jennifer!

Carl is in New York. A five-minute February spot for Ed Sullivan. Helga writes him there, "Dear Sophocles Papa—I love your letter and what it says and I love you. . . . Whoever is responsible for the technical end of the photography on the Sullivan show should get a citation. I've never seen you done that way. . . . There was a plastic quality to the face and yet it was like a statue, somehow transcending the 'human' look. You came over so beautifully. Care for yourself. . . . Swipes."

How is my little father being looked after there in the big city in those cold February weeks in his eighty-fourth year? There is the kind of band of aficionados who tend him and escort him about, guiding him to television appearances, radio interviews, press conferences, a Carnegie Hall date where Kostelanetz again directs "A Lincoln Portrait," to their little clubs, to guitar-playing private fests.

The "hostesses" are honored when their guest (the Grizzly occasionally raging but essentially tame) praises their establishments and their food and their skill at taking down his dictation or transcribing his shorthand into the poems or pieces he works on. He gives them his books inscribed with long elaborate grateful loving dedications.

These aficionados that he is using keep Jack Daniels on hand and a favored brandy, a little rug for his aging knees, a special welcoming corner ready for an unexpected visit. And some, besides enjoying the private performances of the Bear, have projects of various kinds going with him and ideas for future collaborations.

But then the darling Bear becomes ill. He is sequestered in one of the special corners and doors are barred to visitors. Why don't they phone Mother and pack him off to her? Does he have a small stroke? Who knows for sure? A mystery.

Helga is planning to be in New York in mid-March and she writes her friend (and Carl's from the beginning of time), Harry Hansen, that she is coming. Harry responds, "Dear Helga: It so happens that I have made no lunch date for March 13 and nothing could help brighten the day more than your presence. Carl has just flown back to Flat Rock. I am afraid he has had a pretty tough time since the Sullivan show. He has a bad cold and was holed up with some people who took care of him and at the same time, I am afraid, exploited him. I think Carl ought to realize now that the time has come for him to curtail some of his many activities. He is so precious to so many of us that he should not endanger his health. Let me know where you would like to eat. Did you like the Italian Pavilion? Best. . . ."

". . . .—The Italian Pavilion, Harry! I'm fond of it. I'm so wounded when you speak as you do about my father. The Sandburg exploiters are recognizable by certain characteristics. I think I'll do a ballad on them—or a cartoon. They'll be the end of him. According to Mama he was in bed in Flat Rock 4 days and now is better—. . . But I'll be talking to you . . ."

Robert Frost's eighty-eighth birthday falls on the sixteenth of that March of 1962. He comes to town to take his turn at the White House and to receive a gold medal from JFK worth $2,500 (authorized in a bill passed by Congress "in recognition of his poetry," etc.). There is a grand party afterwards at the Pan American building with 400 guests, including Helga. And a black tie dinner, hosted by Stewart and Lee along with the publishers.

Are these aging poets indestructible? Frost greets the long line of guests, but misses the lavish dinner (he's resting up for his reading later which will go on and on into the small hours). I write the Udalls to thank them and, "Just between us, I did not think Robert looked well. And if it had been my father, I would have made them bring him a chair and not let anyone shake his hand. I was afraid they were killing our poet."

Briefly, I have a look at my nearly indestructible father a week later in a sandwiched visit to the farm. He does not come out with the family but waits in his chair, his feet up on the extension. He seems shrunken, small. His gray beard bristles. Ashes from his dry cigar spill on his shirt. "Once there were two Irishmen," he says, "now there are millions." And he is off, in charge.

The next look-in is in early May. This time I bring a sweet-toned guitar. I do not like the sound of the one he has (I have become a judge of guitars). The children each pay a third and Sophocles throws in the case (so he'll be in on the present). Carl unexpectedly growls, "The lake looks like Judgment Day!" And, "Why should Adlai Stevenson plug for Frost! You tell me." And as suddenly is gentle, "Girl, will you watch your polysyllabic words?" "Yes, sir, I will!"

Then, "Spick? What is my name for her?" "Snick." "Ya. Um. Things I used to have slip away from me." He hands

Helga the analects. "Thanks, Buppong." Two minutes later, "I've got an extra one. Have you seen this?" "Thanks."

I tell Mother that I've given him the new "It Is April" poem. "Is your name on it? Better be sure. Or he'll think he wrote it." Well. I say, "Humphrey took Joe Glazer with him." "Who's Humphrey? There goes my m—my memory." Later, after doing correspondence, he turns, "Will you take a walk, Marne?" "No, I'm tired today." One moment later, "Would you like to take a walk, Margaret?" And then, "There used to be a key to Al's place around here." It is disconcerting.

Paula says he began to do this after the trip to New York. He is more tender than ever. "You know how we adore you. . . ." And, "Sit here a few minutes. Your dress. I don't think I've ever seen it. How becoming. Your gold watch. Your glasses. I had forgot your hair was that color!"

My mother, at seventy-nine, broods over her charge. She calls me in Washington, "He asks, 'Did I ever win the Nobel Prize?' And yesterday, leafing through the *Ever the Winds of Chance* manuscript, 'Did I get an award? Did I write that?' " And she tells me, "We don't go all the way to the front gate on our night walks. We go half way and rest four times. It is like a walk in a cathedral. The dome and the stars!" My mother.

THE GLASS SHATTERS

PAULA WILL not let my healing father away from the farm for a while and when a Watergate concert takes place on the eighth of that July, the press, "Helga Sandburg explained that she was speaking for her father who was unable to attend because he is deeply engaged in writing a book. . . . Miss Sandburg then pointed up to the lighted monument above the Watergate and said that 'whatever part of the evening is to honor Sandburg is really directed at the tall man up there.' "

It was a Lincoln affair and Helga sends the clipping to Carl, "Take care of yourself. I am coming for a couple of weeks at the end of August, and hope to help you with mail and to have some lazy talk too. Here are three poems just for the fun of it. I love you I love you I love you. . . ."

Golden is a help. He comes to visit Carl and Paula likes that. The two men march over next door to the Flat Rock Playhouse on August 13 where an overflow crowd of 700 wait. In one seat is a "Miss America," who gets no attention when the "craggy, white-topped poet and his rotund friend and biographer" arrive! An ovation.

Then, for more than an hour, holding in his hands the heavy *Complete Poems,* he reads, enthralled with his words. And Harry, "On a day when two spaceships are circling the earth at fantastic speeds, it is something that there should be a standing-room audience here listening to some poetry."

The two of them are promoting new books. Golden's *Your Entitle'* (his fifth) is just out. Harcourts is publishing *Honey and Salt* and will release it the next sixth of January on Carl's eighty-fifth birthday. There are unpublished new poems in it. He reads the title poem to the crowd here.

Can love be locked away and kept hid?
Yes and it gathers dust and mildew
and shrivels itself in shadows

unless it learns the sun can help,
snow, rain, storms can help—
birds in their one-room family nests
shaken by winds cruel and crazy—
they can all help:
lock not away your love nor keep it hid. . . .

There are sanctuaries
holding honey and salt.
There are those who
spill and spend.
There are those who
search and save.
And love may be a quest
with silence and content. . . .

His new sweet-toned guitar is along. He strums and begins and "the folk song which should have followed faded into an uncertain growl. He made his apology and abandoned the songs. The audience sighed its regret. . . ." Afterwards "Miss America" poses on the stage for the cameras with the two men and Carl engages "in a brief larking waltz" with her before the pair of entertainers head up the hill to the white-pillared house at Connemara.

A few days later, I arrive. John is here, "Hi, mommy cool. I get up at 5:30 and quit at 5:30. I'm a farm boy on a twelve-hour day!" Chekhovian, returning home. Here is the son one seldom sees, brown, foreign. Here the strange loved father. Here the adored mother, the sisters. Grateful that all are present. One goes to the Cherry Orchard.

In the next afternoon, Carl is reading his own poems aloud at the dining table (cigar in the corner of the mouth not removed). He hears that I like a man, "I'll come to Washington and have dinner with you some evening." Paula, on the news that I may live with the man, "I'm glad he's sensible and doesn't want to get married." Adding, "You may decide to live for years that way, unmarried."

She comes to me, "Sometimes I think, let him go. Why should I worry so and try to keep him sensible." Carl becomes angry, "You're trying to make me believe I am ill!" "On the contrary, I am trying to keep you well."

Out on the porch, he, "She is a great daughter we have." She, patting his cheek, "Ah, indeed, Buddy." His shirt has a new burned hole between his arm and chest. And he has things spilled on the front. He walks rather in a stagger, doesn't see the extra step and nearly falls.

He stands at the window. "That's a great back yard. And you can't sneeze at the front yard." Out there are all the varied birds about the feeders, immature cardinals (the babies sometimes rosy or orange-pink), and doves, chickadees, sparrows, nuthatches, a mockingbird, two young quail, chewinks, yellow-billed cuckoo, scarlet tanager pair. And then suddenly a huge brown rabbit finally climbs up on the stump where Margaret puts feed. Then a squirrel there too, holding the grain in little paws.

On the first day Helga has the feeling of the daughters who slept with Lot. His beard is soft, his flesh so thin. The bones so weak. One wants to lie with him, warm the coldness out.

Up here in the dining room looking over the bird stations, my father smokes a cigar and downstairs at the workbench, John Carl does the same. John, "I'd come up and listen to you and Buppong, but I can't take it. You are just like him." "I know. I'm kooky." "Yes. You are both removed from reality."

My sister Janet. "The moonlight is beautiful at night," she tells me. As she goes through life, Janet does good just by touching people. When we drive into town to shop, a girl stops by our car. She speaks of Biblical affairs (a "Watch-tower" in her hand), "Samson was a great man. He held up the church. We cannot understand why he was so strong." "That's right!" Janet agrees with enthusiasm. The girl informs us that the two magazines (one for each) are five cents apiece. "That's one dime!" Janet declares.

Once she wrote a series of poems.

Roses

There are roses that climb.
There are roses that grow on bushes.
Pink roses, yellow roses,
White roses, and red roses.
Roses smell so sweet.
Bloom on, roses, bloom on.

Tulips

There are red tulips, white tulips,
Pink tulips, and yellow tulips.
Tulips bloom in gardens.
Ah, tulips you smell so sweet.
Tulips bloom in the springtime,
So keep on blooming, tulips. Bloom
On! and on! and on!

Whippoorwills

Ah, I hear your call in evening dusk.
I like to hear them a-far off,
I don't like to hear them when they sound near.
So when you call, do it far away.
Call, whippoorwills, call!

What can Helga say of this sister? That she cherishes her because she knows no meanness of mind or spirit. Charity is

Janet's essence. She notes the way of a sparrow, a flower, a sun, a season.

Fall

Fall is the time of the year the leaves fall.
There are red leaves and yellow that fall.
Fall, you are one of my favorite seasons.

And then late in the evening, into the small hours. We are having a bit of wine and singing every song we know. At last Carl to his daughter, "Do you have a way to go home?" "Yes." And later, "Are you staying?" "Yes." "That's good." And then, "How long are you staying?" And, "Do you have your car?"

He says too, startling me, "I, like Marilyn, wanted to commit suicide. I got a revolver, but your mother there took it away and won't tell me where it is."

The world, shocked, had lost Marilyn Monroe on the sixth of that August. The New York *Times* said, speaking of the funeral arrangements, "Mr. Sandburg was surprised to learn he was writing a eulogy. He said that he had no intention of writing such a eulogy and was mystified about the origin of the news report."

Look did an interview at Connemara, illustrating it by the photographs taken a couple of years before in the studio of a New York photographer aficionado (reaping rewards now) of Carl and Marilyn dancing, drinking champagne, he playing his guitar for her. The article is in the *Look* on the table here. Paula takes it up and leafs through and views the pictures of the two with admiration, "You look like a priest, Carl!"

A day or so later. House guests arrive. They present Carl with a box of his favorite cigars and make a noise about it.

They leave the room and he turns to Paula, "That was nice of John to give me those cigars." Catching on, I go at once to the great bottle of Benedictine I brought and label it, "To Buppong with love from Helga and John Carl and Karlen Paula!"

Mother explains. He's fine at conversation. Remembering is the problem. He comes to her, "What am I calling my book?" *"Honey and Salt*, Buddy." "Oh yes. That's a good title. Is it a poem of mine?" And on receiving a letter about Marilyn and himself the next day, "Did she do away with herself?"

Helga has not done a lick of work with Carl. Mail to him now is a diversion. He reads it like the daily paper. The good ones twice. Nothing is answered. I have my manuscript on the juvenile with me and so have plenty to do.

The air of happiness here. The spirit of exercise and replenishment underlying all. And the dominating surrounded male. Washington seems another time. Another country. Here everyone shouts and talks and something is always going on. Helga stands bewildered, half-participating, trailing after others. One sister is following birds with binoculars. My son is playing guitar duets and whistle-and-guitar ballads with the male guest who has arrived. The other sister comes with a cup of coffee she has just brewed. I am a part in a play, a character. Only nothing happens and time is suspended. It is away from reality.

Helga is glad to leave. And looks forward to a schedule of work. On the way home, stops to see Harry Golden in Charlotte. I have a present for him, a "Birthday Song" that is going into the music book and with a blues beat.

I'll tell you about a fellow
That the whole darn country knows,
Prints a paper down in Charlotte

In a special kind of Golden prose.
He's the egg-head's joy
And strictly no goy!

He's always pitching into issues,
Big and little, here and there,
He waves his arms and grins his grin,
And bites down on his long cigar.
He's the teen-agers' joy,
America's boy! . . .

And more of the same. Harry thinks it is time to get my divorce and I agree. He knows the local lawyers and puts me in touch with one and we set a date that suits both our lecture schedules. The hearing takes place. The proceedings go fast. Helga gloats, silently shouting over the paper handed her. Asks Harry to give it to the press. She wants it known that she is free!

I describe to Harry my father coming upon Mother leafing through my *Blueberry* (the juvenile horse story) manuscript. "What are you reading?" "Helga's book." "What is it? How many has she written? Three? One? I haven't read any of them." "It's a juvenile." "Are there any polysyllabic words in it?" "Well, er, ..." "Because my Rootabaga. . . ." "Oh, it's nothing like yours! The Rootabaga stories are for all ages—children and adults, Carl. This one is for just a limited age group." Harry says, "It's for red-headed boys only, between the ages of nine and eleven!" Wonderful.

We talk of the folks' planned trip together to Seattle and Los Angeles. Carl has high-paying appearances out there that have been arranged. Harry, "He doesn't want her to go and she doesn't want to go, but she's going. Yeah!" And it is true. Paula is terrified by the change in Carl. "I do not want him waking up in some strange city and saying, 'Where am I?' "

And then there he is out in Seattle at the World's Fair

Opera House, reading "for more than two hours." When he finishes, he removes his glasses and steps away from the lectern. The audience rises with a crash of applause. "Thank you, comrades, thank you. I never . . ." And Carl pauses and controls his voice, "Comrades, I'll never forget this. It is the finest. . . ." And according to the press what he says next is "buried in another crash of applause."

At the same time, Helga, in her role of aficionado, is at a party for Robert Frost. At the Udalls'. Louis Untermeyer and the young poet, William Meredith, are there. Robert asks about the goats and what they are like and as always speaks of my father. He mocks the present work, "I heard they changed the lead character to a woman, Mary Magdalene!" And Louis, "I understand they altered the ending. Charlton Heston comes galloping up with an army and demands, 'Take down that man!' "

Frost is just back from Russia. He went with Stewart, visited around, read his poems and on the premier's request, flew to Gagra on the Black Sea where Khrushchev was staying. He arrived exhausted, running a fever. Khrushchev sent his own doctor to his bedside. Later the Soviet leader came himself. They talked. Robert gave him his book, inscribed, "From a rival, in friendship." The "good gray poet" is full of his trip and whether or not anything comes of it, he has spoken his piece and he is pleased.

How startling, just before Christmas, to hear of Robert's heart attack in the Peter Bent Brigham Hospital in Boston. He tells his daughter Lesley, ". . . . Life has been a long trial yet I mean to see more of it."

Helga feels the likeness of this poet to Carl. Each continually wants his political piece to be known and felt. Each has striven to shake the world a little. Each wants to stir the heart and with confidence preaches from his lifework of poems endlessly. And their audiences are vast.

On the twenty-ninth of the next January of 1962, the world finally gave up on the "good gray poet." In two months, he would have been eighty-nine. Helga shuts herself in her study and writes an emotional elegy, ending,

See the sun withdraw within the whirled clouds,
And all the disturbed elements misbehave.
Let living men mark a cross on their calendars
That on this day a certain event occurred.
Robert Frost goes once again to earth!

I mourn Robert and when a public memorial service is held in three weeks at Amherst College, Stewart sends his car and I go in their morning plane, somber, with the others. My father is four years younger than Robert. I trust that we will have him, the wheel on which our lives turn, for a while yet. Who can tell?

Christmas. Helga is at the farm. The ponds are frozen. The pasture is snow-drifted. Carols flow out from a hi-fi set that John put together in the summer. Carl says, "That thing turns this room into a cathedral!" He looks fine, is beautiful, in almost foreign dress—black suit, soft deep blue shirt, black bow tie at an angle. Paula comes into the room. He takes her hand, "What luck, getting your mother, Swipes."

For the first time I can play the guitar and sing for them. He praises and, "You're doing all right. You sing them your way. I don't mind. A lot of those songs you've picked up from me!"

More treasures. I have a new poem and want him to know and to let me read it. "It's for your granddaughter!" "Go ahead," he says, "shoot!" And they listen. For the first time!

Someone should say it to you, daughter: love.
Daughter, I loved you when you were three
The way I loved the golden spaniel pup,
Who scampered sunny-tempered on the porch.
You never cried, you laughed;
You never walked, you ran;
You never liked, you loved;
You never spoke, you sang.

Someone should say it to you, daughter: love.
Daughter, I love you best now at nineteen,
The lines of worry there where you have frowned,
You quiet way of going from a room.
You cry too much, you laugh too much,
You walk too much, and run;
You like too much, you love too much,
You speak too much, and sing.

Yesterday I saw in you no part of me,
Although I knew that you were of my blood
And had my smile and had my mother's eyes.
Sister, today you stood before the glass
And took the comb and ran it through your hair
And looked into your eyes and there saw me
And my mother and her mother and hers.
Let someone say it, daughter, sister: love.

And then the lovely child herself arrives, the day after Christmas. And a reporter the next day. Asking about the black tie party coming up, the one for Carl's eighty-fifth birthday and the publication of *Honey and Salt.* The U.P. man deals questions and Paula hangs about in case she is needed. When the interview is printed, ". . . for a moment the title of the new book slipped his mind. His wife, Lilian, had to remind him."

The press is there, of course, for the party, cameras clicking, light bulbs flashing. And Buppong? "Being a poet is a damned dangerous business," he tells the 150 assembled guests (among them John Gunther, Alfred Kazin, Mary Hemingway, Malcolm Cowley, Harry Golden.)

The encomiums. Justice William Douglas mentions that Sandburg will be remembered as long as Abraham Lincoln and he plans to return on the ninety-fifth birthday. John Steinbeck, "Carl, all of us could learn from you and some of us have. Thank you for living." A letter from Jessamyn West is read and one from Adlai off in the Caribbean, "Please give the young man my affectionate regards." Mark Van Doren has a dramatic declarative prose poem to offer. And Uncle Ed (he is lean and well, the angel radiant), "Carl, Sweet Little Sister and Distinguished Guests, etc . . ." (All about the first time he met Carl at Oma and Opa's farm.)

Carl stands to cut the cake. And then (a little out of place, low shoes, the dress from a Hendersonville shop, shy, laughing, handling it all, looking forward already to returning home), Paula comes to cut a piece too. And now, sure enough, my father has commenced to read from the book, beginning with the "Honey and Salt" love poem that leads it. This one was once called "Most Any Father and Most Any Daughter" and was written twenty years and more ago, back at Connemara. I was between marriages then and kept the copy he gave me. It is good advice.

. . . forget everything you ever heard about love
for it's a summer tan and a winter windburn
and it comes as weather comes and you can't change it:
it comes like your face came to you, like your legs came
and the way you walk, talk, hold your head and hands—
and nothing can be done about it—you wait and pray. . . .

Honey and Salt, the book, is an assemblage, brought together by Carl's new editor, Hilda Lindley, with the help of Mother and Margaret, out of the reams of poems, some very old, in the papers in the house. Now and then a little poem is put with others to make a long one ("I was born in the morning of the world, So I know how morning looks, . . ."). Carl is not consulted. They are his words, though. And he recognizes them as he reads them over. The "First Sonata for Karlen Paula" is there, and one not used until now, "Out of the Rainbow End—For Edward Steichen" ("A delphinium flings a shadow . . ."). There are seventy-seven "new" poems in all.

Carl presents Helga with a copy inscribed in his new frail hand.

Helga

You saw most of
these pages in the
writing—and the
spirit of you is
here & there in
many a line—

Papa alias Dad
1963 A.D.

The press ends its report on the evening, "Mahalia Jackson, a Chicago girl, puts her heart into 'I'm Grateful' and everyone returned home to wait for Mr. Sandburg's 95th birthday."

And so the days pass. Paula goes along if Carl leaves Connemara. Fanny Butcher, in writing of the birthday party, "Lilian says she is going to try to keep her poet for a little while. You might as well try to keep Ariel in a plastic bag . . ." André Kostelanetz in May will again do "A Lincoln Portrait" and again wants Carl. Who arrives with Paula at his side.

Joe Wershba reports on the rehearsal in his column, how Paula tells Carl, "You were good, Buddy, but tomorrow night I want you to wear your lower incisors so that your voice will be clear as a bell." "But I couldn't find them." "I have them right here in my pocketbook." "They hurt!" "We all have to suffer in this vale of tears!" So there.

Mrs. Kostelanetz is at the rehearsal. She tells a story about Ira Gershwin presenting Carl with a pre-Castro Havana cigar. When Carl takes out his penknife and begins to cut the cigar into three parts, "Ira almost collapsed." Kostelanetz himself embraces Carl, "Dear friend!" They have performed the "Portrait" again and again over the years since their premiere on CBS Radio over twenty years ago. Both performances now have long been sold out.

And then in July, another trip away from Connemara. It seems that out in Glen Canyon, Utah, on the backwaters of the Colorado River, George Stevens at last begins the filming of the ten (twenty?)-million-dollar, ultra-wide-screen, four-hour production, *The Greatest Story Ever Told*. The cameras are rolling on Christ's (von Sydow's) baptism by John (Charlton Heston).

Stevens has been over to the actual Holy Land and decides (to the relief of the Hollywood guilds and unions) that the terrain of the wastes of Utah and Arizona and California are more like the long-ago landscape of Nazareth than the present one. Also that Nevada's Pyramid Lake suits him better than the true Sea of Galilee. So, Carl is wanted. For consultation on his job. They will depart on July twelfth. It will be Mother's first look at Carl's quarters at the Bel Air.

Helga is heading west for lectures at the University of Idaho and then Seattle. Afterwards, I plan some work up in the Kootenay region of Canada where a painter-Lochinvar has asked me for a couple of months. I am on a deadline for a follow-up juvenile (on *Blueberry*'s blind foal, to be called *Gingerbread*). My books are selling. Three out in 1963. *Blueberry* ("For my daughter, Karlen Paula"). A small children's *Joel and the Wild Goose* ("For my sister Janet, who understands geese and children"). The songbook that now has a final title, *Sweet Music* ("For my elder sister, Margaret, who always remembers the words").

But first I slip down to Flat Rock on the way for a day or two before their Hollywood jaunt. I have a magazine under my arm. *Redbook* paid a thousand for "The Innocent" (all about a retarded child and how her family accepts her). Mother reads it at once, "I agree with your agent. You were underpaid!" So!

A walk with my family. Janet, "Feel my hand. I am so strong!" She is. Carl picks up a leaf from the road, "A little soiled. But interesting." And later, "The trees are scarcely moving. There is a little breeze. As if they are breathing." How I treasure him!

Would he like to answer some correspondence? "Not now. Perhaps later." Mother says he hasn't dictated or started a letter for a year. Out on the pillared porch, he is catching two quarters, balancing them on the back of his hand and flinging them in the air. "You are a prestidigitator," says Paula, pleased. He flips an open jackknife and catches it. Helga gasps, "Mother!" (That flashing glinting dangerous blade!) But that one is serene, "I never tell Carl what to do."

"I am a man," says my tender father, "who was almost a juggler." He catches half-dollars too, two at a time, "If they're quarters, it's easier!" And then spending time guessing the years of flipped coins. After a while, it is time for supper. "What would you like?" asks Paula. "I don't need any special attention. I eat any food. I've been a kind of a bum all my life. . . ."

Well, and then I am gone and the two of them are out there entering the Bel Air lobby, where everyone jumps to attention. They are expected. She wears her print dress and a little white sweater (from the Hendersonville shop). He in overcoat with a gray sweater looped about his neck like a scarf. Then settling into the camp chairs on the movie lot. Carl smokes—just a tiny bit of a cigar in his fingers.

The Biblical portrayers come up to talk in their long white "authentic" cowled robes. Ed Wynn (the blind beggar whose sight is restored). Van Heflin, Joseph Schildkraut, John Considine, Peter Mann, Roddy McDowell. Thirty Academy Award winners are in Stevens' cast. Von Sydow spent six months learning passable English. Stars are all about from John Wayne (a western voice of doom from the Centurion at the Cross). Dorothy McGuire (the Virgin Mary). Sidney Poitier (Simon of Cyrene, the African Jew who helps to carry the cross). Pat Boone (the youth at Christ's tomb).

My parents do not remain long. In a week they are back at Connemara with no engagements scheduled anywhere ahead for Carl. Does George Stevens see the difference in his friend? Does he tell Paula to take Carl home and care for him? Mother writes a friend, ". . . he does not have a pain in his body but just has to slow down. He takes shorter walks now. . . . Our granddaughter, Karlen Paula, is with us. . . ."

On my return from Canada, *Gingerbread* in hand, I stop for a look-in. And also I have a mission. *Sweet Music* is scheduled for fall production. My editor hopes along with me that my father can be persuaded to write the words he put in *The American Songbag* for me when I was nine. It seems too good to miss.

And so here goes. Helga approaches him in his chair. He has the hiccups. "Even kings hiccup," he says and adds, "That is a three-word proverb." He ignores my question, rather lost and drowsy. Life here has a dreamlike quality. I wander about. The barns seem worn and unused. The old Horse Barn is cobwebbed.

I think I will give up the mission. Who cares if he does or does not do it? Mother insists and perhaps the moment will come. It is an independent crowd. Margaret self-occupied and bright. Janet grave, greeting her father (with her strong hands), "Good evening." "And good evening to you!" What an odd marvelous group they are.

Buppong sits on the sunny balcony with his whiskey and water (Helga has coffee). His little beard is soft and white. "Why did those trees ever grow so tall?" He makes toasts to the trees. "Here's to longwinded preachers. May they lose all their listeners. . . . Here's to the dead evil ones. May they roast forever on the fiery spits of hell. . . ."

He turns to me, "Are you writing any poetry these days?" Well. Mother says later that he complains, "Others write and ask my advice on writing. Why doesn't she?"

Helga is watching the old ones. How those two adore each other. With pure unerotic love. Like small children. They are so chastened and fervent.

He is inimitably whimsical. "Here," he says, "is a young

woman who knows her way around." He takes the *Sweet Music* manuscript apart phrase by phrase, word by word, song by song. It is difficult for Helga. But still she is contented, amused.

At last in the evening just as the light goes, she almost has it. It is a hard labor. She waxes sweet as honey. Mother is nodding approval of it all. And he turns, knowing, "I am yours to command in these matters."

may you ever be near
to the hearts of a thrush
and a mockingbird is
the loving wish of your
everloving father: so
be it = Carl Sandburg

Now, after writing the words exactly as prescribed, more is being asked of him and he cries (half anger, half trepidation), "What have I done? What do we want?" Helga is only asking for a date at the bottom! And now the entire family is enlisted and dashes about and and at last finally and absolutely ascertains that 1963 is Roman MCMLXIII. He then proceeds.

Connemara Farm
1963 AD

And he mocks, pleased with himself, kissed, "Sugar Music is a sugar title for a sugar book. . . . May you ever be a father is the mockingbird wish of your thrush. . . . May you ever thrush is the father mockingbird of your ever loving wish!" And quite a bit more of the same.

Ah! And going back through the years to that child. Looking into the glass darkly at nine-year-old Helga receiving the heavy volume from her father, his songbook. And with never a care, thrusting it on a shelf to be rescued by my mother and held over the years for me, now knowing it for a treasure.

For Miss Helga Sandburg
– and may you be a thrush,
a mockingbird – is the wish
of your ever loving
Father

Helga is back in the Garden, dashing straight to the Tree and the Apple. Eve. The beating heart, the frantic loins, the wild adoration. With never a look back. Lost again, dreaming, wandering through Eden.

Barney. Stunningly handsome, graying hair and wild blue eyes, aggressive determination in all ways. A surgeon! An author. A four-star Lochinvar (They are rated in the back of Helga's journals. Some get no stars, but are loved just the same. Four stars is tops.). I plan to give up all my Lochinvars for Barney (but not immediately).

It is late in October then of that year when Helga writes to the farm, "Dear Mama and Buppong—This is the poem I wrote for Barney when I decided I THINK I will marry him. . . . Your loving child— . . ."

Dear love, I said to you from in the dream,
Say what makes the willow tree so green,
Say what makes the light on pale skin gleam,
Say while we lie together in the dream.

Your mouth on mine I heard your heart repeat,
The willow's roots are long and dark and sweet,
The pale light is the space where voices meet.
Then where is love? I heard my quick heart beat.

Love, you said, is of its own self wove,
It is not us; there is no act to prove.
In its green time this thing will choose to move,
And then into the dream stood love.

And he sends his letter, "Dear Mr. Sandburg, I am Helga's Barney—Dr. George Crile, Jr., head of the department of General Surgery at the Cleveland Clinic. I am one of the ones who want to marry your daughter. To be more precise I am the one whom she is thinking of marrying. Helga has asked me to visit you and Mrs. Sandburg at your farm. I hope that this can be arranged, for I want to discuss Helga's and my plans with you and have your approval of our marriage. . . ."

It is the ninth of November when we arrive at Connemara. "And where will you sleep?" asks Janet clearly. "Here in this big room on the ground floor where I used to be!" "But, you're not married." "True. Well, I'll put Barney next door in that little one." "Okay."

The supper table. Champagne is brought out. The evening is wonderful. Carl understands who Barney is and that Paula is crazy about him. He gets to his feet (rising to the occasion in style and like a ship's captain), "Swipes, do you want to marry this man?" "Yes, sire!" "Then do you take him for your lawful wedded husband?" "I do." "And do you, Barney Crile . . . ?" And he does.

"Now, Janet," says Barney, "I'm your brother-in-law. Is it all right if Helga and I sleep together?" "Okay!"

And forever after, that is where Helga considers that she was properly married. (There is another civil business in Washington to stop Barney's daughters from weeping!)

The press is happy, "SANDBURG BLESSES CRILES" is the headline. My friends handle it, startled because of the sincerity of Helga's consistent proclamations of the joys of the single girl.

And then the days move and it is the twenty-second of that November. Helga has not yet come to Cleveland. The move is accomplished. All is packed. I still have lectures, engagements. I am in New York to help my book. John Barkham on the *Saturday Review* takes me to lunch. Barney will be flying into Washington in the late afternoon and will meet my shuttle plane there. It is difficult working out our times together. I need him! My heart. My loins. I need my love by my side. There is a Washington Book Fair on Saturday and the plan is to drive to Cleveland together on Sunday as the New Life in the Garden begins.

A strange stark wounded day starts for the nation. I leave the Italian Pavilion with my girl friday to take a cab to Dial Press to autograph *Sweet Music* for their list. A woman accosts us, "The president was just assassinated. In Texas. Shot by a sniper. He is dead!" She excuses herself, "I had to tell someone."

Feeling the slight disarray of the city, the hidden hysteria, the girl friday heads back to Dial and I share a taxi with a rather wild woman to the East Side Terminal. At first when I had heard the woman say, "Something terrible has happened!" I had thought of Barney and then of half the world perhaps destroyed in some incidental holocaust.

The widow, the deprived children, their photographs everywhere in the papers in the terminal, swarming over their father's desk, holding his hand. Waiting for Barney. Leaning on the cold wall of the Washington terminal until his plane comes to ground. Assailed by the violence (rape, murder, fire, the four horsemen, death). My sweet president! My country!

Barney at last comes (he was overhead in a circling pattern of priority planes). His arms! Helga heals a little. As we head for his car, Lyndon Baines Johnson has left the Dallas Parkland Memorial Hospital and taken the oath of office on Air Force One with blood-stained Jackie at his side.

Night comes on. A storm is building itself. Soon high winds prevail with rain. The funeral will be on Sunday and the burial Monday. In the morning, we stop in at the subdued book fair, change plans and drive on to Cleveland. It is a bittersweet ending to my Washington days, holding fast to Barney's enormous love.

The sixth of January 1964, and our new President Johnson phones the farm with birthday greetings, hoping that when he reaches eighty-six himself, he will have done "half as much for the country." At the same time, he invites Carl to come with Paula to the White House in April. He has asked Uncle Ed and Joanna too.

And then here they are. Mother, just eighty-one and not giving a fig for fashion, in her nice practical loose-fitting blue dress and her low black shoes (she enchants Lady Bird with her definite opinions, waving her hands). Uncle Ed with the beautiful young wife on his arm and the strange beard (Helga never does get used to it), smoking his cigarette in the Rose Garden. Carl spiffy, his black suit brushed, his bow tie straight.

Lynda Bird is here with a girl friend, coming over from George Washington University in bobby socks and skirts to get a look at their poet. The Lincoln Bedroom is visited and tea and coffee are served on the Harry Truman Balcony. The three men (our president towering in the middle with wide grin), line up for the cameras. LBJ enjoys his role, feeling the statesman (in the distance is the Washington white marble obelisk and the Jefferson rotunda).

The New York *Times* headlines, "JOHNSON STAGES A BALCONY SCENE." And, " 'Hey down there!' called the President from the two-story Truman balcony. . . . 'Hey! Here's Carl Sandburg. Don't you want to ask some questions?' . . . Somebody asked what Mr. Sandburg's next book would be. . . . Mr. Sandburg's reply was inaudible, but the relay wasn't. 'He says he's going to write a volume of poetry.' Then Mr. Sandburg apparently announced that 'I was in the Spanish–American War.' After all this showmanship, including an active display of the LBJ baseball arm, his guests were escorted to the Cabinet Room for a brief glimpse at the railroad strike negotiations working around the clock there. . . ."

On their return to Connemara, Mother phones Helga in Cleveland to report. Our conversations are long. Helga wants to know! "Well, he asks, 'Aren't we going to visit our youngest daughter soon?' And a little while later, 'When are we going to see Helga?' " It seems he no longer exercises by lifting a chair up over his head and replacing it. She has her brother's photo on the mantle of Carl doing that on the Umpawaug catwalk. "Last time he tried it here in the dining room, his hands started shaking and the chair nearly went out the window!"

And they are going back to the White House for a visit in September. The announcement will be made on the fourth of July. Carl is to be awarded the Presidential Medal of Freedom, "the highest civil honor conferred in time of peace." Her brother got it last year from Kennedy. She adds, "I don't think Johnson needs any help but it doesn't do any harm for him to give this to Carl. And he really likes Carl. He's a good politician. He got the civil rights bill through when Kennedy couldn't." And also, "Johnson used the right moment to bring those two boys into the meeting and it didn't do any harm. He settled the strike all right!"

My mother! As a young wife in 1910, marching in a suffragette parade in Milwaukee. Now her voice comes over the phone to me sweet and clear, "My brother marched in the NAACP parade at Redding! Joanna brought a stool but he refused to sit. 'I came all this way to march and not to sit,' he told her!"

She phones again on the tenth of July, just before their four-day visit to see my new home and to let the doctors at Barney's clinic check over my father. Mother says that if the clinic wants to charge she won't mind. This is the last year when it will be deductible. This year they get the final $45,-000 on that $175,000 that *The Greatest Story* paid him. The government took sixty percent and Lucy ten percent. "Now, as for *Honey and Salt*, it made $30,000 in two years and it's just a small book of poems!" Adding that Carl's first two books out in 1916 and 1918, made $500 in two years.

Young Paula is living with us now and going for her B.A. at Western Reserve nearby. ("You will be happier with her here and she can take care of the house," said Barney, firm, "when we go around the world a few times.") I am enchanted with my New Life and want my family to be a part of it. Already I have sent them a recent poem for Barney, "Letter To a New Husband Away In Los Angeles" (later it wins the Chicago *Tribune* Poetry Award).

Stranger, to your house I came two moons ago,
Where great bird stands erect on clumsy feet
Outside our door and pecks upon the pane
To tell me something I don't understand.
His beak opens to take the bread I proffer;
Bending his long neck, his eye meets mine.

He is recalling other hands and eyes;
I know no other swan. In the mirrors of our house
Tremble faces now and then, shadowless ghosts,
Whose gaze I meet with love I manufacture out of need.
Moths flutter from old rugs and skins brought down
From attic rooms and holding cocoons
Spun in another time. Nothing remains the same.
If your dreams are invaded by wandering presences
Who are gentle and place the keys and turn the locks,
Are you learning, like me, to welcome them where they belong?

Husband, light the lamps and take me to your arms.
In the dawnlight the swan walks to the door,

His neck upstretched, impatient his call.
The wind through the winter window smells of spring.
Let tomorrow come. I sit before the mirror
And run the comb through my hair and wait upon your return.

And then they are here! My husband and my father are smoking their cigars. I put a tape on the recording machine and let it run (I will dwell on it later). "I have been here one and a half hours and I haven't been insulted yet," says Carl. And Mother, "You have been here one and a half hours and haven't insulted anyone and that is more remarkable."

He asks questions, "Well, Swipes, are you all through with schools or are you going somewhere?" And later, "As to publishers, anyone interfering with you, unjustly and evidently unjustly, you tell me and I'll give them a kick in the pants!" "Thank you." "I'll do it. I've had to do with your upbringing and I know what you've got." And so on.

Paula brings him the old lute-shaped guitar that he gave John long ago. He finds chords that suit him. I want the sound in this house! Night is coming on. He stops abruptly, "Well, Buddy, I'll finish this last bit in my glass and we'll be going." There is much conversation before he reluctantly gives up, lets Mother convince him that he is staying, "Let's go up to the hay now. Have I got everything I need?" "Yes, everything is upstairs." "Have I got my bag?" "Yes." And his voice singing on the stairs as the two Paulas see him to his bed.

The Cleveland *Plain Dealer*, "Sandburg, 86, took tests at The Cleveland Clinic and found he was in tip-top shape. . . ." Then, time passes and Helga is driving the two to Hopkins Airport. Carl says it again and again and once more, "First the missus decides that we're going to stay in Cleveland for a long time, and then all at once we're going to leave!"

And then soon from Connemara, Mother, "He says, 'Do

you think sometimes we might go back?' And, 'I believe he'll make Helga a good husband.' And, 'I have a feeling I'll be going to visit Helga soon.' "

The Presidential Medals of Freedom are awarded two months later. Ed Murrow gets one, John Steinbeck, Walt Disney, John L. Lewis, J. Frank Dobie, the Lunt and Fontanne team, T.S. Eliot, Aaron Copland, Helen Keller, Walter Lippmann. Thirty in all. "Our glory is peace, not war; our greatness is in people, not power," says LBJ.

And the press, "When Sandburg's name was called the 86-year-old poet-historian stood beside his chair and asked the President: 'I salute you here and then walk up?' The President beckoned him. Sandburg then moved in front of Mr. Johnson, saluted smartly and said, 'Sixth Illinois Volunteers.' Mr. Johnson smiled warmly and pulled Sandburg around beside him in the spotlight. . . ."

Mother on their return, "Carl always does something special. He thought it was a war (not peace effort) medal. So he saluted! He refused to move! President Johnson really smiled and seems tender and warm with Carl." Mother talks for hours over the phone to me.

Another call from the White House. LBJ landslided into office in the November elections with the largest popular vote plurality in the country's history. Inauguration plans are under way. Will someone fill the shoes that Robert Frost did at Kennedy's swearing-in? Will Johnson invite Carl? Secretary of the Interior Stewart Udall, Carl's fast friend, is for it. But perhaps LBJ does not want to seem to be imitating JFK.

Mother's sweet voice, "They are trying to get my husband to be the poet of the Inauguration. I don't see why not. He just loves to read. Hum. It's too bad they can't have it in April. Hum. It's a shame it can't be indoors . . ." And more. (As for Helga, she feels that Robert, at eighty-seven, had been a different man than Carl at eighty-six. But I do not protest this to my beautiful mother.)

Instead of asking him to come to Washington, the president sends a birthday present to Flat Rock in January, color photos of the White House visit, "To Carl Sandburg, the golden voice of the men who toil in field and mill." And, "Happy 87th birthday to Carl Sandburg, a legend in American Literature, from his friend, Lyndon B. Johnson."

An Inaugural invitation also arrives. (Uncle Ed and Joanna accept theirs at once!) My father, "Do I have a talk to make, Buddy?" "No." "Then I wouldn't think of going!"

A new happening. My father has a beard! Paula says, "Carl recognizes himself on the color prints I took, while he thought it was Opa, not himself, who was the bearded one on the black-and-white prints!" She mails the pictures. It is white and shaggy with sideburns up to his uncut hair. Mother is not about to trim it the way Joanna does Uncle Ed's gray full-flowing one. My father has given up shaving for a while and the family accepts it. He resembles an aged Hemingway, Helga thinks. "A John Greenleaf Whittier!" says Mother.

At the same time now in 1965, at long last *The Greatest Story Ever Told* ("The Gospel According to George Stevens," headlines the *Saturday Review*) is released. A glittering $100-a-ticket premiere opens on Broadway at the Warner Cinerama Theatre on the fifteenth of February. Lady Bird comes in on the arm of our U.N. Ambassador Adlai. It runs three hours and forty-one minutes with a fifteen-minute intermission and is a box office success. At the very end, after the long listings of the stars and the bit players and the various complicated credits and before "GEORGE STE-

VENS, PRODUCER" (in full screen by itself), there is (full screen also and in color!) "IN CREATIVE ASSOCIATION WITH CARL SANDBURG." And there you are. Carl never views the final product of his Hollywood days.

These are his twilight years. Mother's calls are filled with tales of his ways, his confusions. Making wrong turnings in the house. And she cries, "He dared to try to do things! . . . He always stood by Pound, poor Pound. . . . Dad is proud of your poems. You are the author in the family now. He says "Itty-bitty Helga" and carries your books about. . . . (There are new ones, *Bo and the Old Donkey*, "For my Mother, who has a way with the earth and small boys"; and poems, *The Unicorns*, "For my husband, Barney Crile"). . . . He doesn't know that's the president on television. He forgets we had an assassination. . . . He doesn't want to listen to the news nowadays. . . ."

Carl doesn't learn for a while of our Adlai's going in mid-July, collapsing outside the London Embassy in Grosvenor Square of a heart attack. He doesn't notice that his granddaughter (a Eurail pass from Barney in her handbag) is gone to Scandinavia and Europe for her summer break. Or that John Carl, now studying in Munich, has fallen proudly and totally in love with a Bavarian girl. We ask them to fly to Cleveland in late August and have a minister marry them, see that they drop in for a visit to the farm so that Carl can bless our Liz also. And the aunts get to take a look.

Early September. My father becomes seriously ill. An ambulance is called and he is taken to Pardee Memorial Hospital in Hendersonville. Paula phones Barney. Helga gets upset, "Don't let my father die!" We take the dawn plane down. It is diverticulitis. Barney and Paula see eye-to-eye on no operation. He approves an intravenous antibiotic approach. In ten days Carl is back at Connemara (by ambulance with Paula beside him) and nurses around the clock.

The *Ladies Home Journal* takes my poem.

When my father decided not to die after all,
My mother asked the hired man to shave his beard.
He sat up nobly in his bed and made no protest,
Amenable to her vanity, her fears allayed.

Father, you were beautiful, your brain on fire!
You lay at eighty-seven on the high white bed,
Bearded, brilliant-eyed, your mind intent upon itself.
Father, lying there you seemed so young.

And I your senior, still the obedient child,
Quelled by the blaze when your eye fell on me,
Hoping, helpless, that I'd been recognized
And not thought some sister or cousin or aunt.

Now, Father, you are going to live yet a while;
You used to prophecy your end would come
When you reached an age divisible by eleven;
We should have remembered and believed and not doubted.

Father, take your time leaving this life;
Go slowly, not for your, but for our sake!

The nurses are dismissed in mid-October and we make a weekend visit. The beard is back. We take walks. He is whimsical, funny, untouched. Sticks his thumbs in his ears and wiggles his fingers at us. Thumbs his nose. Makes wonderful faces! Tells Barney, "I know you. You're the man who married my daughter." And to Mother, "We'll have to watch about her growing up. She could get wild if we don't watch her and educate her properly. She'll need superintending!" "She has a husband," says Paula, "who will see to that." "That so? Nevertheless, I think you and I are going to have to watch over her all the same."

In the long evenings, there is talk. And music. Helga goes to find the guitar and gives it to Carl. He fumbles awhile, hunts chords, returns it to me. I am happy with the sweet-toned instrument. Barney roars out a Yale version of "Abdul, The Bulbul Ameer" at the same time as my family sings the *Songbag* way. It works amazingly well and there are a number of reruns.

Helga feels that when the visit ends after the long readings, the shoutings, the emotions unleashed, that a sense of the Cherry Orchard again comes through. And Barney says in the night, "I've never before been to a house with an undivided feeling of peace!"

Back in Cleveland, Mother's calls come regularly, "Carl is always in good humor and sings as lustily as ever, never forgetting to include in his repertoire 'Jesus Christ and Saint Peter Went Out For a Walk.' . . . We have a very nice licensed practical nurse . . . Carl has no pain in bed until he tries to get up. . . . We have an RN nurse now 7 in the morning until 3. And another from 3 until 11. I take care of Carl the rest of the time. . . . Oh, and we are expecting Joe and Adaline and their children any minute now!"

By the next birthday, 1966, Carl is up again and about, wearing his green eyeshade, taking little walks. His president does not forget, "SANDBURG IS HAILED IN JOHNSON TRIBUTE ON 88th BIRTHDAY." The telegram comes, "YOU SANG TO THEM OF THEIR TRADITIONS YOU WROTE TO THEM OF LINCOLN'S GREATNESS AND OF THE GREATNESS OF THE LAND THAT PRODUCED HIM AND NOW IN RETURN WE SAY HAPPY 88TH BIRTHDAY TO YOU IT DOES NOT RING WITH POETRY BUT IT COMES FROM DEEP WITHIN A NATION'S HEART." There.

And when the press asks for a comment on the state of the nation, Paula tells them, "Mr. Sandburg has never liked wars and he hasn't kept up with the situation in Vietnam. He doesn't even want to express an opinion about it."

Does my father's wandering mind ever turn back upon the busy last days in Hollywood and New York before the New York incident at the apartment of the aficionado? There is a little scrawled note in his shorthand that I come upon, "Pls know y ar oftn in my thots—" (Please know you are often in my thoughts). Does his mind go onto all those people who had loved him and tended him and used him, their performing Bear?

Uncle Ed is fine, vigorous, taking Joanna to Europe in the summer, visiting the Pablos Casals and Picasso, viewing "The Family of Man" exhibit in Luxembourg at the castle in Clairvaux, having more decorations *de l'Ordre de Merite* hung about his neck (just below the beard), visiting his birthplace house, smoking his cigars and cigarettes with abandon.

He is developing a new type of oriental poppy at Umpawaug, "When you get a new plant, you get almost the same feeling, I imagine, that a woman gets when she bears a child." He takes visitors about his farm, shows them a large perpendicular boulder where he wishes his ashes to go (it is there that he photographed Carl long ago, when they were both in their prime and power). Home-grown vegetables are served at his table and good wine. Joanna curls on the sofa beside him.

He says, "Carl is an old man—he's eighty-eight and I'm only eighty-seven." And, "Taking liberties with the last lines of a poem by James Whitcomb Riley, the Hoosier poet, I'd like to say, 'When God made Carl, he didn't do nothing else that day but just sit around and feel good.' "

And so there is Helga's uncle. Why does her father fade before him? Mother says he loves John's hi-fi music. And,

"He reads as beautifully as ever and sings as beautifully! . . . He does not like *Honey and Salt,* 'I didn't give them that title and half of the poems in it were not written by me!' . . . He wants to go back to Galesburg and rather thinks that his mother has just died and that there is a wake. . . . He says, 'I don't believe I'll go to Adlai Stevenson's funeral. I don't want to see him in a casket.' 'That was some time ago, Carl.' But he mentions it again."

The year is ending. "Last night your father thought he was on a train. I heard him cough and went to get him a Kleenex. He asked, 'When do they serve lunch on this god-forsaken train?' 'It's not time yet,' I told him, 'It's nap time now.' 'And what are you doing here?' 'We're traveling together.' 'So?' And in great voice he began to sing half a dozen old songs! He really doesn't recognize me. He's the world's greatest poet. He's the Spokesman for the Common Man. . . . He is weaker."

The week before Christmas, we go to Connemara. Helga wants to see for herself. It is a lovely time. We bring out champagne as an evening wears on. Persiflage. Love. The guitar, the one he never uses any more, soft-toned and inlaid with mother-of-pearl. Paula whispers that Helga may take it back to Cleveland with her. On into the night the songs. On and on and on. He never forgets the songs. They are in his blood.

The wine and the noise of our coming make my father seem the old Buppong. He rallies and questions and declares and compliments and salutes. I think how he is still with us and how grateful I am for my family here, treasuring him and holding their breath.

July 1967. Helga, up there in Cleveland, does not like it when the phone rings. She is expecting a message from the farm.

Stand here with me in the dimness of now and look back into the brilliance of the scene. Carl's great white front room at Connemara, where the windows look to the mountains off there, blue and smoky. He is in a hospital bed with high sides. Note the beauty. The serenity. Chopin comes from John's hi-fi (Remember? Carl said, "That thing turns this room into a cathedral!"). Young Paula is at the farm this summer. She's graduated and plans to stay awhile. She has a way with words and is about to begin a book, telling her story of the family and her life here. Harcourts wants it. Hilda Lindley is her editor.

Carl is gaunt and often incoherent. Propped up on the pillows now. The beautiful quiet-faced black nurse sits in the chair across the room. When he opens his eyes, he likes to see her there. She waves her fingers at him and he smiles and waves back. Mother calls to young Paula to come with her into the room. An enormous magnolia blossom has been picked from the towering tree outside the balcony. It is on the mantel and its heavy lemon scent fills the room, blending into the magnificent encompassing music.

Death is on its way. Young Paula writes to us of the scene and, "Gramma is quite unchanged. She is philosophical and says very staunchly that he is still the most important figure in the house and that all she can do is make things as comfortable as possible. . . . I went in the other day to get his records, to wash the dust off them so they would play better, and he took my hand very sweetly and praised my green Mexican dress, saying 'Jeeeeesus Christ, what have we here . . , etc.' just as he used to do. . . ."

Mother at midnight goes in to see him. She's been up late in the Farm Office with things to do. She looks down at him and he doesn't see her. She feels he makes an effort and slowly his eyes focus on her. He understands and knows her! Says clearly, "Paula!" He is acknowledging her presence and their understanding. And becomes vague again, floats away.

Death itself in the morning. Many calls to make. One to us from young Paula. Mother and the doctor want to talk. They say it simultaneously. Mother, "Carl passed away." The doctor, "Mr. Sandburg expired this morning." Our Barney replies, "It's the end of an era!" Mother likes that. We take the first available plane, arriving in the evening.

Already the house is changed. The nurses have gone home. My daughter has a broom in hand. The rooms have been cleaned, the baths scoured, all the beds made up freshly, the medicines thrown out, the hospital bed to storage. The tenor is almost gay, except when young Paula verges on tears now and then in her recitation. In the white front room where he was, the magnolia flower is on the mantel (brown now and like a sculpture). It is removed. The wheelchair in the corner is folded and put away. Fresh flowers from Paula's garden are set about.

Janet, "I won't go to the funeral! When I heard, I put my head down and cried a little. Sometimes a cry does a person a lot of good!" Margaret says that quite a while back Mother had told her with tears, "The man I love is not really here now. He is gone already." Margaret sighs.

The phone rings continually. The clan is assembling. Disposition of the bedrooms is decided. Uncle Ed and the angel to the white front room where the death came. John Carl and Liz, the "Younger Steichens," to the bedroom upstairs next to Janet (Liz is now carrying Helga's first grandchild!). Young Paula to the little cellar room by ours. Cousins, others, to the crows' nest and Carl's bedroom upstairs. It is a full house, an odd collection with varieties of love among them.

In the center of it all is Paula. Again and again on the telephone, "I love you because of what you were and did for

Carl, not for what you can do now! . . . Ah, Carl's voice seemed to change. To be weaker a day or so ago. The nurses noticed it too. When he cursed and swore as they moved him, his voice did not have the strong ring, but was almost a whisper. . . ."

Helga will see the body! It is a confirmation. I must view the shell so I can relinquish the living creature. Not having witnessed the death, feeling him somewhere about. The shell placed so serenely in its coffin and dressed in the double-breasted gray suit that young Paula helped Mother pick out. A red and black broad tie that he wore often. He looks quite spiffy and I am sure would approve of it all. Helga stands there (a little intimidated) with white gloves (Mother likes that), formal. His veined broad speckled blacksmith hands are quiet, one crossed on the other. I am satisfied.

Joe Wershba calls. There is a television program dealing with his life. Mother falls asleep to Carl's reading voice. Margaret wakes her, "Oh, thank you!" He is singing "September Song" and his voice is strong, sweet. The cadence.

Discussions on funeral arrangements. The New York *Times* man, Alden Whitman, will be arriving. He says there is a poem at the end of *Smoke and Steel* that should be used. "Finish."

Death comes once, let it be easy.
Ring one bell for me once, let it go at that.
Or ring no bell at all, better yet.

Sing one song if I die.
Sing John Brown's Body or Shout All Over God's
Heaven.
Or sing nothing at all, better yet.

Death comes once, let it be easy.

And that we should obey. Helga, "How about the 'better yet' part?" And Mother, "No songs! No. None of that." A little later she comes to Helga, "I remember those songs. They should be played. He always sang them!" The bearded young selected Unitarian minister arrives, George Tolleson, new, honored. It is agreed. He will start the service with the poem and the first song. The last one will come at the end.

Our Barney drives Mother to the airport to pick up the Steichens. The brother and sister meet. Joanna stands aside with Barney. Uncle Ed so tall and Paula so small. She in almost a whisper, "It was so peaceful. He breathed more and more slowly and then he was gone. He didn't suffer at all!" The one bends to embrace his sister strongly. (Their lives are changed now.)

At the farm dining room, Helga brings the chilled champagne bottle (she and Janet have just washed and dried the eleven dusty glasses that seem never to be used except on our visits!) for Barney to open. Uncle Ed and Mother sit in the two big armchairs, glasses in hand. Mother's laugh rings out. And his follows. It is a celebration!

Helga is assigned the arranging of the meals. Slowly the house fills. The dining room table is taken apart and the three extra leaves brought up from storage. A long yellow damask cloth is unfolded and spread, found in the bottom of a drawer among others. The front doorbell rings and a chocolate cake, yellow-iced, is there, left by some neighbor who has come and fled.

Uncle Ed is caught marching down the hall to his room, holding onionlike stalks in his hand and rejoicing, "Piracy on the high seas!" He is taking a souvenir back to Umpawaug. He has been visiting Mother's bed of lilies. One is in bloom, white-and-crimson-speckled and striped. He wants that one and Mother whispers to me, "We were waiting for it! To bring it to your father as soon as the bud opened. That was the morning he died!"

By eleven, the *Life* people are here. They are allowed to do as they please. "Carl belongs to the people," Paula declares. And the *Life* man, Mike Silva, "This is the happiest house I have ever been in!" There is a strong soft gaiety, a holiday air.

The family goes, as Helga did, to view the body. The press is with them. Mother takes a brief look (She's been used to him) and steps aside. John Carl has no desire to look (like our Barney). Young Paula is there and Joanna, standing aside as Uncle Ed (cameras rolling) stomps up, with his heavy cane for support, and stands with feet apart for many moments, gazing down. Perhaps he, as happened with Helga, is taking in the reality of the shell.

The plethora of flowers steadily flowing into the house! At first, the strange statuesque pyramids are separated and made up into vases. As the crescendo mounts, they are left as they come, placed here and there in their baskets, jars, as wreaths.

At noon, as Paula orders, the meal is served up. A sliced roasted rare beef. Macaroni pies prepared by the maid. A salad from the farm garden and zucchini dishes. There are sixteen at the table. The *Life* man sits (uninvited) in the center of one side. John Carl is pushed out and sits by the window in a chair. Mother and Uncle Ed are side by side at the table's head and at the foot, Liz and Harry Golden. He and Uncle Ed raise glasses of goat milk high in toast.

Later there is coffee and the neighbor's cake. The cameramen are roaming about and no one heeds them. Uncle Ed smokes a long fancy Havana in a "humidor holder." Harry, immaculate and classy in black suit, lights his own fat one. *Complete Poems* is brought out and one and another reads aloud one or more that he likes. Do you feel Carl there? As his words are spoken by these men in honor? "The Junk Man."

> *I am glad God saw Death*
> *And gave Death a job taking care of all who are*
> *tired of living:*
>
> *When all the wheels in a clock are worn and slow and*
> *the connections loose*
> *And the clock goes on ticking and telling the wrong time*
> *from hour to hour*
> *And people around the house joke about what a bum*
> *clock it is,*
> *How glad the clock is when the big Junk Man drives*
> *his wagon*
> *Up to the house and puts his arms around the clock and*
> *says:*
> *"You don't belong here,*
> *You gotta come*
> *Along with me," . . .*

Mother meanwhile sits out on the white pillared porch with the New York *Times* man. She looks off to the mountains, "I thought it was a wonderful way of going. . . . He had a beautiful passing. . . . Carl now belongs to the world! . . . You know, he used to go to a library when he came into town and ask how many of his books had been stolen. He was pleased because he had more of his taken than any other writer!"

It is one o'clock. Some go off to change clothes. There is a breeze out on the porch. Everyone is gathering, pulling on gloves, hats. Talking of something that connects them with Carl. Blue sky. Blazing sun. Stunning thick-boled towering pines with lighted green boughs. The black nurse (like an actress, with presence, in lavender) arrives and asks to see his room again. Helga takes her in. The Steichens are finishing dressing. ("I'll button it," says Joanna. He strikes her away, "No, don't button it! The beard will cover it!") And everyone is assembled.

The quick decision as to who will go in which of the two waiting funeral cars. "You go with your mother," says Barney. "I go with my husband," states Helga. Mother, Uncle Ed, Margaret and Joanna are in the car in front of us as we start down the drive. At the turn, by the white farm gate, it halts. Out clambers Uncle Ed, cane in hand, to walk slowly to a white pine. He deliberately tears off a low small branch. And makes his way back to the car and we are off.

Why does he do this? It is a long time before I learn that almost twenty-one years ago to the day, on the thirteenth of July of 1946, Uncle Ed had been one of the few mourners at a small service for his old mentor and *maestro*, Alfred Steiglitz, in New York City. At Steiglitz' wish, no eulogy was spoken or music played. My uncle had placed a similar green pine bough on the black-draped casket. What does it mean? Is he remembering that other day? Did he think of it when he stood over Carl's body at the funeral home?

A white police car, red flashing on its roof, guides us to the old St. John in the Wilderness church. And here is Uncle Ed, slowly emerging from his car, the cane clutched in his right hand along with the pine spray, his left tightly holding to Mother's hand as they mount the steps. Joanna grips his right arm. (Does she think he may stumble?) How extraordinary Paula is! She wears no jewel. She has changed into a fresh loose green-flowered dress. No hat or gloves. Her dark shoes are heelless. She will not even weep, as Helga is prepared to.

I tell my Barney, "Call John over. I want my children with me!" All in a line, entering the hushed place where the gray-white pearl pall with its black and gold trim covers the coffin where he (his shell!) lies inside with feet to the altar in the stained wooden nave.

There goes Uncle Ed, leaving Mother and Joanna in their front-row pew (with its polished nameplate) to place his green mysterious offering on the pall and in his majestic way, the cane helping, return impassive, to them.

My son's quiet face and steady low voice, "I'm sorry, Helga," as he goes into the pew after Liz. And young Paula with one of her beaus, who has come to be with her.

The little pipe organ suddenly trumpets into the Union army's marching tune, "John Brown's body lies a-mouldering in its grave! John Brown's body lies . . ." And all are joining in. Not Helga!

And then the minister, how ". . . Each of us has died a little with the death of Carl Sandburg. . . ." Helga is not listening, gazing at the pall, the green bough.

His time is up and the voice ceases its readings from Carl's books and the organist launches into the spiritual (again as required by Carl's little poem "Finish") about "God's children" and their "shouting all over God's heaven! . . ." And (as also directed by "Finish"), the bell tolls one time and everybody troops out.

Back at Connemara, the *Life* man, "Can I tie up the phone?" "First," says Harry, "let me take it just a moment!" And Helga wants the green pine branch and a cousin is sent to find it at the funeral home where the body is about to be shipped to Atlanta for cremation and they are wondering what to do with it.

Barney must get back to the Cleveland Clinic and I will

join him in a few days. I need to follow Mother's direction to pilfer a bit from his rooms. Little pen-knives and green eyeshades. Old cigar boxes filled with notebooks and pencils and a golf ball or two and clips. Barney calls from the airport and I retell his story to Mother and Uncle Ed. A little girl was getting on the plane and she wouldn't tell her mother why she had cried at the funeral. Finally she came to Barney and whispered, "It's because he won't be writing any more stories for children now!" Barney's voice catches in the telling. My uncle, "That's the story of the day!"

One by one, everyone is leaving. The "Young Steichens" by their car. Harry an hour ago with a press man. Young Paula will take Uncle Ed and Joanna to the airport. But first my uncle comes to me. He is emotional now on leaving Connemara and kisses strongly, familial, the beard old-fashioned and brushy, "My little love! . . ."

During the day, roaming about, in an upstairs closet, Helga came upon an old thin mahogany guitar with a worn green ribbon. She tunes it and the tone is not good, but it feels strongly his. We have a song fest that evening. It begins when I feel the need to sing the two songs I could not at the funeral. I go to his chair in the other room. I am alone and sing them over for myself.

Then the others wander in and get to looking up the right words in songbooks and finding other songs forgotten. Janet, "How about 'Where Oh Where Is Old Elijah'?" And later, "Sing 'The Boll Weevil'!" Margaret sighs and says that that is the one as a child that Janet always asked for. After everyone is gone to bed, Margaret stays. We sing and sing!

At breakfast, the television is on and there is the funeral again, Mother and Uncle Ed going up the stairs, he sort of blindly forging forward and holding her hand in a fierce way, she luminous. The pall-covered casket with the pine branch leaving the church.

At mid-morning, the phone rings. It is the *Life* people, "We can't find the poem Harry was reading!" Helga leafs through and gives it to them, " 'Upstream' in *Slabs of the Sunburnt West.*" The voice cries, "I'm ecstatic!"

The phone again. The New York *Times* man wants to read his piece to be sure it is approved by all. It is!

And then it is five o'clock in the next morning and Helga is sleepless. I go into the Farm Office. I can hear Janet heating milk for the newborns in the kitchen. She is brewing coffee and brings me a cup.

Then for hours wandering about the house and pulling out drawers in his rooms and (Mother urging me on!) collecting worn coin purses, buckeyes, a tooth (gold-filled), ancient pennies, a pearl-handled pocket knife, a little blue inscribed booklet, *A Cabin In the Clearing, "Carl!* At Christmas 1951 a new poem comes to you with Holiday Greetings *somewhat wistful* from Robert Frost *preferably called Robert."*

Another day is spent going through tall storage cupboards in the living room, taking out books for expected grandchildren. "If there aren't enough for them all," says Margaret, "I'll give them some of mine." Over twenty great boxes are packed and addressed and ready to be shipped (in one is his old brass spittoon) to Cleveland.

Mother is having little cards prepared with her new name. She says clearly, "Now I am Lilian Paula Sandburg." After a lifetime, the return to a single life. "Lilian Paula Sandburg, her daughters and grandchildren, appreciate your expression of sympathy." So there!

A few days later, at breakfast in my home, weeping suddenly and unexpectedly. The powerful urge to write the poem for him. Helpless before the important gesture. Being a bard's daughter. Having some knowledge, feeling the nearness to his old close spirit, Helga must.

And Barney, by now used to his wife's ways, "Why not stop doing that and write it!"

The poem begins and in some days is finished. *McCalls* wants it for a thousand, says my agent. Carl would like that! A poet needs to be heard. It is a long grieving poem and starts

Father, once you said that in the grace of God you might,
As did Hokusai, live to the age of eighty-nine;
I thought my own thoughts about the prophecy:
Take your time leaving this life,
Go slowly, not for your, but for our sake.

Father, when you went away finally
The striped lily, waiting to bloom, bloomed,
Taking up your going breath,
Standing among other-colored lilies and crimson dahlias
In the old garden's morning fog.

I was not there, but the others told me
Of your favorite nurse, the beautiful Mrs. Green,
Putting Chopin on the record player a few evenings before
And bringing you a Magnolia Grandiflora flower,
White-petaled and a foot across, as was her custom
From the great tree outside your balcony,
And how you were sleeping and night began coming on
And how the room became like a cup brimming over
With that music and the heavy lemon scent of the enormous
flower
And how everyone then somehow felt better
And more able to endure your inevitable leaving. . . .

The sound of his footsteps, his knock at Helga's door, his voice in that particular timbre, "And would you be so good as to let me come in for an idle moment?" are lost, figments in the wind. Or are they? His first great-grandson is born six months after his going—Sascha. And before long another—Tristan. After a while a great-granddaughter, Helga Sky, and then Birch and then Marcel Andreas.

A memorial? Yes, on the steps of the Lincoln Monument on a Sunday in September of that 1967 with LBJ climbing the steps and walking to Paula, bless her, luminous still. And he holding her hands and Lady Bird kissing her cheek while the rest of us stand and wait.

His ashes? At dusk on a Saturday at the end of September, being placed by Mother and Margaret beneath a boulder called "Remembrance Rock" in the back yard of the birthplace in Galesburg.

The remaining goat herd? In that October, Paula runs a notice in the *Dairy Goat Journal.*

And another in December.

CHIKAMING HERD

OUR HERD REDUCTION SALE IS COMPLETE
WE CANNOT ACCEPT ANY MORE ORDERS FOR STOCK
WE WISH TO THANK ALL OF OUR FRIENDS IN THE
DAIRY GOAT INDUSTRY FOR THEIR PATRONAGE
AND WISH THEM ALL CONTINUED SUCCESS IN
THE FUTURE

Mrs. Carl Sandburg, Flat Rock, N. C. 28731

Connemara? In February of 1968, under the aegis of our Secretary of the Interior Stewart Udall, an option is taken by our government, to purchase the farm as a National Historic Site. A year and a half later, a check for $200,000 is presented to Paula in exchange for her deed of the land to the National Park Service. The Golden Place is open to the public in October of 1972.

Young Paula's book? *My Connemara* is out in May of 1969, dedicated ". . . to all that has been a part of Connemara—the fields and mountainland, the 'million acres of sky,' and the white house, the wild flowers, crops, trees, creatures and people. . . ."

Helga's walk into the Garden with Barney? It remains Eden. And with Adam himself, a place to wander, fearless of the fall of an Apple, the hiss of a Snake, a loud voice from Heaven.

My family's new home? It is a few miles away in Asheville,

where there are maples, tall pines, firs, room for Paula's garden and a few fruit trees. There she goes in July of 1969 with Janet and Margaret. In no time, the latter has installed feeding stations and the news is out and birds come flocking.

Uncle Ed? At his ninetieth birthday party at the Plaza Hotel in New York in March of 1969, ". . . I don't see how my sister can stand life without Carl. I can hardly stand it myself. I didn't see him too often in the last years, but there was always the telephone and we talked. I miss him terribly. I loved him."

Four years later, a poem for him too, with a long title, "Reflections On the Night Express from San Sebastian to Barcelona on Steichen Who Died In His Sleep Just One Day Under Ninety-four."

Your young wife's cable reached us in the nick of time
In Madrid, the uniformed child flying down the street,
As we were climbing in the Fiat, bound for Burgos
And the finest cathedral in Spain, the Spaniards repeat. . . .

We toasted you that night with vino tinto,
In which sweat and vine and sun and red dry land
Contrive to work a local miraculous blessing.
We spoke of love and your Family of Man.

We mentioned how your life was fields and flowers,
Complex cameras or simple, pigment, paint,
Women, two wars, strong heart for certain men;
We saluted your humility, arrogance; we named you sinner, saint.

Next day we came to Castillo and Altamira,
Those glorified caves of prehistoric man,
Where wild creatures crowd and curl about the ceilings
And time stands still. There you were born again.

Steichen, on this your first and ninety-fourth birthday
You lit the torch and assembled all your skill

And took the pigment and laid it on the ceiling
And the mystery of Art started in the cave in the hill.

As Uncle Ed has directed her, Joanna comes with a friend or two and scatters his ashes by the great boulder at Umpawaug that he has named "Topstone."

Paula? As she fades and the dragon is gentled nowadays, Margaret takes on the duties of householder. She and Janet care for Mother in their home until her end in February of 1977. On May Day of that year she would have been ninety-four. Helga goes to join Janet and Margaret at the same birthplace "Remembrance Rock" so her ashes may mingle with her husband's.

Her tribute poem was done long years before. "Eloge to My Mother."

This small-boned powerful life-loving woman
Views the world and us her children introspectively.
With disheveled chatter and disposition even
To us she is certain sanctuary.

And when she goes with odorous straw to make
A bed for those small goats she loves,
They fall kneeling among her beautiful hands that take
Strongly apart the oat bales interwove.

They adore her! And when they set about
To drop their young, they press against her side,
Their calls of agony not so great a shout
As if she were not there to hear they cried.

I would send her all my love this way,
In a ranting and incompleted poem,
Attempting with industry not as a small child to say,
"Love!" But as a woman not too well or wisely grown. . . .

When time moved and she came once to visit me,
We had to buy a dozen varied saplings for she said,

"You can't have a yard without a tree!"
From the cellar I got up a pick and a man's stout spade;

The rocks had been created one with the soil
And to make a root-basin properly
Took a half hour's steady toil.
"Here," she said, and grasped the tool, "Let me

Dig that hole. My body's old
And doesn't matter longer. You are young!"
Helpless, half-astonished I stood;
She heaved and chopped, the boulders flung,

The cave was built forthwith. I would send
Her all my love, knowing she has no patience or place
In her valiant person for tribute. Still I would commend
To her retiring self enormous processionals of praise.

How about the nation that Carl has cared for? A thirteen-cent First Class Commemorative stamp is issued in his honor on the centenary of his birth on 6 January 1878. There are speeches and songs and television shows and Margaret's *Breathing Tokens: One Hundred and Eighteen Previously Unpublished Poems* and Helga's *A Great and Glorious Romance: The Story of Carl Sandburg and Lilian Steichen* are released.

It was a wondrous romance. Early in their life together, Carl wrote a letter to Paula, ". . . . I don't know what your fingers are working at nor what problems your brain is feeling its way about. But all last night your heart beat close to mine. . . . I remembered your low-voiced talks to me as we lay close to each other, between kisses,—the rarest, highest thing I ever touched in life or work or books—your talk of what life is & what life may be. . . .

"Down whatever road your soft eyes look & your little feet go today, they go with beauty and sweetness & poise. And always and always and always I am with you and I love you and I love you. Foolish and rough & often thoughtless I have been & may be again but what there is of me loves and loves. Two children turning pages in a big book under a high tree. May all the gods of luck watch & speak wisely with them. Love and love. . . ."

And so the pilgrims have arrived at the end of their journey. Helga's tale is done. The moonlight of the present meets the sunlight of the past. The window, the glass of memory we have been looking through, shatters and is no more.

INDEX

INDEX

INDEX

INDEX

INDEX

INDEX

INDEX